Laws of Chaos

Laws of Chaos

A Probabilistic Approach to Political Economy

Emmanuel Farjoun
Moshé Machover

VERSO
London · New York

This paperback edition published by Verso 2020
First published by Verso 1983
© Emmanuel Farjoun and Moshé Machover 1983, 2020

The moral rights of the authors have been asserted

1 3 5 7 9 10 8 6 4 2

Verso
UK: 6 Meard Street, London W1F 0EG
US: 20 Jay Street, Suite 1010, Brooklyn, NY 11201
versobooks.com

Verso is the imprint of New Left Books

ISBN-13: 978-1-78873-648-0
ISBN-13: 978-1-78873-703-6 (UK EBK)
ISBN-13: 978-1-78873-704-3 (US EBK)

British Library Cataloguing in Publication Data
A catalogue record for this book is available from the British Library

Library of Congress Cataloging-in-Publication Data
A catalog record for this book is available from the Library of Congress

Typeset in English Times The Thetford Press Limited
Printed in the United States of America

Contents

*Dedicated to
the memory of
Robert H. Langston*

No one but man himself—with his own hands—produces these commodities and determines their prices, except that, here again, something flows from his actions which he does not intend or desire; here again, need, object, and the result of the economic activity of man have come into jarring contradiction.

How does this happen, and what are the black laws which, behind man's back, lead to such strange results of the economic activity of man today? ...

In the entity which embraces oceans and continents, there is no planning, no consciousness, no regulation, only the blind clash of unknown, unrestrained forces playing a capricious game with the economic destiny of man. Of course, even today, an all-powerful ruler dominates all working men and women: capital. But the form which this sovereignty of capital takes is not despotism but anarchy.

And it is precisely this anarchy which is responsible for the fact that the economy of human society produces results which are mysterious and unpredictable to the people involved. Its anarchy is what makes the economic life of mankind something unknown, alien, uncontrollable—the laws of which we must find in the same manner in which we analyse the phenomena of external nature. . . . Scientific analysis must discover ex post facto *that purposefulness and those rules governing human economic life which conscious planfulness did not impose on it beforehand.*

Rosa Luxemburg, *What is Economics?*

Foreword

This book is an attempt to construct a non-deterministic theoretical framework for the foundations of political economy. It relies on probabilistic and statistical methods, of the kind used in the modern foundations of several other sciences.

Originally, we were motivated to embark on this undertaking by our deep dissatisfaction with the various attempts to resolve or dodge the so-called transformation problem in Marxist political economy. The arguments around this problem over the last hundred years have changed in form, but very little in economic or mathematical essence. We took an interest and became thoroughly familiar with the technicalities of both the input-output approach and the various re-interpretations of Marx's notion of *price of production*. But we were unhappy with both.

In an essay by the first-named author,[1] criticizing Steedman's exposition of the Sraffa-von Neumann input-output method,[2] it was pointed out how utterly sensitive this method is to the slightest variation in its cornerstone: the hypothesis of a *uniform rate of profit*. It was further pointed out that this hypothesis is quite unjustified. To a person versed in the mathematical technicalities and aware of the fact that one can often 'cook' the right assumption to get to a desired conclusion, this must seem a very fundamental weakness. Nevertheless, it was equally clear that *within a deterministic framework* there is no reasonable alternative to the uniformity assumption as a way of theorizing competition. Thus it seemed to the author that in order to dispense with the unjustified uniformity assumption a *non-deterministic* framework might well be necessary. In such a framework, rates of profit are allowed to move at random according to an inherent *probabilistic* law.

This idea seemed to go hand in hand with the view of the late R.H. Langston,[3] concerning the inherent and irreducible oscillations of prices, and together they led to the conceptualization of prices themselves as a random variable, as presented in chapter V.

When we examined these rudimentary ideas together, it gradually became clear to us that they form a basis for a far-reaching critical review of the entire foundation of political economy. The assumptions that we criticize and reject are by no means peculiar to the Marxist school, or to those who have taken part in its internal debates; they are shared by the most diverse schools of economic thought, classical and neo-classical alike. Thus, what began for us as a preoccupation with a purely internal problem of Marxian economics was enlarged into a general conception that bears on the foundation of the whole science. The transformation problem has become for us almost a side issue; in this book it is discussed only in chapter VI.

We believe that what we have to say should be of interest both to Marxists and to those interested in the foundations of economic theory but not particularly familiar with the Marxist tradition and its internal debates.

The idea that probabilistic methods can and should be applied to economics, and that verifiable economic laws can be derived by means of statistical considerations, is far from new. On the conceptual level, it can be traced back to Adam Smith and, more particularly, to Karl Marx, who stressed the essentially statistical nature of economic laws. Actual applications of probabilistic methods to practical economic and financial problems are quite common in the field of insurance and, more recently, in stockbroking. At a more theoretical level, certain schools of mathematical economics have developed and applied the probabilistic approach in econometrics and related fields of economic theory. In this respect, the work of the Austrian economist Josef Steindl is especially noteworthy.[4]

However, when it comes to a mathematical modelling of the *central* categories of political economy—such as price, profit, value, capital intensity—an extremely rigid deterministic approach is invariably taken. In this respect Langston broke new ground: he was acutely aware that the oscillations of prices are an inherent and irreducible part of their very nature in a capitalist economy, and he therefore tried to develop a price theory that would incorporate the indeterminacy of prices as part of their very definition. But his project was overtaken by his sudden and untimely death. In Farjoun's essay[5] it was stressed once again that one must somehow try to reconstruct the very foundations of the political economy of capitalism on concepts that incorporate the insecurity and non-deterministic nature of the market.

The present book is an attempt at such a reconstruction. If it has any claim to novelty, it lies not in the use of probabilistic methods as such, but in their systematic application to the *foundations* of political economy.

One result of the present work to which we wish to draw particular attention is the theoretical derivation of the *law of falling labour-content* (or of *rising productivity of labour*), which we regard as the archetypal law of all capitalist development. We define the *labour-content* of a given commodity as the total amount of human labour required (directly and indirectly) to produce that commodity. Thus our notion of labour-content is similar, if not completely identical, to what Marx calls *value*. It must be stressed that this important law cannot even be formulated, let alone explained or derived, in a theory that does not incorporate a notion of labour-content or value. Indeed, one of the central theses of this book is that labour-content, as a basic common measure of all commodities, is an indispensable theoretical concept in political economy. This thesis is diametrically opposed to that advocated by many adherents of the input-output school, particularly Ian Steedman and his followers, who see no role whatsoever for labour-content (or value) in the foundations of economic theory.[6] However, Steedman and his co-thinkers are right about one thing: their conclusions are indeed logical consequences of the hypotheses they postulate—the most powerful and unrealistic of which is that of the uniformity of the rate of profit.[7] We are convinced that political economy can advance only if it rejects this hypothesis, which has ruled it since its inception.

We are acutely aware that we what we have at this stage is not a worked-out and well-rounded theory, but a skeleton of a research programme, which only long years of theoretical and empirical investigations can flesh out. Nevertheless, after some hesitation we have decided to publish our ideas in their present imperfect state. We do so in the hope that public discussion may contribute to the clarification of the fundamental issues raised, and that others—more competent than we are in economic theory, the theory of probability, and statistical methods—may join in and help to advance the project that is outlined here.

Being a first work in a new direction, this book does not presuppose a high level of mathematical knowledge. On the other hand, our new approach does employ concepts and results from the theory of probability that are not normally used in books on economic theory (although they may be familiar to students of economics who have done a course in statistical methods). We have written the book in such a way that it requires of its readers only a modest knowledge of elementary algebra and calculus; much of it requires even less, and can be read by a person with very rudimentary mathematical knowledge. Also, we have thought it best not to presuppose detailed familiarity with probability theory. The probabilistic concepts and theorems that we employ are therefore presented in appendix I, in sufficient detail to make their use comprehensible.

In the course of writing this book we have had the benefit of useful criticism from the many friends and colleagues, too numerous to name here, who read earlier drafts of parts of the manuscript, or with whom we discussed our ideas.

We are especially indebted to two people. The late Robert H. Langston played an important role; in particular, the basic notion of specific price is due to him. During the long period of gestation and writing Jon Rothschild encouraged us to develop some initial arguments into a more presentable form. His criticism and ideas have been especially valuable for the elaboration of the topics discussed in appendix II.

Introduction

Critical political economy finds itself today in a paradoxical position. On the one hand, the prolonged crisis of capitalism has thoroughly discredited the dominant economic schools, neo-classical and Keynesian alike. Their illusion that they had captured the basic structure that underlies money, prices and profit, and could therefore successfully prescribe how to manipulate the economic system towards stability, has been shattered by reality.

On the other hand, the persistent inability—despite great efforts —of the Marxist school to clarify the apparently basic notions of price levels and general rate of profit (in money terms), and to integrate their quantitative determination in a consistent way into the labour theory of value, has led many critical socialists to conclude that something fundamental must be wrong with the whole approach. *Value*, the basic concept of critical political economy, seems to have lost its credibility. The doubts are familiar: they touch not only the problem of 'transforming' values into prices and the secular tendency of the rate of profit, but also the coherence and usefulness for political economy of the very concept of value.

This paradoxical state of affairs is marked by fierce controversies over the meaning of, and relations between, seemingly simple magnitudes such as price, profit and wage, and their connection (or lack of one) with the concepts of value, organic composition, utility functions, supply and demand, and economic equilibrium.

However, upon careful examination of these debates, it emerges that there is a far-reaching general agreement among the various schools—Marxian and non-Marxian, left and right—which circumscribes the arena of their sometimes bitter struggles. In fact, this common ground was marked out by Adam Smith and has changed very little since his day. This consensus concerns two closely related central concepts: *natural prices* and the *general rate of profit*. It is almost universally accepted that *in an economy with perfect competition, one can associate with each commodity an 'ideal' or 'natural' equilibrium price, and that in a state of equilibrium all commodities are sold at their ideal prices, which are so formed as to guarantee identical uniform rates of profit to all capitals invested in commodity production.*

Fierce battles are fought over such questions as how to compute the numerical magnitude of this equilibrium rate of profit theoretically, and what is its real source; can it be related to labour-values, or to utilities, or is it (as Sraffa maintains) implicitly determined by the very notion of natural price and uniform rate of profit. But, at the same time, there is a broad agreement that the *reality* of capitalist competition, as well as the internal economic *logic* of capitalism, can be captured by positing a model with uniform rate of profit and ideal natural prices corresponding to it.

Our main aim is to show that this generally accepted belief rests on a fundamental theoretical misconception: there is no way in which the logic of the capitalist system—let alone its reality—can be encapsulated by a model in which the rates of profit accruing to all productively invested capitals are assumed to be equal. Further, we shall argue that there is a relatively simple, though hitherto disregarded, alternative theoretical framework for dealing with the concepts of profit and price, which is mathematically manageable and captures with far greater realism the essence of the actual phenomena.

It is quite remarkable how the idea of a uniform rate of profit was passed virtually unchanged from Adam Smith through Ricardo and Marx to modern economic schools, Marxian and non-Marxian alike.

Marx writes: '. . . there is no doubt, however, that in actual fact, ignoring inessential, accidental circumstances that cancel each other out, no such variation in the average rate of profit exists between different branches of industry, and it could not exist without abolishing the entire system of capitalist production.'[1] And further: '. . . capital withdraws from a sphere with a low rate of profit and wends its way to others that yield higher profit. This constant migration, the distribution of capital between the different spheres according to where the profit rate is rising and where it is falling, is what produces a relationship between supply and demand such that the average profit is the same in the various different spheres, and values are therefore transformed into prices of production. Capital arrives at this equalization to a greater or lesser extent, according to how advanced capitalist development is in a given national society: i.e. the more the conditions in the country in question are adapted to the capitalist mode of production.'[2]

This is essentially a reiteration of the statement with which Adam Smith begins chapter X of his *Wealth of Nations*: 'The whole of the advantages and disadvantages of the different employment of labour and stock must, in the same neighbourhood, be either perfectly equal or continually tending to equality. If in the same neighbourhood, there was any employment evidently either more or less advantageous than the rest, so many people would crowd into it in the one case, and so many would desert it in the other, that its advantages would soon return to the level of other employments. This at least would be the case in a society where things were free to follow their natural course, where there was perfect liberty, and where every man was perfectly free both to choose what occupation he thought proper, and to change it as often as he thought proper.'

While these formulations are somewhat loose and open to interpretation, they have in practice always been taken to imply an ideal, if not actual, uniformity of the rate of profit.

The position on these matters has not changed to date. Sraffa and his followers, along with the whole input-output brigade, base their entire conception of the price of commodities on the assumption that an equal rate of profit is generated in the production of each and every commodity.

Thus J.T. Schwartz, a noted mathematician and mathematical economist, states in his lucid exposition of the input-output model: 'We have here taken an essential step in assuming the rate of profit to be the same for all types of production. This corresponds to the ordinary assumption, in the theory of prices, of "free competition"; it can be justified in the usual way by arguing that a situation in which the production of different commodities yields different rates of profit cannot be stable, since investments would be made only in the industry yielding the highest rate of profit to the exclusion of other commodities yielding lower rates of profit. Long-term equilibrium, of which our simple theory is alone descriptive, would be reached only when all such rates of profit became equal.'[3] And, in an even more recent survey article, he repeats this 'usual' justification and concludes: 'Thus over the long term we must expect the rates of profit on all types of production to converge to a common value. When this "investment equilibrium" is reached, the price of each commodity will be the price which yields the normal [common] rate of profit on its production.'[4]

It would be possible, though tedious, to quote hundreds of similar statements by a host of theoreticians. The proposition that free competition leads the rates of profit to converge to a common equilibrium rate (and prices to their respective 'natural' equilibrium levels) has come to be regarded as a truism.

Of course, it is perfectly well understood by most (as indeed it was repeatedly pointed out by Marx) that in reality rates of profit are never actually uniform. This is always explained by a deviation of reality from the ideal of perfect competition, or (even if perfect competition is assumed) by the perpetual perturbation of the system away from its ideal state of equilibrium. But while such a state of equilibrium, with a uniform rate of profit, is known not to exist in reality, it is generally regarded as a legitimate simplifying assumption. The Sraffians, and the input-output theoreticians in general, take this assumption as their point of departure, while Marx, whose deeper-level value theory is independent of it, introduced it in the third volume of *Capital*, and attempted to reconcile the two.

The alleged legitimacy of this assumption rests on two vital suppositions. First, that a state of equilibrium with a uniform rate of profit, towards which the system of free competition is assumed to have already converged under market forces, is a *theoretically* coherent construct, which reflects, albeit in an ideal form, the real logic of free competition.

Second, that the actual system oscillates around such a state of equilibrium and is usually more or less close to it, and therefore that deductions made under the assumption of a uniform rate of profit yield reasonable approximations to the actual phenomena. In other words, that the assumption of such a state of equilibrium, while not absolutely correct, is nevertheless correct as a first approximation. (For example, that 'prices of production'—that is, 'natural prices'

—computed under the assumption of a uniform rate of profit are 'the centre around which the daily market-prices revolve, and at which they are balanced out in definite periods'.[5])

We shall argue that both these suppositions, normally taken for granted, are fallacious. A state of equilibrium with a uniform rate of profit is a chimera that not only fails to exist in practice but is a theoretical impossibility. The assumption of its theoretical existence is illegitimate inasmuch as it negates certain vital, essential and fundamental aspects of a system of free competition. The forces of competition, which drive capital out of spheres of production with low rates of profit into spheres with high rates, are real enough. But they do not, and *cannot*, drive the rates of profit to converge to a common equilibrium *magnitude*. Rather, the drive is towards an equilibrium *probability distribution*, whose general form (at least) is theoretically ascertainable and empirically verifiable. Consequently, any deduction made on the basis of the assumption of the uniformity of the rate of profit (which, technically speaking, amounts to the counter-factual and theoretically absurd assumption that the probability distribution just mentioned is degenerate) is *in principle* suspect, and any result derived in this way cannot be taken even as a valid first approximation, unless detailed special arguments to the contrary are provided.

Apart from the usual justification—of the kind quoted above—another argument is sometimes put forward in favour of the assumption of the uniformity of the rate of profit at equilibrium. Thus, Joan Robinson writes in a recent book that this assumption is essential since 'if the rate of profit is not uniform, prices may be all over the place, as they usually are.'[6] This revealing statement amounts to a recognition that something may be fundamentally wrong with the uniformity assumption, which is nevertheless recommended, if not for its empirical or theoretical validity then at least for lack of any alternative other than theoretical chaos.

We shall argue that this counsel of despair is unjustified; fallacy and lawless chaos are not the only possible choices. This seeming dilemma is merely an expression of a methodological prejudice that recognizes only fully deterministic theoretical models. What it overlooks is the possibility that although prices (and rates of profit) may indeed be 'all over the place', not only in reality but also in theory, their distribution may be subject none the less to definite laws.

There is no doubt that the free movement of capital is an essential feature of capitalism. It is therefore reasonable to incorporate an assumption of perfect competition into a theoretical model of this mode of production. Unofficial monopolies or oligopolies, whereby one firm or a small number of firms may corner the market in a particular commodity, both crystallize and dissolve out of competition and through it; *they are a facet of the competitive process and do not negate it in any way.*[7]

Legal monopolies conferred by the state are a different matter; like some other forms of state intervention in the economy, they do constrain competition and deform the unfettered play of market forces. However, we believe that so long as the system is basically capitalist, these deformations may be disregarded at a first approximation. We see no clear evidence that such a simplifying assumption is illegitimate as far as the major modern capitalist countries are concerned. And we suspect that claims to the contrary are, at least in part, an attempt to explain away the divergence between reality and some predictions of the conventional models of perfect competition. However, it seems to us that this divergence is in fact due not so much to the unrealism of the assumption of perfect competition itself, as to the erroneous theorization of the concept of equilibrium in those models. In any case, it is quite clear that capitalism in its 'pure' form implies perfect competition, and it therefore seems correct to make this assumption at the first stage of analysis.[8] Exogenous constraints and deformations can be introduced at a later stage. In the present work we shall therefore base our analysis on the assumption of perfect competition.

Our principal claim, then, is that the *divergence* of the various rates of profit from uniformity, and their *non-convergence* to a common magnitude is an *essential* feature of perfect competition, rather than a deviation from it that can be ignored at a first approximation. This is not to say that *any* pattern of 'deviation from uniformity' can be stable. Under perfect competition, the system gravitates to a sort of dynamic equilibrium with a characteristic distribution of the various rates of profit among various capitals.

A probabilistic analysis of the 'chaotic' movement of large collections of relatively independent portions of capital can reveal the shape of this distribution. The trouble with the old conventional models is that the shape of the economy, which emerges out of the chaotic movement in the market of millions of commodities and of tens of thousands of capitalists chasing each other and competing over finite resources and markets, cannot be captured by the average rate of profit, any more than the global law of the apparently random movement of many millions of molecules in a container of gas can be captured by their average speed.

From the point of view that we advocate it will be seen that the labour theory of value was led into a theoretical crisis not because of the supposed incoherence of the concept of labour-value, nor because it assumed free competition, but because it attempted to reconcile value categories with the fallacious assumption of the uniformity of the rate of profit. Thus our critique of the Marxian theory is diametrically opposed to that of those critics who, taking the uniformity assumption as gospel, use it to discredit the labour theory of value.

The Uniformity Assumption

In order to prevent misunderstanding, we must point out that the assumption concerning the uniformity of the rate of profit has two principal versions—one 'soft', loose, flexible and hazy; the other 'hard', strict and far-reaching. The former we regard as innocuous and, if properly interpreted, quite reasonable; but we reject the latter version as fallacious.

In order to explain these two different forms of the assumption, let us start from the definition of the rate of profit. To this end, we consider some convenient time interval, say one year. If the rate of profit per annum of a given firm is denoted by R, then the magnitude of R is determined by the equation

$$P_o = P_i + R \cdot K, \tag{1}$$

where P_o is the total price received by the firm for its annual output, P_i is the total price paid by the firm for all inputs *used up* during the same period (cost of raw materials, energy, labour and so on, including also wear-and-tear of machinery and other fixed stock), and K is the invested capital that is employed (but not necessarily wholly used up) in the process. Here R is measured in units per annum,[9] and P_o, P_i and K are measured in some fixed monetary unit.

For the soft version of the uniformity assumption, one divides the economy into 'branches' or 'sectors' according to some convention, theoretical considerations or actual economic relationships. Each branch is an aggregate of a number—presumably a *large* number— of firms. Little or nothing is said about the distribution of rates of profit *within* each branch. Instead, one considers the *average* rate of profit for a whole branch.

If we now denote by R the average rate of profit of a given branch (rather than the specific rate of a single firm) then this R must again satisfy the same equation (1), except that this time P_o, P_i and K must be interpreted as the *aggregate* price of outputs, price of inputs and employed capital for the *whole* branch. Next, one considers the average magnitude of R over a period T of several years. Let this average be denoted by $\bar{R}$. Note that this $\bar{R}$ is an average of averages: first, R itself is a *cross-sectional* average, over all firms belonging to the given branch; then $\bar{R}$ is taken as the *time*-average of R, over the period T.

The soft version of the uniformity assumption claims that *in a competitive economy, the values of $\bar{R}$ for all different branches must be very close to each other, and for theoretical purposes can be taken as uniform across the whole economy.*

If Marx's remarks quoted above[10] are read in context, then it becomes clear that this is what they are intended to mean.

This version of the uniformity assumption is loose and open-ended inasmuch as it does not specify the size of the branches into which the economy is sub-divided, nor the length of the period T. But the plausibility of the assumption depends crucially on these questions. It can be shown, both empirically and theoretically, that if the branches are large enough, so that the economy is sub-divided into a small number, say a dozen, of major chunks (such as 'steel', 'textiles', 'construction'), then the soft uniformity assumption becomes quite realistic and plausible, provided one takes the period T to be sufficiently long, say twenty or thirty years. (In the limit, if the whole economy is considered as one single branch, the assumption becomes a mere tautology.)

But just because of its open-endedness and looseness, the soft version of the uniformity assumption is insufficient for a formal algebraic model of prices and profit, of the kind proposed by input-output theory. Such a model is concerned with the 'ideal' (or 'natural', or 'equilibrium') unit price of each type of commodity. Here, by a 'type' of commodity one means a species of individual commodities, which can be regarded as mutually indistinguishable, and therefore as having the same ideal unit price. (For example, cars of a given model may constitute a single commodity-type, but a Mini and a Rolls-Royce cannot plausibly be regarded as being of the same type.)[11]

For this purpose, an aggregation of the economy into a small number of major 'branches', each comprising a large number of firms, is of no use. One must set up a separate price/profit equation for each commodity-type. It is meaningless to talk, in this context, about the unit price of 'steel'; one must take each kind of steel-product separately. Besides, even if one turns a blind eye to this problem and decides to consider large 'aggregate types' (however implausibly defined), then it turns out that the result (the solution of the price/profit system of equations) depends in a crucial way on the number of 'branches' and on the method of their aggregation.[12]

For this reason it is now generally accepted that in setting up an algebraic input-output model for the theory of prices and profit, one must allow a separate 'branch' for each specific commodity-type. The number of these 'branches' is enormous, each branch comprising a small number of firms, perhaps a single firm. In practice, one usually takes each 'branch' to be simply one firm.

One then proceeds as follows. Turning back to equation (1), we interpret it again as a relation between the profit, price of inputs, price of outputs and capital of a single firm (or of a small 'branch' consisting of a few firms producing one commodity-type). Suppose that during the year in question n units of the given commodity-type were produced and sold. Dividing equation (1) by n, we get

$$p_o = p_i + R \cdot k, \qquad (2)$$

where $p_o = P_o/n$, $p_i = P_i/n$ and $k = K/n$. Thus, p_o can be interpreted as the unit price of the output, p_i as the cost of inputs used up per unit of output, and k as the capital employed per unit of output. R, as before, is the rate of profit per annum.

Equation (2) is a summary form of a price/profit equation. (In order to subject it to algebraic treatment, it must be re-written in fuller detail by breaking up p_i into a sum of prices of inputs of different types; k is similarly broken up into a sum of prices of different types of capital commodities.[13]) An equation like this can be written for each commodity-type. In this way, a large system of price/profit equations is obtained.

In dealing with this system of equations, the input-output theorists postulate the *hard* version of the uniformity assumption; namely, *that the rate of profit R is the same in all the equations of the system*. In other words, *the production of every type of commodity yields the same rate of profit*. This assumption is clearly included in Schwartz's statements quoted above;[14] it is also made, quite explicitly, by Steedman and his co-thinkers.

Marx also postulates the hard version of the uniformity assumption in the theoretical model of prices and profit that he sets up in the third volume of *Capital*. In this model, each type of commodity has an ideal price, called its *price of production*, which is defined in such a way that if every commodity were to be sold at its price of production, then the production of all types of commodities would yield one and the same rate of profit, called the *general rate of profit*. In fact, the assumptions made by the input-output theorists concerning their 'equilibrium' prices and rate of profit are made also by Marx concerning his prices of production and general rate of profit.[15] Indeed, this is hardly surprising, since input-ouput theory arose largely out of attempts to provide Marxian economic theory with a rigorous algebraic framework.

Now the gulf between the two versions of the uniformity assumption is very wide indeed. The soft version is concerned with the average rate of profit in each branch of production (where a 'branch' can, indeed should, be taken as a major chunk of the economy, comprising many firms). And it does not claim that the average rates in different branches are equal at any given time, but only that the *time-averages* of these branch-averages, taken over a sufficiently long period, are equal or nearly equal. The hard version of the uniformity assumption, on the contrary, postulates a state of affairs in which at one and the same time the rates of profit across the whole economy (in the production of each and every type of commodity) are all equal.

On the other hand, while the soft version may perhaps be regarded as a statement about the real behaviour of a competitive economy, the hard version purports to describe not a real state of the economy but a purely hypothetical one. However, both the input-output theorists and Marx claim that the hypothetical state described by their models, based on the hard version of the uniformity assumption, is an 'equilibrium' or an 'average' state, around which a real competitive economy continually oscillates.

It is this claim that we reject. Our arguments against it will be presented in the following chapters, especially chapter I.

From now on, whenever we refer simply to the *uniformity assumption*, we have in mind its hard version.

The Probabilistic Method in Economics

For convenience of exposition, the first few chapters of this book are devoted largely to a critique of the uniformity assumption and to a construction of the rate of profit as a random variable. The treatment of price as a random variable is undertaken only in chapter V. For this reason, the reader may first gain the false impression that our departure from conventional economic theory consists *merely* in our rejection of the uniformity assumption. A few words must be said here in order to forestall such a misconception.

First, it must be pointed out that once the uniformity assumption is removed, much else in the conventional treatments of the foundations of economics crumbles to the ground. In the Marxian theory, magnitudes that depend only on *value* categories do not require the uniformity assumption, but without this assumption the concept of *price of production* can no longer be defined.[16] In input-output theory, if a uniform rate of profit is not assumed then the price/profit system of equations becomes indeterminate, and equilibrium prices can no longer be defined. The uniformity assumption is here not merely a side issue, but the linchpin of the whole model. The same holds, with even greater force, for neo-classical macro-economics.

But our departure from conventional treatments does not consist merely in a denial of one particular statement, however central. It consists rather in replacing a deterministic methodology by a probabilistic one. This methodological difference requires some explanation.

Economists, just like ordinary people, are well aware of the fact that some economic phenomena are very messy and irregular. To be more precise, *market* phenomena are disorderly. While the process of production is highly regimented, the process of exchange is typically rather chaotic. Most people in the capitalist world are aware of this, partly from direct experience and partly from accounts they see and hear. (Think of documentary films you have seen on TV—some depicting a modern Japanese electronics factory, others showing a scene from the stock exchange or the commodity exchange.)

In particular, profits and prices are notoriously highly variable, both in time and in 'space' (that is, cross-sectionally, at a given moment of time). Anyone who has ever been to a vegetable market knows that the price of tomatoes varies not only from day to day (indeed, hour to hour), but also from stall to stall. If you have just bought 1 kilogram of tomatoes for 50 pence, you know that the price of *your* kilogram of tomatoes is 50 pence. But you are not really entitled to make the statement: 'The price of tomatoes today in this town is 50 pence per kilogram.' Other people may have paid 45 or 55 pence for an identical quantity of similar tomatoes. Strictly speaking, there is no such thing as *the* price of tomatoes, even if it refers to a particular day in a particular town. For this reason, all economists would agree that concepts such as prices and rates of profit are statistical, and that the laws governing them must be at least partly statistical in nature. But the question is, *at what stage of the theoretical analysis should explicit statistical considerations be brought in?*

The traditional approach starts by looking for *deterministic* laws. Since such laws cannot apply to real-life prices, profits etc., one invents idealized theoretical concepts, to which deterministic laws are believed to be applicable. Thus we have the *ideal* unit price (sometimes referred to, rather misleadingly, as the 'natural' price) of each type of commodity. For example, the ideal price per kilogram of tomatoes is the price that *everyone* who bought a kilogram of tomatoes would pay, if life were not so messy and unpredictable.

In this way one sets up a deterministic theoretical model, in which laws governing ideal prices, profits etc. are derived. The ideal quantities of the model are supposed to be deterministic approximations to the real statistical quantities; the latter are supposed to be obtained from the former by the addition of an indeterminate random (or 'noise') term. For example, the different prices actually paid for commodities of one and the same type are considered to be equal to the ideal price of such a commodity, plus a variable random term, which can be positive or negative and which assumes a different value for each particular commodity.

Likewise, the deterministic laws derived within the theoretical model are supposed to be approximate idealizations of real phenomena. A better representation of the real economic phenomena can (hopefully) be obtained by adding a random statistical 'error term' to the deterministic equations of the model.

Thus, the deterministic approach does not, in principle, deny that economic categories and phenomena display in reality an indeterministic behaviour. But it hopes to capture this behaviour by superimposing a statistical 'disturbance' on a deterministic model. The probabilistic element is thus admitted at a second stage, as an afterthought following the deterministic first stage. In fact, most economists dealing with general economic theory never actually bother with this second stage; they are content to develop their deterministic models, and merely observe (either freely, or when challenged) that statistical 'disturbance' or 'noise' factors should be added to those models if one wishes to obtain a reasonable fit to reality.

Nevertheless, there is a rich literature concerned with the superimposition of probabilistic elements onto deterministic models. A great number of the applications of the theory of probability to economics are directed at this sort of exercise.[17]

The probabilistic methodology adopted in this book is entirely different. It does not search at all for deterministic models incorporating ideal determinate prices, ideal states with a uniform rate of profit and so on. Indeed, it denies that such models provide a reasonable approximation to the reality of a capitalist economy. (And if one starts from a misconceived 'first approximation', then the superimposition of a random element as an afterthought will not do much good either.)

Instead, we *start* with a probabilistic model, in which price, the rate of profit (and other economic parameters, such as capital intensity) are treated from the very beginning not as determinate numerical quantities, but as random variables, each having its own probability distribution. The results derived in such a model are concerned with characterizing these distributions and with finding statistical inter-relations between them.

Of course, *after* one knows something about the distributions of variables such as price and the rate of profit, and their inter-connections, one can *derive* results concerning global numerical quantities such as average price and the average rate of profit. But the important point here is that the distributions are taken as primary, and the numerical quantities come in as constructs derived from these. If any determinate relationships are to be discovered, they must emerge *ex post*, out of the probabilistic disorder; not the other way around.

The probabilistic methodology is not entirely new; it has been applied in several areas of economic theory, most particularly in econometrics.[18] In this context, J. Steindl's book[19] deserves special mention. 'It deals with a kind of "equilibrium" exemplified by the size-distribution of firms and its statistical law . . . ; this equilibrium, however, is not the one to which economists are accustomed, but is the "steady state" of statistical mechanics which results from the balance of actions of a great number of particles.'[20] It is true that Steindl directs his inquiry at rather narrow and technical (albeit interesting) questions such as the most probable size or age of a firm. But his general introductory discussion of existing and potential applications of probabilistic models in economics, and his explanation of the notion of random variable in an economic setting, transcend that narrow range of problems and can serve as a good introduction to the probabilistic methodology in economics as a whole.

What we attempt to do in this book is to apply the probabilistic methodology, inspired (as Steindl points out) by the paradigm of statistical mechanics, to issues that lie at the core and foundation of political economy.[21]

The General Plan of this Work

We start by arguing that in a free market economy a state of equilibrium in which the rate of profit is uniform cannot exist. We introduce the alternative concept of dynamic equilibrium, in which the rate of profit is a random variable on an appropriate probability space. In developing this concept, we draw on an analogy with statistical mechanics—the classical analysis, due to Maxwell and Boltzmann, of the mass behaviour of large ensembles of randomly moving corpuscles. We discuss, under certain broad assumptions, the general form of the probability distribution function of the rate of profit. In fact, theoretical and empirical evidence suggests that the rate of profit has a so-called *gamma* distribution. We draw some interesting consequences from this conjecture.

Our next task is to set up a framework in which prices are represented as numerical values of a single random variable on the space of all commodity transactions. For this purpose we must first introduce the notion of *labour-content* as a measure of commodities, to which prices will be referred as ratios. We discuss the general conditions that such a measure must satisfy and, after considering various candidates for such a measure, we conclude that labour-content is the best, and in some sense the only reasonable candidate. We then take the ratio of price to labour-content—which we term *specific price*—as our random variable representing the price structure in the economy.

We then attempt to determine the general shape of the probability distribution of the specific price variable. We use here powerful theorems of probability theory that characterize probability distributions by means of their independence properties. We outline some arguments to suggest that specific price has a normal (Gaussian) distribution.

The probabilistic considerations outlined above lead to certain consequences and applications that are empirically testable. Some economic variables are seen to be strongly constrained in ways unforeseen by deterministic models. For example, the distribution of capital intensity is seen to be quite narrowly restricted, although in the conventional deterministic models it could theoretically assume any shape. A probabilistic relation between capital intensity and wage levels can also be derived. These and other conclusions are strongly corroborated by actual economic data.

Finally, we indicate directions and problems for further research —work that should help to put more flesh on the theoretical skeleton set up in the present essay.

Chapter One
Non-Uniformity of the Rate of Profit

We have seen that the assumption of a uniform rate of profit, as an idealized expression of equilibrium under perfect competition and of equality among the various portions of capital, is basic to all classical theories of prices and profit, including the traditional Marxist theory. The same is also true of neo-classical theories. Before we offer an alternative theorization of the rate of profit as a *random variable*, we would like to examine and criticize the uniformity assumption from both the mathematical and the economic points of view.

Ever since Adam Smith, economists have put forward various explanations for the observed deviation from uniformity. But most of those explanations associate differences in the rates of profit accruing to different firms or branches of production with some important but contingent structural *inequalities* between them, such as inequality of 'risk', or differences in the degree of monopolization. Explanations of this sort are of no interest to us here. Rather, we are interested in those random but necessary differences in rates of profit that must arise even if all firms are assumed to compete on an equal footing, in the sense that no lasting structural bias of the system favours any branch or firm.

We shall try to explain why the uniformity assumption is in principle incompatible with a theorization of the capitalist system as a system of free competition and private property in the means of production. Our objections are of two principal kinds—mathematical and economic. Each of these, by itself, would be sufficient to undermine the uniformity assumption as a legitimate reasonable abstraction from reality.

Mathematical Objections

In the following two chapters we shall see that the mathematical tools for dealing with a large and disorderly collection of moving objects are well developed, and that these methods can be adapted to the study of an economy comprising a multitude of economic units, acting in an uncoordinated way to secure their survival and to improve their relative position. In that connection, we shall illustrate by means of examples from physical science the fact that, in general, the short and long-term behaviour of such a system cannot be captured correctly by assuming that the movement of its constituent parts has reached a uniform average.

Here we shall raise a few preliminary elementary objections to the uniformity assumption. Let us assume that the *long-term average* rates of profit in different branches of production are equal or approximately equal. Does it then follow that at any *particular time* the rates of profit in different branches are clustered close together? By no means.

To illustrate this simple mathematical point, consider the following—admittedly, drastically simplified—example. Suppose there are just two branches, A and B, each with a capital of £1,000. Let us assume, moreover, that the amounts of capital remain the same over a period of ten years. During five years (not necessarily consecutive) out of the ten, branch A yields profit at 5% per annum, while branch B yields 35%. In the remaining five years the position is reversed: branch A yields 35% and branch B only 5%. The long-term average rate of profit (over the whole ten-year period) is the same for both branches: 20%, which is also the yearly average rate of profit of *both branches, taken together*. Yet, each year the rates of profit in the two branches are wide apart.

Is it, nevertheless, legitimate in a theoretical calculation to replace the different rates of profit by a single figure (their average) and pretend that there is just one uniform rate? The answer is that it depends on the precise use to which such a simplifying assumption is put. If—to continue our example—we want to calculate the *total* yearly profit, we get the same result, £400, whether we assume a uniform rate of 20% for the total capital of £2,000, or whether we take £1,000 at 5% plus another £1,000 at 35%. The result in this case is the same, because the total profit is a magnitude that depends solely on the average rate of profit and on the total amount of capital, but does not depend on the dispersion of the different rates of profit among the various portions of capital.

However, certain quantities are very sensitive to the dispersion of the rate of profit. Suppose that our A and B are not branches but individual firms. Suppose also that a firm must pay tax at the rate of 50% on all its annual profits, except on the first £150, which are not taxed. Therefore, a firm that makes a profit of 5% on its capital of £1,000 will pay no tax; while the other firm, which makes a profit of 35% in the same year, will pay £100 tax. (The firm's profits for the year amount to £350, of which £150 are tax-free and the remaining £200 are taxable at 50%.) The total tax paid each year is therefore £100. But if we assume that both firms make profits at a *uniform* rate of 20% per annum, then the yearly profit of each is £200, of which only £50 are taxable, so that each firm would pay £25 in tax, and the total tax paid (by both together) would be £50. We see that in this case the final result is drastically altered by assuming, contrary to fact, that the *average* rate of profit actually prevails as a *uniform* rate.

This last example merely highlights a simple mathematical fact, ignorance of which is a common source of fallacy. The fact is this: *a mathematical relation that holds among variable quantities does not, in general, hold between their respective averages.*[1]

The moral of this is that one must exercise extreme care in considering an ideal 'average' state as though it were a real functioning state, with the usual relations between various quantities. Without such care, one can fall into the same error as the poor statistician who drowned in a lake whose *average* depth was six inches.[2] To sum up this point: Even on the hypothesis that the *long-term* average rates of profit in different branches of production are equal,[3] it does not follow that at *any given time* there is a uniform, or nearly uniform, rate of profit. The uniformity assumption is an *additional* assumption, and a very drastic one at that, because it distorts those phenomena and relations that are sensitive to the dispersion of the rate of profit.

Our second objection is closely related to the first. Technically speaking, it concerns the question of *stability*—a question that mathematicians have been studying, in various forms and contexts, at least since the time of Laplace, who investigated it in connection with Newtonian celestial mechanics. In very general terms, it is a question about the behaviour of a system that is perturbed away from a state of equilibrium (as every real system usually is).

Suppose it is proved that some variable that describes the behaviour of a given theoretical system (model) assumes a particular numerical value (or, more generally, that a particular relation between several such variables holds) when the system is in a state of equilibrium. Does this result remain at least approximately correct when the system is slightly perturbed away from equilibrium? It turns out that—perhaps contrary to naive expectation—the answer is often negative.

Therefore, even if it were reasonable to assume the uniformity of the rate of profit for a state of equilibrium of a system with perfect competition, one must not jump to the conclusion that results deduced from this assumption remain approximately true for a non-equilibrium state. This caveat is especially pertinent in view of the undeniable fact that in reality the rates of profit of different firms, and even of different branches of a capitalist economy, are always quite far from uniformity.

Yet, as far as we know, none of the input-output theorists, for example, who use the uniformity assumption to deduce the prices of commodities 'at equilibrium', has ever attempted to show that the resulting prices are not strongly sensitive to slight variations in the rate of profit between branches. Had they raised this question, they would have found that in general their models may be quite sensitive to such variations, so that the results they prove have doubtful validity, even as first approximations, for the real world, in which rates of profit are not uniform.

Economic Objections

We must now raise another question, essentially economic rather than mathematical: is it theoretically sound to suppose that in an ideal state of equilibrium rates of profit would be uniform?

The concept of *economic equilibrium* is, of course, a construct of economic theory. What we are questioning is not the usefulness of such a construct in general, but a particular way of theorizing it. Whatever conditions are postulated for a state of equilibrium, any disparity between them and empirical reality must be explainable by the intervention of disequilibrating forces. Yet, even a cursory glance at the detailed economic statistics of an advanced capitalist country reveals that at any moment in time the disparity between rates of profit of different firms, or in different branches of production, is so large, that one begins to suspect that it cannot be explained by external constraints on free competition, or by mere deviation from equilibrium. Surely, the external inhibitions upon the mobility of capital cannot be so strong as to produce such an enormous 'deformation'. And what is the meaning of a putative state of 'equilibrium' if the real economy is *always* so very far from it?

One's suspicions are aroused still further upon closer examination of the real data.[4] It transpires that in reality rates of profit are at least as widely dispersed as certain other important economic parameters, such as the *rate of labour costs* (as measured by the ratio between a firm's total annual wage bill and its invested capital). Moreover, at least one parameter—the ratio of profits to labour costs (= the ratio between a firm's annual gross profit and its annual wage bill)—is much more narrowly distributed, and therefore much closer to uniformity, than the rate of profit. Yet, while economists since Adam Smith have repeatedly argued that the rate of profit must tend to uniformity, and at equilibrium must actually be uniform, their theories do not impose any limit on the dispersion of rates of labour-costs; nor do they explain why the ratio of profits to wages should be so close to uniformity.[5] What happens in reality is not explained by theory, while what theory tells us to expect does not actually occur.

Leaving empirical observations aside for the moment, let us take a closer look at the traditional theoretical argument that purports to show that in a state of equilibrium (under perfect competition) the rate of profit must be uniform. The argument consists of two parts, a premiss and a conclusion.

The *premiss* is that if the production of a particular type of commodity yields an abnormally high rate of profit, then competition will set in motion countervailing forces: capital will tend to crowd into the production of that type of commodity, leading eventually to its being over-produced; competition among its producers will then become fiercer, and its price will be forced down, bringing down also the rate of profit. Exactly the opposite process will operate if the initial rate of profit is abnormally low. The *conclusion* that is supposed to follow from this is that, as these processes play themselves out, the economy will tend towards (or oscillate around) a state of equilibrium in which all rates of profit are equalized.

While we do not wish to dispute the premiss of this argument, we claim that the supposed conclusion does not follow from it at all, and is in fact false. To see this, we must consider what is meant by a *state of equilibrium* of any system whatsoever. Stated in very general terms, a system is in a state of equilibrium when all its internal forces neutralize each other, so that if left to its own devices the system will continue in the same state, and will be perturbed away from it only under the influence of *external* forces.[6] If the state of equilibrium is stable, and the system is subjected to a small perturbation by external forces, the internal forces of the system create a negative feedback effect, pulling the system back towards equilibrium. The system will then either converge to that state of equilibrium or oscillate around it.

A simple and familiar mechanical example of such a system is provided by the pendulum. When at equilibrium, a pendulum hangs vertically downwards; and it remains at rest in this position unless it is subjected to external perturbation.[7] If externally perturbed, it will start to oscillate around its state of equilibrium. In the absence of friction, it would continue its oscillation for ever; but due to friction its oscillation is gradually dampened and the state of equilibrium is eventually restored. In the case of the pendulum, this state of equilibrium makes good sense *not* because such a state is necessarily ever reached—for, on the contrary, a real pendulum may perhaps be continually subjected to perturbations, and may therefore never come to rest—but because any departure from this state can always be ascribed to the action of *external* forces, different from the internal forces that tend to pull the pendulum towards equilibrium. The point is that this concept of equilibrium, ideal though it may be, does not violate the fundamental laws of motion of the pendulum itself.

Let us now return to a capitalist system in conditions of perfect competition. At first sight, this case may seem analogous to that of the pendulum, with a state of equilibrium here characterized by a uniform rate of profit. And so it has seemed to economic theorists since Adam Smith. The fact that in reality rates of profit are not uniform does not, in itself, seem to refute the assumption that in an ideal state of equilibrium they *would be* uniform—just as the oscillations of a continually perturbed pendulum do not refute the physical law that, in an ideal state of equilibrium, it would hang down motionless.[8]

But in fact there is a crucial difference between the two cases. For in a capitalist economy the very forces of competition, *which are internal to the system*, are responsible not only for pulling an abnormally high or low rate of profit back towards normality, *but also for creating such 'abnormal' rates of profit in the first place*. To make this crucial difference clearer, let us consider the following two 'thought experiments'.

The first thought experiment is concerned with a pendulum. Suppose that the pendulum is pinned down, by an external constraint, to its vertical position. Then imagine that the constraint is removed and the pendulum is left to its own devices, free from the intervention of external forces. What will happen? Clearly, the pendulum will persist at rest in its vertical position. *The persistence of this state is guaranteed by its being a state of equilibrium.*

Now consider an analogous thought experiment with a perfectly competitive capitalist economy. Suppose that, due to the intervention of some all-powerful planning authority, rates of profit are forced to be absolutely uniform throughout the economy for a couple of years; suppose also that other conditions which are traditionally thought to characterize a state of equilibrium are enforced. Then imagine that the external constraint is removed, and the economy is left to its own devices, shielded from external intervention. Perfect competition will then resume its unfettered operation. Will rates of profit then remain uniform for any length of time, or will the uniformity be rapidly scrambled by competition itself? Clearly, the latter; but then it follows that the initially enforced state could not possibly have been a state of equilibrium!

Indeed, under any reasonable theorization of the concept of competition, the competitive forces that tend to scramble rates of profit away from uniformity are at least as real and powerful as those that pull towards uniformity. For one thing, even if rates of profit were to start from an initial uniform level, this would not prevent the flow of new investment capital from one branch of production to another. This flow is motivated not only by past differences in rates of profit in different branches, but at least as much by conjectures about future demand for various products. For example, firms in the coffin-making business may decide to invest their profits in another branch, say in furniture-making, rather than expand the manufacture of coffins, not because that other branch is at present more profitable, but because they do not anticipate a growing demand for coffins.

But even leaving such considerations aside, there are various competitive strategies that have a 'scrambling' effect on the rate of profit. For example, a large motor-car manufacturing firm, wishing to maximize its profits *in the long run*, may actually price its products *down* in order to encourage demand, or in order to drive its competitors into bankruptcy. Such a price war may, in the short term, reduce rates of profit in this branch of production well below the general average. Nor can technical innovations be left out of account; after all, their introduction is motivated by competition. But such innovations, taking place at an uneven and uncoordinated pace, would clearly tend to scramble any putative uniformity in the rate of profit.

The general point to be grasped is the following: competition, by its very essence, is a disorderly process—and the freer it is, the more disorderly. Because of this, it would tend to destroy rather than preserve a uniformity in the rate of profit if such uniformity were ever imposed on the system. To expect competition to preserve an initial parity in rates of profit is as unreasonable as expecting all horses in a race to finish together just because they started together.

Therefore the lack of uniformity of the rates of profit that exists in reality cannot be wholly ascribed to the presence of constraints upon free competition; disparities would necessarily arise even in the absence of all constraints.

At first sight we might seem to contradict ourselves by accepting, on the one hand, that competition tends to reduce extremely high rates of profit and to boost rates that are very low—while at the same time asserting, on the other hand, that competition also tends to prevent the creation of uniformity. But in fact there is no contradiction. In the next chapter we shall make this clearer by showing how analogous, *seemingly* contradictory, behaviour is theorized in the science of statistical mechanics. Here we shall be satisfied with the following rough description of the 'contradictory' effect of free competition: Due to competition, *at any given time* the amount of capital yielding extreme rates of profit (whether extremely high or extremely low) is *relatively* small, and most chunks of capital that find themselves in such a position do not endure in it for very long; but at the same time competition continually gives rise to *new* disparities.

In conceptualizing economic equilibrium we must decide whether we wish to treat competition as an external perturbation or as an internal force. If it is the former, then one cannot invoke it to argue that in a state of equilibrium rates of profit would equalize. But if competition is regarded as internal—as it must be, since we want to capture the essence of a *competitive* system—then we cannot ignore its 'scrambling' effects.

An ideal state of equilibrium with a uniform rate of profit is a chimera—not merely because such a thing never happens in reality, but because if it did it would violate the basic laws of motion of the capitalist system and negate some of the very processes that make it tick. To posit such a state is tantamount to regarding competition as an internal force when it pulls in one direction (towards uniformity) and as an external perturbation when it pushes in the opposite direction (away from uniformity). This makes no more sense than if, in considering a pendulum, we were to regard the force of gravity as internal when the pendulum swings to the right (and gravity pulls it back towards the left), but as an external perturbing force when the pendulum swings to the left. Any conclusion drawn from such a hypothesis is likely to be not merely wrong, but wrong in a way that runs counter to some essential feature of the system in question.

If a competitive market economy has a state of equilibrium, it must be a state in which a whole range of profit rates coexist; it must be a *dynamic* state, in the sense that the rate of profit of each firm keeps changing all the time; it can only be a state of *equilibrium* in the sense that the *proportion* of capital (out of the total social capital) that yields any particular rate of profit remains approximately constant. (For example, one-eighth of the total social capital may steadily yield profits at rates under 3% per annum, but any *given* firm may belong to that unfortunate eighth one year, and to the remaining seven-eighths in the following year.)

This requires a new conceptualization of the whole system, which we shall undertake beginning in chapter III.

To conclude the present preliminary discussion, we must address ourselves to a question that may have occurred to the reader: given the great strength of the arguments against the assumption of uniformity, why has this assumption rooted itself so deeply in the economic tradition, and why is it still so widely used even by very modern schools, such as the Sraffians and other input-output theorists? While we do not have anything like a complete answer, we would like to mention, rather tentatively, some of the reasons that may have contributed to the persistence of the uniformity assumption.

First of all, while the traditional argument that purports to deduce the uniformity of the rate of profit from the assumption of free competition is fallacious, the fallacy is rather subtle and not easily detectable. It does become more obvious against the background of an alternative paradigm, of the kind provided by statistical mechanics; but statistical mechanics itself developed only in the second half of the nineteenth century, so the alternative paradigm was certainly not available to the old classical economists. Of course, even today knowledge of physical science is not too common among economists.

Moreover, it is no good objecting to the uniformity assumption if one is at a complete loss to propose a more reasonable alternative. Such an alternative is suggested by the paradigm of statistical mechanics; but, as we have just pointed out, it has remained beyond the ken even of most modern economists. Be that as it may, the fact is that although some economists have challenged the uniformity assumption, their objections were not (as far as we know) accompanied by an alternative theoretical framework, and went largely unheeded.

Another possible reason for the popularity of the uniformity assumption is its technical simplicity. The mathematics of input-output matrices with a uniform rate of profit is very attractive indeed, and so is the mathematics of the corresponding production function of the neo-classical school. This mathematical simplicity and elegance must have attracted economic theorists who were looking for a closed and neat algebraic or analytic model.

Another important factor may have been the lingering confusion concerning the very notion of the rate of profit. Historically, while the distinction between *profit* and *rent* (land rent) was well established in early classical economic thought, the *rate of profit* (on capital employed in production) has often been confused with the *rate of interest* (on loans or on financial assets). Now, the rate of interest, while never absolutely uniform, is clearly much closer to uniformity and much more secure than the rate of profit on industrial capital. The strong tendency to uniformity of the rate of interest may have fostered the illusion that a similar phenomenon would occur also with the rate of profit, provided that free competition were allowed to take its own course. Since interest is often regarded as the 'purest' form of profit in general, it is easy to fall into the error of believing that any deviation from uniformity in the rate of profit is an aberration of the system away from its ideal state, rather than an intrinsic feature of the system itself.[9]

The rate of profit is also easily confused with the *rate of return on stocks and shares*. In reality, however, they are quite different, since the value of a firm's operating capital (on which the rate of profit is computed) is quite different from the total stock-market value of its shares. Some stocks and shares pay a fixed rate of return, and are in fact just a form of ordinary *financial* capital. Equities, on the other hand, pay a variable dividend, but their *price* is determined in the light of expected future dividends, so as to yield an expected 'normal' rate of return. If the rate of profit is confused with these things, it is easy to form the illusion that in an ideal state of equilibrium rates of profit would equalize.

In addition to all these reasons, there is of course the weight of tradition itself. The uniformity assumption has such a distinguished pedigree, and has been repeated so often, that it has turned into a kind of obvious 'truth', which few people bother to question.

Leaving all this aside, let us turn to consider a radically different theoretical framework.

Chapter Two
A Paradigm: Statistical Mechanics

At the 'microscopic' or 'molecular' level, a fair-sized competitive capitalist economy presents a picture of enormous complexity and disorder. Tens of thousands of firms and tens of millions of workers and individual consumers are engaged in producing and exchanging a huge assortment of commodities. It is estimated that about 60,000 different chemicals are regularly produced for the market; the number of different commodities of all kinds must run into millions. The actions of any two firms or consumers are in general almost independent of each other, although each depends to a very considerable extent on the sum total of the actions of all the rest. Each investment of capital, each transaction in the market, is affected by a great variety of social, technical and economic causes, influenced by innumerable individual motives and volitions and subject to countless imponderable accidental circumstances.

The global 'macroscopic' behaviour of such a system therefore emerges as the summation of a vast number of uncoordinated individual 'microscopic' processes and events, each impelled by many causes and motives. Even if we assume—an assumption of extreme determinism—that *in principle* it ought to be possible to trace each of the microscopic processes, events and causes and by summing them arrive at the global laws governing the macroscopic phenomena, it is clear that such a task is in practice beyond human capability: the number of microscopic components and processes is simply far too large, the individual events cannot be observed with sufficient precision, and the causal relations governing them are far from being completely known. Besides, such a deterministic procedure of summation, even if it were feasible, would be very wasteful indeed; a complete description of the microscopic state of the system must involve the determination of an astronomic number of parameters, while its macroscopic state involves only a small number of parameters. One and the same macroscopic state is produced by a large set of different (but in some sense essentially similar) microscopic states. Therefore, from the macroscopic point of view, a complete description and analysis of the system down to the last microscopic detail is largely irrelevant.

It is therefore generally admitted that any global 'macroscopic' laws governing profits, prices and other economic magnitudes must bear a statistical character, and that probabilistic considerations must be used in deducing such laws. Indeed, this is recognized even by the various traditional economic theories. Thus, the very notions of average ('equilibrium') rate of profit and natural ('equilibrium') prices are avowedly statistical in nature. However, those theories do not introduce explicit probabilistic elements into the quantitative-mathematical models that they set up. Statistical arguments appear only verbally, in the preliminary discussion (for example, in justifying the notion of an ideal uniform rate of profit); but once a quantitative or mathematical model is set up, these arguments disappear from the foreground, and the model itself is completely deterministic.[1] Inevitably, the probabilistic element in such theories is always crude and very often quite erroneous.

In order to remedy these defects we must set up mathematical models in which probabilistic considerations play an explicit central role, so that, for example, profit and price appear not as quantities that are fixed at any moment of time, but as so-called random variables, each with its own probability distribution.

In setting up such a theory, it will be instructive to look at another branch of science, in which similar methods are long established, well developed and highly successful; we are referring to *statistical mechanics*, first developed by Maxwell and Boltzmann over one hundred years ago. Of course, we do not propose simply to transcribe the theorems of statistical mechanics into economic language. Rather, we would like to use the methods of that science as a rough and general guide, and to point out broad analogies that can serve to illuminate certain economic problems and arguments, including some of the points discussed in the introduction. We shall also use this setting to introduce some of the probabilistic ideas and techniques, which we shall later apply in an economic context. (A reader who is unfamiliar with statistical mechanics need not panic: no detailed knowledge of that subject will be required, and the ideas referred to will be explained in an elementary way.)

The purpose of statistical mechanics is to explain the macroscopic physical properties and behaviour of material systems consisting of a very large number of elementary constituent particles. The simplest (and oldest) example of such a treatment concerns the physical behaviour of gases under various (and varying) conditions of temperature and pressure. (The theory in fact reduces these macroscopically observable parameters, temperature and pressure, via a statistical analysis, to the microscopic behaviour of the molecules of which a gas is made up.) The theoretical model used for this purpose is that of an *ideal gas*, to which we shall now turn.

Consider a quantity of 'gas' enclosed in a container, which for the sake of simplicity we imagine to be cubic in shape. The ideal gas is supposed to consist of a vast number of particles, or 'molecules'. In the simplest cases, that of a simple monatomic gas, which is the only one we need to consider here, these particles are all identical and have no constituent parts of their own.[2]

Let us suppose that the system is isolated: the container is hermetically closed and thermally insulated; the volume and temperature of the gas (and hence also its pressure) remain constant. Even if initially perturbed, the system will eventually reach a state of equilibrium. This does not mean, however, that the particles of the gas will come to rest; on the contrary, they persist in vigorous motion, ever colliding with each other and with the walls of the vessel. Thus each particle continuously changes its position, and frequently (many thousands of times each second) also its speed and direction as a result of these collisions.

The heat energy of the gas (a macroscopic quantity) is explained as the sum total of the energy of motion of its particles, so that (roughly speaking) the hotter the gas, the more frantically they rush about. Another important macroscopic quantity, the pressure exerted by the gas on the walls of the container, is similarly explained in microscopic terms: the pressure is the sum total of the impact of the vast number of particles continually colliding with the walls.

This so-called thermal motion of the gas particles is totally disordered and uncoordinated: at any given moment the motions of any two particles are quite independent, except if they happen to collide at that very moment. Nevertheless, what any one particle is doing depends very much on what all the rest, taken together, are doing at the time. This is because of the law of conservation of energy, according to which the total energy of motion of the system remains constant. (If the thermal insulation is not perfect, the total energy may change, but if this happens comparatively slowly the effects of energy seepage may be neglected at a first approximation.) Thus all the particles compete with each other for a share in the same pool of energy. If one particle moves unusually fast, appropriating an unusually big share of energy, other particles must move more slowly. The energy of any given particle at a given moment must be equal to the total energy of the system minus the sum of the energies of all the other particles. (Here there is a broad analogy with the disordered and uncoordinated microscopic behaviour of a competitive capitalist economy. As we shall see in chapter VII, the protagonists in such an economy compete with each other over a common—constant or slowly changing—pool of productive resources and purchasing power.)

As we shall see, there is no way in which the macroscopic behaviour of our gas can be described, even in broad qualitative terms, by a theory that assumes that in a state of equilibrium all particles travel at the same speed. On the other hand, it is neither feasible nor necessary to follow the detailed motion of each particle. We shall therefore outline the development of a *probabilistic* theory, which takes into account the diversity of the particles' motions, without, however, having to treat them individually.

Let us consider how the microscopic state of our ideal gas may be described. Suppose there are n particles altogether (where n is a very large number); let us label them with numbers: $1, 2, \ldots, n$. The set of particles (or, equivalently but somewhat more abstractly, the set of labels) will be our *sample space*. (The word 'space' here has no connotation of physical or geometric space; the term *sample space* is taken from probability theory, where it is used to denote the population of objects under study.) Let us fix a point of time, t. Unless otherwise stated, this t will remain fixed throughout our discussion.

As a first step towards describing the microscopic state of the gas at time t, we must specify the position of each particle in three-dimensional space (ordinary *real* space). The position of a *single* particle may be specified by means of a triple of coordinate-numbers (x, y, z), where the first coordinate, x, is the (shortest) distance of the particle from the left ('western') wall of the container, y is similarly the distance of the particle from the front ('southern') wall, and z is the height of the particle above the floor of the container. However, we need to specify the position not of one particle but simultaneously of all n particles. For this purpose we use, instead of a triple of *numbers* (x, y, z), a triple of *mappings* (X, Y, Z).

Let us explain in detail the meaning of the mapping Z. (The other two, X and Y, are entirely analogous and can be explained in a similar way.) Our Z is not a number, but a mapping (that is, a function, a law of correspondence) that assigns to each of the numbers 1, 2, ..., n a particular real number. Namely, if i is any one of the numbers 1, 2, ..., n, then the number assigned to i by Z—denoted by $Z(i)$—is the third coordinate (the height) of the i-th particle at the fixed moment t. Similarly, $X(i)$ and $Y(i)$ are respectively the first and second coordinates of the i-th particle.

In technical jargon one says that Z is a *real-valued mapping over the sample space*, or a *real-valued mapping whose domain is the sample space*. This simply means that $Z(i)$ is defined whenever i represents a member of the sample space (that is, in our case a particle) and that the value of $Z(i)$ is always a real number. The same applies, of course, to X and Y.

The triple (X, Y, Z) is not yet sufficient to describe the microscopic state of our gas. But before proceeding to complete the description we pause to introduce some basic probabilistic equipment. Again, we shall deal in detail with the mapping Z; the other two, X and Y, can be treated in an entirely similar way.

For any set A of real numbers, we can talk of the *probability* that Z falls in A, briefly: $\mathbf{P}(Z$ in A$)$. This has the following meaning: Suppose we are going to select at random one particle, say the i-th, out of our sample space—imagine for example that out of a well-shuffled pack of n cards bearing the labels 1, 2, ..., n, we intend to pull one card, and let i be the label on this card—then $\mathbf{P}(Z$ in A$)$ is the probability that the real number $Z(i)$ will happen to belong to the set A.

Since every particle has an equal chance of being selected,[3] it is clear that

$$\mathbf{P}(Z \text{ in A}) = \frac{m}{n},$$

where *m* is the number of those particles for which $Z(i)$ does belong to A. In other words, $P(Z \text{ in A})$ is equal to the *proportion*, out of the whole sample space, of those particles for which $Z(i)$ is in A.

In most, if not all, cases that we shall come across, the set A of real numbers will be defined by means of inequalities. In this connection we use a fairly self-evident notation, which we shall now illustrate by a few examples. If *r* is any real number, then by $P(Z \leq r)$ we mean the same as $P(Z \text{ in A})$, where now A is specifically the set of all real numbers less than or equal to *r*. Similarly, $P(Z > r)$ is the same as $P(Z \text{ in B})$, where B is the set of all reals greater than *r*. If *s* is another real number, then $P(r \leq Z \leq s)$ is the same as $P(Z \text{ in C})$, where C is the set of all reals in the range from *r* to *s*, inclusive. Thus, to take a more specific example, $P(0 \leq Z \leq \frac{1}{2})$ is the probability that if we select a particle at random, its height (from the floor of the container) will be between 0 and $\frac{1}{2}$ units of length. By the way, since the height of a particle cannot be negative, $P(0 \leq Z \leq \frac{1}{2})$ is clearly equal to $P(Z \leq \frac{1}{2})$.

We now define the *cumulative distribution function of Z*, *denoted* by F_Z. This is a real-valued function of one real variable, defined by the identity

$$F_Z(r) = P(Z \leq r) \quad \text{for all real } r.$$

With these definitions, our *Z* is now elevated to the status of a *random variable*. In general, a random variable is any mapping over a sample space, for which a cumulative distribution function (c.d.f.) can be defined in the same way as we have done for *Z*.

In exactly the same way, we can regard *X* and *Y* as random variables, and define their cumulative distribution functions F_X and F_Y. All the information concerning the *macroscopic* state of the system is contained in such distribution functions. On the other hand, these functions tell us nothing about the state of any individual particle.

Certain simple properties of the function F_Z follow easily from its definition.

First, for any *r*, $F_Z(r)$ is a probability of some event, and must therefore be a number between 0 and 1, inclusive. Second, F_Z is a *non-decreasing* function: if $r \leq s$ then $F_Z(r) \leq F_Z(s)$. This is because if $r \leq s$ then any particle that satisfies the condition $Z(i) \leq r$

must also satisfy the condition $Z(i) \leq s$. (This property in fact expresses the *cumulative* character of F_Z.)

These two properties hold, quite generally, for the cumulative distribution function (c.d.f.) of any random variable (defined over any sample space whatsoever). The following three properties, however, depend on the particular nature of our present sample space and the random variable Z, and do not necessarily apply to other cases.

Since the gas particles are all assumed to be *inside* the cube-shaped vessel, the height of a particle (measured from the bottom of the vessel) cannot be negative. It follows that if r is any negative number, then $F_Z(r) = 0$. Similarly, if the edges of our cube are d units long, then the height of every particle is at most d, so that $F_Z(d) = 1$. Hence also, if r is any number greater than d, we have $F_Z(r) = 1$.

Finally, since our sample space is finite (the number of particles, n, is finite, albeit very large), Z can only assume a finite number of different values (in fact, at most n) at any time. It follows from this that F_Z must be a *step function* : it has a finite number of jumps, and between two consecutive jumps it is constant. Let us illustrate this by means of a simplified example: Suppose that the number of particles, n, instead of being vast, is just 4, and suppose that (at the moment t under consideration) the heights of these particles are 0, $\frac{1}{3}$, $\frac{1}{2}$ and 2 respectively; then the reader can easily verify that F_Z has the graph shown in fig. 1.

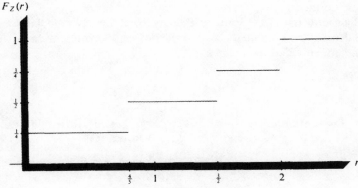

Figure 1.   Graph of a c.d.f. ($n = 4$)

The step-like shape of the c.d.f. creates a technical-mathematical difficulty: we should like to make use of the powerful techniques of the calculus, but these are very poorly adapted to dealing with functions having too many discontinuities. Fortunately, for very large n —which is the case we are interested in—the shape of F_Z very closely approximates a smooth curve, because (unlike the simplified case of fig. 1) the number of steps is very large, while the jumps between successive steps, as well as the width of each step, are extremely small. The graph of F_Z will look perfectly smooth to the naked eye, and its step-like shape can only be detected by a powerful microscope. We shall therefore pretend that F_Z is smooth; the error involved in making this assumption is for all practical purposes quite negligible.[4]

The new assumption we have just made enables us to introduce our next probabilistic concept: the *probability density function* (p.d.f.) of Z, denoted by f_Z. We define $f_Z(r)$ to be the derivative of $F_Z(r)$ with respect to r.

The meaning of f_Z is the following: for each r, the value $f_Z(r)$ measures the average density of the particles at height r. More precisely, for each r and for small[5] positive h, the product $hf_Z(r)$ is the best first approximation to the probability $P(r \leq Z \leq r + h)$. Another way of putting it is that if a and b are any two numbers[6] such that $a \leq b$, then

$$P(a \leq Z \leq b) = \int_a^b f_Z(r)\, dr. \qquad \text{(See fig. 2.)}$$

The *mean* or *average* value of Z, also called the *expected* value of Z, is denoted by EZ and defined in the obvious way: it is the sum of all the $Z(i)$ divided by n. Thus

$$EZ = \frac{\Sigma Z(i)}{n},$$

where the summation is from $i = 1$ to $i = n$. Let us note that EZ can be expressed in terms of the p.d.f. f_Z as follows:

$$EZ = \int_{-\infty}^{\infty} rf_Z(r)\, dr.$$

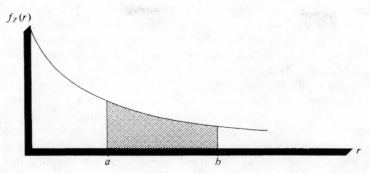

Figure 2. The curve is the graph of the p.d.f. f_Z of some random variable Z. The darkened area is the integral of f_Z from a to b, and is also equal to the probability $P(a \leq Z \leq b)$.

(Such a formula holds in fact for any random variable for which a p.d.f. can be defined. However, in our case, since $F_Z(r) = 0$ for all negative r and $F_Z(r) = 1$ for all $r \geq d$, where d is the length of the edge of our cube, it follows that $f_Z(r)$ vanishes everywhere except in the interval from 0 to d, so that in our case it is enough to take the integral in this formula from 0 to d rather than from $-\infty$ to ∞.)

Our discussion so far has referred to a fixed instant of time. However, as time flows, the particles move in the vessel, so that for each i the height $Z(i)$ changes with time. Thus the random variable Z and the functions F_Z and f_Z all vary in time. (The same of course holds for X and Y and their c.d.f.'s and p.d.f.'s.) Similarly, the means EX, EY and EZ also change with time.

However, if our gas has already reached a state of equilibrium, then macroscopic changes of density in any part of the vessel are highly improbable. This means that if A is any non-microscopic portion of the interior of the vessel, the number of particles in A remains virtually unchanged in time. By saying that A is *non-microscopic* we mean that although it may be quite small, it still contains a very large number of particles. By saying that the number of particles in A remains *virtually* unchanged we mean that any likely *change* in the number of particles in A is negligible in relation to that number itself; thus if at one moment there are m particles in A and after some time the number has increased to $m + k$ or fallen to $m - k$, then k will in all probability be negligibly small in proportion to m. This does not mean that the same *particles* remain in A; quite the contrary, even at moderate temperatures the turnover of particles will be very fast (if A is not too large). It is only their *number* that remains virtually constant.

It is not difficult to show that what we have just said amounts to the following: *In a state of equilibrium, the c.d.f.'s F_X, F_Y and F_Z remain virtually unchanged in time; at the macroscopic level their variation in time is negligible, and they can therefore be regarded as time-independent.* Indeed, this italicized statement may be taken as part of the definition of the term 'equilibrium' in relation to the system under consideration.

It follows from this that in a state of equilibrium the corresponding p.d.f.'s f_X, f_Y and f_Z, as well as the averages $\mathbf{E}X$, $\mathbf{E}Y$ and $\mathbf{E}Z$, remain virtually unchanged in the same sense.

It is important to understand that, for a system such as the one we are dealing with, the very concept of equilibrium is purely macroscopic. In a state of equilibrium the system is macroscopically placid, but at the microscopic level there is pandemonium. (Microscopic agitation would cease, according to classical theory, when the temperature is down to absolute zero, which is about $-273°C$, but absolute zero is not attainable.)

Thus, for each i, the height $Z(i)$ of the i-th particle will continue to change, and at times will change very fast, even if the system as a whole is in equilibrium. The same applies of course to $X(i)$ and $Y(i)$.

Let us now fix i; that is, we choose an arbitrary particle, say the i-th, and focus our attention on it for a time. We wish to consider the average of the values that $Z(i)$ goes through in a given duration T of time, say from $t = 0$ to $t = T$. This *time average* is conceptually very different from the *space average* of Z, which we have called $\mathbf{E}Z$. In the former, i is held fixed, t is allowed to vary, and the averaging is performed over all t from 0 to T; in the latter, time is held fixed and i allowed to vary, so that the averaging is performed over the whole sample space. (The term *space average* thus refers to the sample space, not to physical real space.)

Mathematically, the time average in question is given by the expression

$$\frac{1}{T} \int\limits_0^T Z(i)\,dt.$$

Statistical mechanics asserts that *if the system is in equilibrium, then for virtually all i (that is, with negligibly few exceptions) this time average will, as T increases, approach the space average EZ as a limit. Thus, for virtually all i and for a sufficiently long[7] time duration T, the time average in question will be as near the space average EZ as makes no difference. The same holds also for the corresponding averages of X and Y.*

This is one of a number of *ergodic principles*, which theories of statistical mechanics either postulate or attempt to deduce from more elementary assumptions.[8]

Note that, as a consequence of this principle, the time averages of the positions of two distinct particles (taken over a sufficiently long duration of time) are in virtually all cases approximately equal. This is a reflection of the fact (or the assumption) that all particles are essentially equivalent *in the long term*, and behave in much the same way, *statistically*.

The reader who has patiently followed us so far may at this stage feel the need for some comic relief. Partly to satisfy this need and partly for a more serious purpose, let us try to ape what the economists do. Let us try to postulate a state of equilibrium in which (in addition to the conditions stated so far, namely that the p.d.f.'s of X, Y, Z and their space averages are time-independent and that the above ergodic law holds) all the $X(i)$, $Y(i)$ and $Z(i)$ actually assume their average values. This is analogous to what the economists do when they posit in their models a uniform rate of profit, which they justify by arguing that the average rates of profit in different branches of production must in the long run tend to equalize. But what would happen in such a supposed state of equilibrium? All the particles of the gas would have to be in exactly the same point somewhere inside the vessel, and hang there motionless for ever!

One does not need to be a physicist to realize that this violates a basic classical physical principle: you cannot have more than one body in the same place at the same time.[9] Several other physical laws are also violated by our hasty postulate; but enough said.

Although our last tentative postulate of equilibrium has proved to be disastrously over-ambitious, and cannot therefore be used as such, we may still hope that it can perhaps be used to yield certain correct results. After all, it is by no means uncommon in science that an assumption that is known to be factually false can nevertheless be used, within proper limits, to yield good approximations to certain verifiable results.[10]

Well, let us see. Let us attempt to compute the (gravitational) potential energy of our gas. (We are assuming that our container is here on Earth rather than in outer space.) The potential energy of a given particle (at a given time t) is equal to the energy that would have been needed to lift the particle, against the pull of gravity, from the bottom of the vessel to its actual position (and the same energy would be released as kinetic energy if the particle were to fall from its actual position to the bottom). Furthermore, energy is *additive*: the potential energy of the whole gas is simply the sum of the potential energies of all its particles.

Now, for a container of moderate size, the potential energy of the i-th particle can be written as $kZ(i)$, where k is a constant that depends only on the mass of the particle, and is therefore the same for all our particles, since we assume them to be physically identical. To obtain the total potential energy, we must sum the expression $kZ(i)$ over all i. We get $k(Z(1) + Z(2) + \cdots + Z(n))$, and since the sum in brackets is $n\mathbf{E}Z$, we find that the total potential energy is $kn\mathbf{E}Z$.

Next, let us suppose—contrary to fact and common sense—that all the particles are simultaneously occupying their average position. Then the height of *all* the particles is the same: $\mathbf{E}Z$, and hence the potential energy of each particle would be $k\mathbf{E}Z$, and the total is n times this, namely $kn\mathbf{E}Z$. We get the same answer, the *right* answer!

Before the reader rushes to the conclusion that our economist friends were right after all, let us hasten to point out that this coincidence of the two results is indeed merely a coincidence; it depends on a very special property of the expression for potential energy, namely its linearity. To explain this, we need to pose the problem in a more general way.

Let g be any real-valued function of one variable. Starting from our random variable Z and the function g, we can define a new random variable U by putting, for each i,

$$U(i) = g(Z(i)).$$

This new random variable may be denoted by $g(Z)$. (A similar procedure can be applied, naturally, to any given random variable, not just to our particular Z.) Let us consider the total value of U, that is the sum $(U(1) + U(2) + \cdots + U(n))$. The *average* value of U, namely EU, is (by definition) equal to this total value, divided by n. Hence the total value of U is nEU.

Now let us try to calculate the total value of U on the (false) assumption that all the particles simultaneously occupy their average position. In this case we would have $Z(i) = EZ$ for all i, and hence $U(i) = g(Z(i)) = g(EZ)$ for all i. It follows that under this assumption the total value of U would be equal to $ng(EZ)$. Clearly, this would be the same as the correct total value of U, which we know to be nEU, if *and only if* $EU = g(EZ)$. Since we have denoted U by $g(Z)$, this last equality can be written in the form

$$Eg(Z) = g(EZ),$$

and it is rather tempting to think that it must be true.[11] However, this is by no means the case, generally speaking. In general the numbers $Eg(Z)$ and $g(EZ)$ are different, and may even be very far apart. Whether they are equal or not depends very much on the particular function g as well as on the shape of the c.d.f. F_Z. There is, however, a special case in which the equality in question can, quite easily, be shown to hold: namely, when g is a *linear* function, which means that $g(r) = kr + c$ for all r, where k and c are constants independent of r.

Looking again at our calculation of the total potential energy, we notice that potential energy is actually a random variable $U = g(Z)$, where g is given by the identity $g(r) = kr$. Thus g here is a linear function (with $c = 0$); and it is because of *this* that we happened to get the right answer for the total potential energy from an incorrect assumption about equilibrium.

We remarked above that the random variables, X, Y and Z are not sufficient for a complete description of the microscopic state of our gas at a given moment of time. The description can be completed using three additional random variables, $\mathring{X}$, $\mathring{Y}$ and $\mathring{Z}$, defined as follows: $\mathring{X}(i)$, $\mathring{Y}(i)$ and $\mathring{Z}(i)$ are (for each i) the derivatives, with respect to time, of $X(i)$, $Y(i)$ and $Z(i)$ respectively. (Recall that, for each i, the coordinates $X(i)$, $Y(i)$ and $Z(i)$ of the i-th particle change in time, as the particle moves.)

It takes only a slight familiarity with applied mathematics to recognize that $\mathring{X}(i)$, $\mathring{Y}(i)$ and $\mathring{Z}(i)$ are in fact the three components of the velocity of the i-th particle in the three coordinate directions: 'east', 'north' and 'up' respectively.

These velocity random variables have, of course, their own c.d.f.'s, p.d.f.'s and space averages. In a state of equilibrium, these c.d.f.'s, p.d.f.'s and averages may be assumed to be virtually independent of time, just as in the case of the position random variables X, Y, Z. Also, ergodic principles similar to those applying to the position variables are taken to apply to the velocity variables.

In terms of the six basic random variables (representing position and velocity) we can define other variables, representing various important physical quantities. For example, *speed* is represented by a random variable V, defined as follows:

$$V(i) = (\mathring{X}(i)^2 + \mathring{Y}(i)^2 + \mathring{Z}(i)^2)^{1/2} \quad \text{for each } i.$$

Thus $V(i)$, the speed of the i-th particle, is equal to the square root of the sum of the squares of the three components of the velocity of that particle.[12]

We have introduced these concepts here for the purpose of drawing a very suggestive analogy. The speed-behaviour of the gas particles is in fact quite reminiscent of the profit-behaviour of firms in a competitive capitalist economy. Because of the incessant collisions of the particles with each other, a particle cannot for long maintain an exceptionally high or exceptionally low speed. If it travels much faster than most of the others, it will soon be slowed down by collisions with them (imagine someone trying to run fast in a slow-moving crowd . . .) and if it moves much more slowly than most, it will soon gather speed as a result of being buffeted by faster particles.

Is it therefore reasonable to assume that in a state of equilibrium all the particles move at the same, or nearly the same, speed? Above we compared the economists' hypothesis of the uniformity of the rate of profit to the totally unrealistic assumption that all the particles of our gas are simultaneously at the *same point of space*. In this we were being somewhat unfair. The economists' hypothesis is really much more similar to the assumption that the particles all move at the *same speed*.

This comparison seems most apt, not only because of the general analogy between profit and speed, but more especially because the assumption of a uniform rate of profit does not seem, on the face of it, to violate any fundamental economic law, just as the assumption that the particles all have the same speed does not seem, to someone unfamiliar with physics, to violate a basic physical law. Indeed, while any non-specialist can see that all the particles cannot possibly be simultaneously in the same place, there is no apparent impossibility about them all travelling at the same speed (though perhaps in different directions).

But in fact the assumption of a uniform speed (at a state of equilibrium) does violate a basic physical law, *the second law of thermodynamics*, known also as *the law of entropy*. This asserts that in a state of equilibrium the *degree of disorder* of an isolated physical system, measured by a quantity called *entropy*, must assume its greatest possible value (that is, the maximum value compatible with the constraints under which the system is operating). A state in which all the particles travel at the same speed is much too 'orderly' to be a state of equilibrium. If the particles were ever compelled, by external intervention, to travel at the same speed, then their collisions with each other and with the walls of the vessel (analogous to free competition . . .) would soon scramble this excessive order, and restore a state of equilibrium in which the p.d.f. f_V has a characteristic form, discovered by Maxwell. The assumption in question is therefore completely untenable.

The economists who assume a uniform rate of profit can be said, figuratively speaking, to ignore the 'law of entropy' regarding a system of perfect competition. This is indeed a rather subtle point and Marx (along with the other old classical economists) may be excused for not noticing the fallacy. But the modern mathematical economists, many of whom must have been exposed to statistical mechanics at least as students, cannot be so easily exonerated.

Returning to our ideal gas, let us show that the assumption of equal speed leads to the wrong result in calculating the *kinetic energy* of the gas. This is a matter of some importance, because a correct determination of the kinetic energy is one of the main purposes of the whole theory.

The kinetic energy of the i-th particle is the energy that would have been needed to accelerate it from rest (speed zero) to its actual speed. Elementary mechanics tells us that this kinetic energy is proportional to the square of the speed, and can therefore be written as $k(V(i))^2$, where k is a constant equal to half the mass of the particle. Since all the particles are assumed to have the same mass, it is easy to see that the total kinetic energy of the gas is

$$nk\,\mathsf{E}(V^2),$$

which is n times k times the average of the square of the speed. However, if we assume (falsely) that the particles are all moving at the same speed, then $V(i) = \mathsf{E}V$ for all i, and the total kinetic energy would be

$$nk\,(\mathsf{E}V)^2.$$

This is different from the correct answer, because $\mathsf{E}(V^2)$ is *not* equal to $(\mathsf{E}V)^2$. (Notice that V^2 is *not linear but quadratic* in V.) In fact, the difference $\mathsf{E}(V^2) - (\mathsf{E}V)^2$ is of great importance in statistical analysis; it is known as the *variance* of the random variable V, and its square root is the *standard deviation* of V.

According to classical mechanics, if we make precise assumptions about the nature of the collisions of the particles with each other and with the walls of the vessel and if the six basic random variables X, Y, Z, $\mathring{X}$, $\mathring{Y}$, $\mathring{Z}$ are completely known at one moment in time (that is, if the values $X(i)$, $Y(i)$, etc. are known for each i at one moment in time) then, using Newton's equations of motion, we could in principle calculate precisely the evolution of these six variables through all time. Starting from an arbitrary initial position, we could follow such a calculation through and would then be able to calculate the c.d.f.'s, the p.d.f.'s and average values of our six variables at a state of equilibrium.

However, such a calculation is far beyond practical possibility. Besides, as we have pointed out, it would require very detailed (and questionable) assumptions about the nature of the microscopic interactions (collisions).

Fortunately, statistical mechanics is able to cut through these impossibly detailed calculations, and by using very broad (and plausible) *probabilistic* assumptions to arrive at the required equilibrium c.d.f.'s, p.d.f.'s and average values of the basic variables (as well as of other random variables defined by means of them, such as speed). For example, it is fairly evident that in a state of equilibrium the particles must be (virtually) evenly spread out as between 'west' and 'east'. From this it follows very easily that the density $f_X(r)$ must be constant for r between 0 and d (where d is the length of the edge of our cube). For negative r and for r greater than d we must always have $f_X(r) = 0$, since all the particles are *inside* the cube. The integral of f_X as r goes from 0 to d must be 1. From all this it is very easy to see that, at equilibrium, f_X is given by the formula

$$f_X(r) = \begin{cases} 1/d & \text{for } r \text{ between 0 and } d, \\ 0 & \text{elsewhere.} \end{cases}$$

And from this it follows that the equilibrium average value $\mathbf{E}X$ must be $d/2$, which is clear in any case.

Exactly the same considerations apply to Y. The case of Z, however, is rather different. Because of gravity, we must expect the particles to be unevenly spread out from bottom to top: there will clearly be fewer of them nearer the top and more nearer the bottom. The calculation of f_Z therefore requires greater effort, but is nevertheless not too difficult.

The equilibrium average values $\mathbf{E}\overset{\circ}{X}$, $\mathbf{E}\overset{\circ}{Y}$, $\mathbf{E}\overset{\circ}{Z}$ must all be 0, for reasons of symmetry. As for the equilibrium p.d.f.'s of $\overset{\circ}{X}$, $\overset{\circ}{Y}$ and $\overset{\circ}{Z}$, they can be shown (using fairly high-powered probability theory, but very weak physical assumptions) to be *normal* (having the familiar bell-shaped Gaussian curve).[13] From this it is not too difficult to deduce that the p.d.f. of the speed V must, at equilibrium, be the celebrated Maxwell function.

The details of these deductions need not concern us here.[14] What we would like to stress is the general message: by means of probabilistic reasoning one can arrive at remarkably strong and informative results concerning the equilibrium behaviour of a 'chaotic' system, without having to rely on unduly strong and questionable assumptions concerning the detailed microscopic behaviour of the elementary components of the system. In fact, the development of statistical mechanics has shown that the macroscopic behaviour of such a system depends surprisingly little—much less than envisaged even by Maxwell and Boltzmann—on the precise nature of the microscopic interactions of its particles, but more on the very fact that the system itself is made up of a very large number of constituent parts and, microscopically speaking, has a very large number of 'degrees of freedom'.[15]

Chapter Three
The Rate of Profit as a Random Variable

Before proceeding to apply probabilistic methods of the kind outlined in the previous chapter in the field of economic theory, we must first forestall a rather obvious objection to the legitimacy of such an approach.

How can methods borrowed from statistical *mechanics* be applicable to political economy, which is a *social* science? Surely, an economy—unlike a gas—cannot be regarded as a mechanical system made up of mindless particles. Economic activity is a conscious activity of human beings, motivated by human aims and impelled by human volition; nothing can be more different from the blind collision of material particles.

This objection is founded on a misunderstanding. As Khinchin observes: 'The specific character of the systems studied in statistical mechanics consists mainly in the enormous number of degrees of freedom which these systems possess. Methodologically, this means that the standpoint of statistical mechanics is determined not by the mechanical nature, but by the particle structure of matter. It almost seems as if the purpose of statistical mechanics is to observe how far reaching are the deductions made on the basis of the atomic structure of matter, irrespective of the nature of these atoms and the laws of their interaction.'[1]

The number of *degrees of freedom* of a system is, by definition, the number of independent parameters whose values and rates of change must be specified by a complete description of a microscopic state of the system.

For example, in the previous chapter we saw that in order to describe the state of our simple model of monatomic gas consisting of n particles, we need to specify the values of $3n$ parameters, namely

$X(i)$, $Y(i)$, $Z(i)$ as well as $\overset{\circ}{X}(i)$, $\overset{\circ}{Y}(i)$, $\overset{\circ}{Z}(i)$ for every i from 1 to n. If a system is subject to a constraint in the form of an equation between the parameters, then the latter are not independent, because the equation may be solved for one of the parameters; that is, one parameter can be expressed in terms of the others. This reduces the number of degrees of freedom by one. (Note that a constraint expressed by an inequality rather than a strict equation does not reduce the numbers of degrees of freedom. Thus the fact that the position coordinates $X(i)$, $Y(i)$, $Z(i)$ must all lie between 0 and d has no effect on the number of degrees of freedom of our ideal gas, although it obviously affects the macroscopic shape of the system.)

Turning to economics, we observe that the number of parameters required to specify the microscopic state of a fair-sized economy is very large indeed. They include, for example, the amounts of the various types of commodity produced and sold (during a unit of time, say one day) by each firm and the prices at which they are sold, as well as the quantities of the various inputs (including labour-power) that each firm buys per day and the prices at which these are bought. Also, for each worker-consumer we must specify the amount of labour-power sold by that worker (that is, the number of hours per day spent in employment) and the daily wage obtained, as well as the quantities of each kind of consumer good bought by the worker and the price paid for each. Many other parameters must also be specified. True, the parameters are not all independent, but must satisfy certain more or less obvious equations. For example, the total amount of any given commodity that is sold throughout the economy during a given day must equal the total amount bought, if the economy under consideration is 'isolated' (that is, if imports and exports can be neglected). Similarly, the total price received by all sellers of each type of commodity must equal the total price paid by its buyers. But in a capitalist economy the number of such constraints is small relative to the total number of parameters describing the state of the system, so that the number of degrees of freedom is still enormous. This is the precise, though very abstract, sense in which capitalism is a *free* market system.

As far as the applicability of probabilistic methods is concerned, the fact that the activity of each economic agent (each firm and each worker-consumer) is motivated or mediated by more or less conscious human aims and volitions is irrelevant, so long as these activities are largely uncoordinated. A very high degree of coordination would of course introduce a large number of additional constraints upon the microscopic economic parameters, thus making probabilistic methods inapplicable. But such a high degree of coordination does not exist under capitalism.

Of course, even a capitalist economy is subject to a certain amount of coordination, whether enforced or voluntary, as a result of government intervention or coalition agreements between economic agents (cartel agreements, policies of employers' federations, trades unions and consumers' organizations). This certainly affects the macroscopic shape and behaviour of the economy, but the number of constraints involved—even if they were all rigorously implemented, which is not quite the case—is still small relative to the total number of parameters. It should also be noted that most of these constraints are expressed not by equations but by inequalities (fixation of maximum or minimum prices for certain commodities, or of minimum wages, or of maximum quotas for the production of certain commodities by certain firms) and such constraints do not reduce the number of degrees of freedom of the system at all.

The existence of an enormous number of degrees of freedom is indeed a unique and fundamental feature—and, in a certain abstract sense, even the most important feature—of the capitalist system. It is this feature that lends the capitalist economy its peculiar opacity: macroscopically, the system behaves in a 'mindless' way, almost as a natural entity, although this behaviour must, in the last analysis, be the resultant of the conscious activities of many human agents. It is this feature that is also responsible for the specific character of economic science, and indeed for its very existence as a separate ('alienated') science.

In traditional, pre-capitalist societies, what we would call 'economic activity' is quite rigidly prescribed and constrained by custom and other forms of social code. The behaviour of such an economy is more or less transparent and largely deterministic; its only major probabilistic element is injected *from the outside*, by the unpredictability of natural phenomena. The study of this sort of economy hardly requires a specialized separate science of economics.

Again, if economic activity in a modern complex industrialized society were regulated and coordinated by a sufficiently

60

comprehensive and detailed plan, then the whole economic system would behave in much the same way as a *single* economic enterprise. Due to the *technical* complexity of such an organism, it would not behave in a totally transparent way. However, its study and regulation would not require economic science as we know it today, but rather a kind of operations research (broadly similar to the methods used today in connection with a single organization).[2]

These ideas concerning the nature of both capitalism and the science of political economy were clearly perceived by Marx and by his best disciples, although they did not use the term 'number of degrees of freedom', nor were they able to see that these very ideas imply that scientific economics must be given a probabilistic foundation. Particularly noteworthy for their lucidity and vigour are Rosa Luxemburg's observations, which deserve to be quoted at some length.[3]

'Today a person can become rich or poor without doing anything, without lifting a finger, without an occurrence of nature taking place, without anyone giving anyone anything, or physically robbing anything. Price fluctuations are like secret movements directed by an invisible agency behind the back of society, causing continuous shifts and fluctuations in the distribution of social wealth. This movement is observed as atmospheric pressure read on a barometer, or temperature on a thermometer. And yet commodity prices and their movements manifestly are human affairs and not black magic. No one but man himself—with his own hands—produces these commodities and determines their prices, except that, here again, something flows from his actions which he does not intend or desire; here again, need, object, and result of the economic activity of man have come into jarring contradiction.

'How does this happen, and what are the black laws which, behind man's back, lead to such strange results of the economic activity of man today? These problems can be analyzed only by scientific investigation. It has become necessary to solve all these riddles by strenuous research, deep thought, analysis, analogy—to probe the hidden relations which give rise to the fact that the result of the economic activity of man does not correspond to his intentions, to his volition—in short, to his consciousness. In this manner the problem faced by scientific investigation becomes defined as the lack of human consciousness in the economic life of society, and here we have reached the immediate reason for the birth of economics.'

After noting the relative transparency and determinism of traditional pre-capitalist economic systems, she goes on:

'Today, we know no masters, no slaves, no feudal lords, no bondsmen. Liberty and equality before the law have removed all despotic relations, at least in the older bourgeois states; in the colonies—as is commonly known—slavery and bondage are introduced, frequently enough for the first time, by these same states. But where the bourgeoisie is at home, free competition rules as the sole law of economic relations and any plan, any organisation has disappeared from the economy. Of course, if we look into separate private enterprises, into a modern factory or a large complex of factories and workshops, like Krupp or a large-scale capitalist farm enterprise in North America, then we shall find the strictest organisation, the most detailed division of labour, the most cunning planfulness based on the latest scientific information. Here, everything flows smoothly, as if arranged by magic, managed by *one* will, by *one* consciousness. But no sooner do we leave the factory or the large farm behind, when chaos surrounds us. While the innumerable units—and today a private enterprise, even the most gigantic, is only a fragment of the great economic structure which embraces the globe—while these units are disciplined to the utmost, the entity of all the so-called national economies, i.e., world economy, is completely unorganised. In the entity which embraces oceans and continents, there is no planning, no consciousness, no regulation, only the blind clash of unknown, unrestrained forces playing a capricious game with the economic destiny of man. Of course, even today, an all-powerful ruler dominates all working men, and women: capital. But the form which this sovereignty of capital takes is not despotism but anarchy.

'And it is precisely this anarchy which is responsible for the fact that the economy of human society produces results which are mysterious and unpredictable to the people involved. Its anarchy is what makes the economic life of mankind something unknown, alien, uncontrollable—the laws of which we must find in the same manner in which we analyse the phenomena of external nature. . . . Scientific analysis must discover *ex post facto* that purposefulness and those rules governing human economic life which conscious planfulness did not impose on it beforehand.'

Hence the historical specificity of the science of economics: 'A science which has for its subject the discovery of the laws of the anarchy of capitalist production obviously could not arise before this mode of production itself, before the historic conditions for the class rule of the modern bourgeoisie were established, by centuries of birth pangs, of political and economic changes.'

Let us now turn to consider the rate of profit and the 'black laws' which govern its distribution.

In a competitive capitalist economy, no business can be guaranteed any particular rate of profit. (Here we are excluding money invested in interest-bearing papers, say, whose rate of return is more or less rigidly controlled; our discussion is confined to capital invested in the production of physical commodities and services for sale in the market.) This uncertainty of the rate of profit is an essential and irreducible feature of the system. We therefore propose to regard the rate of profit as a random variable and to investigate the structure of its distribution.

Our first step is to define a suitable sample space. We choose some moment of time, t, which will remain fixed throughout our discussion, unless otherwise indicated. We suppose that at time t there are n entities, called *firms*, in the economy. We assume that n is a very large number. We label the firms (in some arbitrary order) with numbers: $1, 2, \ldots, n$. Our sample space (at time t) is, by definition, the set of all firms (or, equivalently but somewhat more abstractly, the set of labels); we call it the *firm space*.

In making comparisons between real economic data and our theoretical model, it must be noted that a 'firm' in our theoretical sense does not always correspond to a whole firm in the real world. In reality, a firm is often composed of several parts, each of which is (or can meaningfully be) taken as a separate accounting unit for the purpose of calculating investments, costs, revenues and profits.[4] Each such unit must be taken to correspond to a separate firm of our firm space. Thus each firm in our present model—like a particle in the model of a monatomic gas—is regarded as an indivisible unit.

However, here (unlike the gas model discussed in the previous chapter) it would be unreasonable to take all firms to be identical. As in real life, some firms may be bigger than others, and must be given more 'weight' in determining the macroscopic behaviour of the system. Below we shall define various random variables over our sample space. If X is such a random variable and A is a set of real numbers, we would like the probability $P(X$ in A) to measure not the proportion of the *number* of firms for which $X(i)$ happens to be in A out of the total *number n* of all firms, but rather the proportion of the *capital invested* in such firms out of the total capital invested in the economy. The latter proportion is, for our purposes, much more significant than the former.

Let us therefore assume that at time t the i-th firm is operating a positive amount $K(i)$ of *capital*. (Note: when interpreting our model in the real world, the capital of a firm must be taken as the total capital assets—valued at present (amortized) prices—operated by the firm, *before* deduction of any outstanding debts and mortgages owed by the firm on these assets.) We now define the *weight p_i* of the i-th firm as $K(i)$ divided by the total value of K:

$$p_i = \frac{K(i)}{K(1) + K(2) + \cdots + K(n)}.$$

It is clear that each p_i is positive and $p_1 + p_2 + \cdots + p_n = 1$. The weights of different firms are proportional to their respective capitals. This simply means that equal sums of money invested in production contribute equal weights. We postulate that if a firm is selected at random out of the firm space, the probability that the i-th firm is the one selected is p_i. (Compare this with our gas model, where all particles had an equal probability $1/n$ of being selected.)

If X is any random variable defined over the firm space and A is a set of real numbers, we define $P(X$ in A) to be the sum of all the weights p_i of those firms for which $X(i)$ happens to lie in A. Thus $P(X$ in A) is equal to the proportion of the capital of those firms, out of the total capital of the economy.

We now introduce the random variable, R, called *the rate of profit*. For each i, we think of $R(i)$ as the current rate of profit of the i-th firm at time t. It equals the amount of profit made by the firm per unit of time (measured in years) per unit of capital. Thus, if h is a short duration of time,[5] the profit made by the i-th firm in the period from t to $t + h$ will be approximately $hR(i)K(i)$. For example, suppose that at time t a firm has capital of £24,000 and rate of profit 0.1 (that is, 10%) per annum. Let h be $\frac{1}{12}$ yrs (that is, one month). Then in the month beginning at t the firm's profits will amount to approximately $\frac{1}{12}$ times 0.1 times £24,000, that is £200. (The approximation is good if *during* that month the capital and rate of profit of the firm do not change much.)

When interpreting our model in the real world, profits have to be reckoned after deduction of all production costs, including rent and amortization, but *before* deducting payments of interest on borrowed capital as well as taxes such as income and profit tax. In other words, just as we take a firm's capital to include capital owed by it to the banks, so also the interest paid on this borrowed capital is taken to be part of the firm's profit; it is the banks' share in the firm's profit. Similarly, taxes imposed on profit are regarded as forming part of the profit; they are the government's share in the firm's profit.

We can now define the c.d.f. F_R of R in the usual way:

$$F_R(r) = \mathbf{P}(R \leq r) \qquad \text{for any real number } r.$$

As in the paradigm of the previous chapter, this c.d.f. is a step function; but to a very high degree of approximation it may be regarded as smooth.

We can therefore talk about the p.d.f. f_R of R; by definition, $f_R(r)$ is the derivative of $F_R(r)$ with respect to r.

Again, f_R has the following meaning. If the curve in fig. 2 represents the graph of f_R, then the darkened area in fig. 2 (the integral of f_R from a to b) is equal to $\mathbf{P}(a \leq R \leq b)$. We recall that $\mathbf{P}(a \leq R \leq b)$ is, by definition, the aggregate weight of those firms whose rate of profit lies between a and b. In other words, $\mathbf{P}(a \leq R \leq b)$ is obtained when we divide the sum of the capitals of those firms whose rate of profit lies in this region by the total capital of all firms in our firm space.

Our aim in this chapter is to make certain deductions concerning the shape of f_R. Of course, very little of interest can be deduced without making some assumptions about our model. However, we shall try to keep our assumptions as weak and as reasonable as possible. In particular, we shall refrain as much as we can from making any assumptions concerning the detailed microscopic interactions in our model. Moreover, our assumptions, as well as the theoretical conclusions we shall draw from them, can be tested empirically.

For example, using economic statistical data published regularly in every modern capitalist country, we can plot the empirical counterpart of f_R in any one year for each of these countries. We obtain a histogram showing what proportion of the total capital of the country was, in a given year, in any rate-of-profit bracket. It is then possible to test how well our theoretical assertions about f_R are corroborated by the empirical graph.

Our first assertion concerning f_R is that *if our model is in a state of equilibrium then f_R is virtually independent of time.*

This assertion can indeed be taken as part of the definition of the concept *equilibrium* for our model. However, it is nevertheless not vacuous empirically. For we claim that our state of equilibrium (unlike the fallacious equilibrium posited by the traditional economists, based on a uniform rate of profit) describes fairly well the normal situation in a real capitalist economy. Of course, we do not claim that any real capitalist economy is usually, or even ever, actually *in* equilibrium. Our claim, rather, is that a capitalist economy during normal times is fairly close to equilibrium.

If we are right, then *while the empirical counterparts of f_R for different capitalist countries may look quite different, the graphs for any one country should change rather slowly from year to year.* (Here we must obviously exclude exceptional years such as times of acute crisis, outbreak of war and so on.)[6] Our—admittedly rather cursory—examination of real economic data tends to confirm this prediction (see chapter VIII). We leave it to the econometricians to test our prediction with the thoroughness to which they are accustomed.

Our prediction amounts to saying that in each capitalist economy the proportion of capital (out of the total capital invested in the economy) which finds itself in any given rate-of-profit bracket will change fairly slowly with time (excluding relatively rare exceptional years). Thus, a certain more or less fixed proportion of the total capital will yield profit at rates less than 1% per annum, another fairly fixed proportion will yield between 1% and 2%, and so on for each bracket.

This does not mean that as time flows the list of firms within each rate-of-profit bracket remains more or less fixed. Quite the contrary, there is a fairly rapid turnover as each firm tries to improve its position and get into a higher bracket. In particular, there is a terrible scramble to get out of the very low brackets, in which the rate of profit is so low as to threaten bankruptcy. But in this desperate game of musical chairs all cannot be winners: since the *proportion* of capital (out of the total capital of the economy) in each bracket must in normal times (that is, at or near dynamic equilibrium) remain nearly steady, any capital moving from a given bracket to the one above it must be replaced by other capital, representing about the same proportion of the whole, moving in the opposite direction. 'Now, *here*, you see, it takes all the running *you* can do, to keep in the same place.' No firm can afford to opt out of this race, because then it would be pushed back by other firms trying to improve their positions.

However, here there is a special role for the intervention of the capitalist state: the state may decide to nationalize certain industries and keep them, say by means of a suitable price policy, in the lower brackets, thus enabling more private capital to avoid this unfavourable position.

Let us now go on to discuss the general form of f_R in a state of equilibrium. The first question we should like to raise is whether it is reasonable to assume that $f_R(r)$ is equal, or very close, to 0 for all negative r. This would mean, in other words, that in a state of equilibrium only a negligible proportion of the total capital has a negative rate of profit (that is, makes a loss). Of course, logically speaking there is nothing to prevent us from incorporating this assumption into our model; but the real question is empirical rather than logical. What we are asking is whether this assumption is at all realistic in terms of the intended interpretation of our model as an approximate description of the behaviour of a real capitalist economy.

At first sight it would seem that this assumption is quite unrealistic. Even leaving aside—as we must do in any case—times of acute economic crisis, when many firms make large losses and are driven to the wall, is it not the case that in normal times there are some firms, representing together a non-negligible proportion of the total capital, that make losses? Are there not some bankruptcies even in times of prosperity?

But upon closer examination we find that in normal times the proportion of capital (out of the total capital of the economy) in the negative rate-of-profit brackets is much smaller than first impressions suggest. Quite apart from the fact that the accounts of some firms are manipulated to show an *apparent* loss where in fact there is no loss,[7] there are two more important circumstances that must be taken into consideration.

First, among the firms that actually do make a loss, there is usually a disproportionately high number of small firms (firms with a small amount of capital). For this reason the *proportion of loss-making capital* (out of the economy's total capital) is considerably smaller than the *number of loss-making firms* would suggest.

Second, and even more important: when a firm is reported to be making a 'loss', what is usually meant is a loss *after* payment of interest on the capital it has borrowed. This is the 'loss' shown in the balance-sheet of the firm. However, for the purpose of comparison with our model, the interest paid by the firm must be taken as part of the *profit*. A firm whose rate of profit (in our sense) is positive but considerably lower than the current rate of interest, and whose capital is partly borrowed, may end up (after payment of interest) with a net loss on its balance-sheet. For example, suppose that a firm with a capital of £2,000 has made a profit at the rate of 1% during a whole year. Its profit for the year amounts to £20. But if half of the firm's capital is borrowed at 10% rate of interest, then the firm owes the bank interest of £100 and its balance-sheet for the year will show a *loss* of £80. If such losses persist, the firm will go out of business. Many, if not most, of the firms reported to be making a loss or to be bankrupt are in exactly this position.

In view of these considerations we believe that the assumption that in a state of equilibrium $f_R(r)$ is negligibly small for all negative r, so as to make $\mathbf{P}(R \leq 0)$ also negligible, is fairly close to reality and may be regarded as a legitimate idealization. Therefore, in seeking a theoretical formula for f_R we shall allow ourselves to assume that in a state of equilibrium or near-equilibrium the probability $\mathbf{P}(R \leq 0)$ is vanishingly small; in other words, that R is a *positive* random variable.[8]

However, because this assumption is only approximately correct, any conclusion derived from it should be regarded as tentative and must, in particular, be subjected to empirical tests.

In seeking a theoretical expression for the distribution of R, a useful heuristic guide is provided by statistical mechanics. In a gas at equilibrium, the total kinetic energy of all the molecules is a given quantity. It can then be shown that the 'most chaotic' partition of this total kinetic energy among the molecules results in a gamma distribution.[9] Now, if we consider that in any given short period there is a more-or-less fixed amount of social surplus (see chapter VII) and that capitalist competition is a very disorderly mechanism for partitioning this surplus among capitalists in the form of profit, then the analogy of statistical mechanics suggests that R may also have a gamma distribution.

This heuristic argument does not, of course, constitute a *proof* that R must have a gamma distribution. (In order to obtain something like a formal proof, we would need to define an appropriate notion of *entropy* in our firm space.[10]) However, a few empirical tests we have made (some of which are illustrated in chapter VIII) do tend to corroborate the hypothesis that R indeed has a gamma distribution. We shall therefore adopt this tentatively, as a working hypothesis.

In order to continue our investigation of the rate of profit and its distribution, it will be useful to introduce some new random variables, which are closely connected with R and which are also very important in themselves. The first of these new random variables will be denoted by Z and called *the rate of wage-bill* or *the rate of labour-costs*. It has the following meaning. For each i, the positive number $Z(i)$ at time t equals the current annual wage-bill (or labour costs) of the i-th firm, divided by its capital $K(i)$. In other words, if h is a short duration of time (measured in units of one year) such that the variation of $Z(i)$ and $K(i)$ during the period from t to $t + h$ can be neglected, then the total labour costs of the i-th firm for this period amount to $hZ(i)K(i)$.

Note that the reciprocal of Z (that is, $1/Z$) is similar to what Marx calls *organic composition*,[11] the only difference being that he measures both labour costs and invested capital in terms of their labour-value, whereas we measure them in money terms.

Using R and Z, we define two additional important random variables, X and Y, by putting

$$X = \frac{R}{Z} \quad \text{and} \quad Y = R + Z.$$

(This notation means that the equalities $X(i) = R(i)/Z(i)$ and $Y(i) = R(i) + Z(i)$ hold for each i. We shall use a similar notational convention throughout, without special mention.)

$X(i)$ is equal to the current ratio (at time t) between the profit and labour-costs of the i-th firm. Thus X is similar to what Marx calls *the rate of surplus value*, except that here, too, we measure R and Z in money terms, whereas he uses labour-values.

As for Y, it may be called, somewhat imprecisely, *the rate of value-added*. In common economic parlance *value-added* includes rent as well as profit; but if we ignore rent then $Y(i)$ is equal to the i-th firm's value-added per unit of time per unit of capital.

The c.d.f.'s of our three new variables, Z, X and Y, are defined in the usual way. As in the case of R, and for the same reason, these functions can be assumed, with negligible error, to be smooth (although strictly speaking they are step functions). We can therefore assume that the p.d.f.'s of the three random variables are defined, in the usual way, as the derivatives of the respective c.d.f.'s.

The same heuristic argument which has led us to the hypothesis that R has a gamma distribution can be applied, *mutatis mutandis*, also to Z. Here, too, the hypothesis that Z has a gamma distribution tends to be confirmed by empirical evidence. Furthermore, as we shall see, empirical evidence suggests that the distributions of R and Z not only belong to the same family, but are equal or very nearly equal. In other words, it seems plausible to assume that R and Z have gamma distributions with the same parameters α and β.

For our own purpose it will be sufficient to assume tentatively, as a working hypothesis, that R and Z have gamma distributions $\mathfrak{G}(\alpha, \beta)$ and $\mathfrak{G}(\alpha', \beta)$ respectively, with the same second parameter β.

We shall now turn to discuss certain remarkable empirical facts concerning the distribution of the random variable X, and we shall then consider how these facts fit in with our working hypothesis regarding the distributions of R and Z.

Let us recall that $X(i)$ is the current ratio (at time t) in which the value-added (excluding rent) realized by the *i*-th firm is divided between capital and labour, in the form of profit and wages, respectively. In other words, $X(i)$ is the ratio between the total gross profit of the *i*-th firm during a short period, and the total gross wages which the firm pays during the same period.

Now, it is a remarkable fact that both in Britain and in the USA (as well as in other developed capitalist countries) the empirically observed values of X throughout manufacturing industry, at any given time, tend to cluster rather close together. In other words, X has a narrow distribution, a small standard deviation.[12] It would seem that the variable X, while not actually degenerate, has a strong tendency to be almost degenerate. This phenomenon is all the more remarkable when the behaviour of X is compared with that of other important variables such as R and Z (defined above) or W (the wage variable, which will be defined in chapter V). None of these other variables has a particularly narrow distribution, although according to traditional economic theory one should expect R, not X, to be degenerate or very nearly so.

Whatever the cause of this curious behaviour of X, it surely must lie beyond the 'purely economic' sphere, for it clearly involves the social relation of forces between capital and labour in their struggle over their respective shares of the value-added. Of course, this does not provide an explanation for the phenomenon, but merely removes it from the sphere of 'pure' economics to the wider sphere of socio-economic relations and struggles. It is not at all obvious why the shove and pull of the class struggle should result—surely unintentionally—in a roughly uniform proportion between the respective shares of capital and labour in the value-added, across virtually the whole of manufacturing industry, irrespective of the different socio-economic conditions in different industries.[13]

To proceed, let us define the index e_0 by putting

$$ e_0 = \frac{\mathbf{E}R}{\mathbf{E}Z} . $$

It is easy to see that e_0 is the proportion in which the *total* value-added (excluding rent) in the whole economy is divided between capital and labour; in other words, e_0 is the ratio between total gross profits and total gross wages. Now, both $\mathbf{E}R$ and $\mathbf{E}Z$ are functions of place and time: they vary from one economy to another; and within a given economy they vary with time. So in principle we may expect e_0 to have different values at different times and places. However, empirical data show that in reality e_0 behaves in the following remarkably stable and regular way.[14]

Fact 1. The value of e_0 has hardly changed over very long periods of time; it does have very mild short-term fluctuations, but in the long term it seems to be more or less constant. This puzzling phenomenon has been pointed out by several economists,[15] but no adequate explanation has been proposed so far.

Before we go any further, let us point out an obvious connection between Fact 1 and the narrow distribution of X. Recall that $X = R/Z$; therefore, if X is almost degenerate, then R must be approximately equal to aZ, where a is a constant that is the same for the whole of industry, but may vary with time. Therefore, $\mathbf{E}R$ is approximately equal to $a\mathbf{E}Z$, so that a is approximately equal to e_0. Hence the values of R/Z must cluster very close to e_0.

Fact 2. The point around which the values of X are closely clustered, namely e_0, seems to be nearly the *same one* both in Britain and in the USA, as well as in other developed capitalist countries. This, too, seems very curious indeed. Why should the ratio in which the total value-added is divided between capital and labour be the same in such different countries with different economies and different relations of forces between the classes?

Fact 3. The empirical data show that this value of e_0, common to Britain, the USA and several other countries, is very close to 1. If this is a mere coincidence, it is a very strange one. Why 1 rather than 5.3, or some other 'messy' number? Even if we accept that capital and labour tend to divide the value-added between them in a nearly fixed proportion, why should this proportion be 'fifty-fifty' rather than some other?

We cannot offer a good explanation of any of these phenomena in isolation. But we can show that if our hypothesis concerning the distributions of R and Z is correct, then the last three facts (concerning e_0) can be derived as consequences from the tendency of X to be degenerate.

Indeed, we shall now prove that if R and Z have gamma distributions $\mathfrak{G}(\alpha, \beta)$ and $\mathfrak{G}(\alpha', \beta)$ respectively, and if R/Z is degenerate, then $R = Z$, so that $e_0 = ER/EZ = 1$.

To prove this, recall that if R/Z is degenerate, then $R = aZ$, where a is a constant. Therefore (see appendix I),

$$ER = aEZ, \qquad VR = a^2 VZ. \tag{1}$$

On the other hand, since R is assumed to have distribution $\mathfrak{G}(\alpha, \beta)$, it follows (again, see appendix I) that $ER = \alpha/\beta$ and $VR = \alpha/\beta^2$. Similarly, we get $EZ = \alpha'/\beta$ and $VZ = \alpha'/\beta^2$. Substituting these four expressions into (1), we obtain

$$\alpha = a\alpha', \qquad \alpha = a^2\alpha'.$$

Hence $a = a^2$, and since a must be positive we have $a = 1$ and $R = Z$.

This theorem means that if R and Z have the gamma distributions assumed by us, and if for some reason or other there is a tendency for X to be degenerate, so that the value-added (excluding rent) is shared between capital and labour in a fixed proportion, then the only value at which such a fixed proportion can stabilize is 1, that is 'fifty-fifty'.[16]

Of course, the model set out in this chapter, as well as the particular assumptions we have made and the specific conclusions drawn from them, must be regarded as tentative. What we are advocating definitely is not the correctness of this or that model or assumption, but the validity of our general methodology. It is mainly in order to illustrate this methodology that we have developed the present model in some detail. In particular, we would like to emphasize two observations.

First, it is a methodological mistake to develop macro-economic theory by starting with a preconceived aggregation of micro-economic quantities, so that the quantitative theory begins only after aggregation is somehow posited. Rather, one needs a probabilistic 'bridging' theory that connects the macro-economic with the micro-economic, and shows *how* to aggregate correctly.

Second, only by means of a probabilistic model—of the same

general type as the model discussed above—can questions concerning the distribution of the rate of profit and other economic variables be posed, let alone solved, as *theoretical* questions rather than merely empirical ones.

Chapter Four
Labour-content as a Measure of Commodities

In chapter I we argued in detail that a valid theoretical model of a capitalist economy must not be based on the presupposition that in a state of equilibrium all types of production yield the same rate of profit. For, this presupposition—which amounts to the assumption that the random variable R of chapter III is degenerate[1]—is not merely unrealistic, but runs counter to an essential feature of the capitalist system.

A similar argument applies to prices. It is well known that prices of all commodities vary in time. But even if we confine our attention to any particular short period, say one day, we find that identical commodities are sold at different unit prices. There are bad buys, good buys and bargains. Moreover, this variation in price is an essential feature of capitalism as a free market system. In this system, every transaction of sale and purchase is a contractual relation between seller and buyer, free from political and other extra-economic coercion; and the price is subject to bargaining between the two parties and is finally fixed by their mutual consent. Nothing —except economic necessity or interest—can force anyone to sell or buy a commodity at a particular price (or, for that matter, to sell or buy it at all). The price that is actually paid is affected by the relative bargaining power of seller and buyer—and this can vary from case to case even for identical commodities.

The buyer is, of course, interested in paying the lowest price possible, other things being equal. But other things are often *not* equal. For example, convenience, accessibility and terms of delivery may affect the price the buyer is prepared to pay. Thus one may prefer to buy several commodities together from a conveniently placed seller, even if this means paying a little bit more, rather than waste time and energy on shopping around separately for each commodity. Or, if one is buying on credit, easier terms of payment may compensate for a slightly higher price. There are many other variable factors, and they affect different buyers differently.

The seller, on the other hand, would like to sell at the highest price possible, other things being equal. But here again other things are often unequal. The profits of the seller depend not only on the price per unit of the commodity, but also on the volume of sales per day. It may therefore be advantageous to charge a bit less in order to sell more. (In particular, it is usual to offer a discount to a buyer who buys a large quantity, so that the price per unit depends on the quantity purchased.) A seller may cut prices even if there is no *immediate* prospect of being wholly compensated by increased sales, in order to undercut other sellers and drive them out of the market.

We must therefore accept the variability of the unit price of any given type of commodity not merely as an aberration of reality from some ideal state of equilibrium, but as an inherent and irreducible feature of circulation in a competitive free market system. We must reject the assumption that in a state of equilibrium the unit price of each type of commodity is fixed, just as we have rejected the assumption of uniformity of the rate of profit. However, once we reject these deterministic assumptions, all the customary theoretical considerations used by the various economic schools for 'determining' prices and their relation to 'the' rate of profit can be applied no longer. For these considerations take as their starting point precisely the assumptions that we wish to reject. The only course open to us is to make a fresh beginning: to constitute unit price as a random variable and then to inquire into its law of distribution and into its *statistical* relationships with the rate-of-profit random variable.

However, if we are to regard unit price as a random variable and we wish to consider several (or all) types of commodity together rather than each one separately, we encounter a difficulty arising out of the diversity of units used for measuring different commodities.

In order to explain this difficulty, we must first draw a conceptual and terminological distinction between *commodity-type* (as a species of qualitatively identical goods or services produced for sale) and each *concrete* article or service belonging to such a species, but sold in a particular transaction, at a particular place and time. We shall use the term *commodity* in the latter concrete sense. Thus, a *commodity* is a particular object or service sold-and-bought on a particular occasion, while a *commodity-type* is a class of commodities that are qualitatively the same but may differ from each other in quantity.[2] For example, the kilo of sugar bought by John Smith yesterday at his local corner-shop is one commodity; the one and a half kilos of similar sugar bought by Jane Brown in the supermarket constitute *another* commodity; but both these commodities *belong* to (or are *instances* of) the same commodity-type: pure granulated white sugar.[3]

Returning to our main theme, let us first suppose that we are dealing with just one commodity-type, say sugar. We may then use the following procedure to constitute the unit price of sugar (at a given time) as a random variable, S. We fix a particular short period of time, say one day. Our sample space will consist of all the transactions that occurred on the given day and in which portions of sugar (that is, commodities belonging to the commodity-type sugar) were sold-and-bought. Let us label these transactions $1, 2, \ldots, n$. If the quantity of sugar involved in the i-th transaction is $Q(i)$, we assign to it 'weight' p_i proportional to $Q(i)$, such that $p_1 + p_2 + \cdots + p_n = 1$. Thus

$$p_i = \frac{Q(i)}{Q(1) + Q(2) + \cdots + Q(n)}.$$

Next, we define $S(i)$ as the price per unit paid in the i-th transaction, so that the *total* price paid in that transaction equals $S(i)Q(i)$. We can now define the c.d.f. F_S in the usual way (see appendix I) and proceed to inquire into its general shape.

Note that each $S(i)$ is a ratio between two quantities: the total price paid in the i-th transaction and the quantity $Q(i)$ involved in that transaction. Therefore the numerical value of $S(i)$ depends on the units of money as well as the physical units used to measure sugar. So in order to define S properly, we must state which units are being used. If we agree that money is measured in pounds sterling and sugar in kilograms, then $S(i)$ is measured in pounds sterling per kilogram. But now suppose that we change our units, and measure money in pence and sugar in pounds. Then we get a different random variable S'. However, the two variables S and S' differ from each other merely by a constant factor: $S' = kS$, where k is a constant (called a *constant of proportionality*).[4] It is of no importance whether we use S or S', because the distribution of one can easily be obtained from that of the other; in fact, it is not difficult to see that

$$F_{S'}(r) = F_S\left(\frac{r}{k}\right), \qquad f_{S'}(r) = \left(\frac{1}{k}\right) f_S\left(\frac{r}{k}\right).$$

The distributions of S and S' are essentially similar, and are related to each other by a simple formula.

However, suppose that we want to deal with several commodity-types simultaneously. For the sake of simplicity, let us consider just two types, say sugar and petrol. Our sample space now consists of all transactions occurring on the given day and involving sugar or petrol, and the relevant random variable is the unit price of the aggregate 'type' sugar & petrol. Obviously, it will be reasonable to use the same unit of money, say pounds sterling, for prices of commodities of both types. But what about the units used to measure *quantities* of sugar and petrol respectively? Surely, it is nonsense to try to measure all commodities by the *same* physical units (that is, to measure both sugar and petrol in kilograms, or both in litres). Besides, this is not even possible in general. (For example, if in addition to sugar and petrol we also have a service commodity-type, such as passenger transportation, then we cannot possibly measure it in kilograms or litres, but in qualitatively different units such as passenger-miles.) On the other hand, if we decide to measure each commodity-type in different (and appropriate) units, then the resulting distribution will be affected *drastically* by the arbitrary choice of units for each type. For example, if we measure sugar in pounds and petrol in gallons we get a totally different distribution from the one we would get if sugar were measured in kilograms and petrol in litres. And the two distributions are not directly connected to each other by any formula.

This difficulty can be overcome if we can find some 'natural'— that is, *economically* natural—unit of measurement that can reasonably be applied to measure all commodities. Using such a common unit, we shall be able to aggregate all commodities (irrespective of the various types to which they belong) into one totality, and define a random variable of unit price meaningful for that aggregate.[5]

The need to apply a common unit of measurement to entities of different kinds arises in various contexts, not only in economic theory, and the common unit appropriate for each case depends on the purpose at hand. For example, if one is faced with the problem of arranging the storage of a variety of objects, then it may be appropriate to measure each object by the volume it occupies (say in cubic feet). Or, if the problem is to arrange the transportation of a cargo consisting of an assortment of items, it may be reasonable to measure each item by weight, or by volume, or by some unit of measurement that combines both weight and volume, according to the method of transportation used.

In economics itself, price is often used as a common measure for different commodities. For example, in calculating a cost-of-living index, one adds up the prices of a sample consisting of different items that make up a 'standard consumption basket'. However, for our present purpose this measure is clearly inappropriate, because it would reduce us to making the tautologous observation that the unit price of *every* commodity is £1 per £. In order to be able to say something significant about the distribution of the unit price of commodities, we must clearly measure the quantities of the commodities themselves by some measure other than price. (Unit price will then be the *ratio* between price and that other measure.)

A whole family of common measures, each of which is theoretically significant and appropriate in its own way, is provided by the conceptual framework of input-output theory.[6] To obtain a measure of this kind, we must first select a particular commodity-type as a 'yardstick'; for the sake of illustration, let us suppose that the commodity-type *petrol* is selected for this role. Any given commodity is then assigned a quantitative measure called the *petrol content* of that commodity, equal to the total amount of petrol required (as direct or indirect input) to produce the given commodity. For example, the petrol content of two kilograms of sugar is equal to the amount of petrol which, according to the standard methods of production of the economy, is used up directly or indirectly in order to produce two kilograms of sugar. In order to explain this more fully, we must describe the underlying *closed production model* in some detail.

In this model we consider a 'closed economy' involving a number of commodity-types. Let $C_0, C_1, C_2, \ldots, C_n$ be a complete list of these types. The order of listing is arbitrary, but for the sake of definiteness we shall assume that C_0 is labour-power, C_1 is petrol and C_2 is sugar. C_3, C_4, ..., C_n are all the remaining types. Next, we fix for each commodity an appropriate physical unit of measurement. For example, we can measure C_0 in worker-hours, C_1 in litres, C_2 in kilograms, and so on for each type. (The size of these units is, of course, purely conventional; for example, we could just as well measure petrol in gallons rather than litres.)

We assume that the production of a unit of any given commodity-type requires definite amounts of commodities of various types which are used up as *direct inputs*. We denote by a_j^i the number of units of C_j used up directly in the production of each unit of C_i. For example, if $a_1^2 = \frac{1}{100}$, this means that the production of 1 kilogram of sugar (from its raw material) uses up directly $\frac{1}{100}$ litre of petrol, say as fuel for some machine in the sugar factory. (Recall that sugar is C_2 and petrol is C_1.) Among the direct inputs we also count machinery and other items of 'fixed' capital. For example, if C_4 is a certain type of machinery used in producing sugar, and if one unit of C_4 is good for producing a million kilograms of sugar (before it has to be replaced) then $a_4^2 =$ one millionth.

The numbers a_j^i are called *input-output coefficients*. By taking them to be determinate numbers at any given time one is assuming, in effect, that at any given moment there is a *standard* method for producing each commodity-type. Similarly, the coefficients a_j^0 constitute a 'standard real-wage basket'. For example, a_2^0 is the 'standard' number of kilograms of sugar consumed by a worker and his or her family for each hour spent by the worker in production for a capitalist.

Such assumptions certainly involve a degree of idealization and over-simplification of reality. The problems raised by all this, especially in connection with the empirical interpretation of the theoretical terms, will be discussed later on.[7] But one point of fundamental methodological importance needs to be mentioned here. Use of the present model of production—and indeed any similar model which may differ from the present one in this or that detail—implies a deterministic view of the sphere of production. This is justified, in our opinion, because the disorderliness, the lack of planning and coordination typical of a capitalist economy resides not in production but in the market, in the sphere of circulation. Indeed, as Rosa

Luxemburg points out in the observations quoted in chapter III, the capitalist mode of production is characterized precisely by this duality, this contrast between the deterministic nature of production and the chaotic nature of the market. For this reason we believe that the production model outlined here, whatever its imperfections and however much it needs to be refined, does not do violence to the essential nature of capitalist production.

Let us return to the discussion of the model itself. The input-output coefficients a_j^i are all non-negative real numbers. If for a particular pair of indexes i and j the coefficient a_j^i is positive, this means that C_j serves as a *direct input* in the production of C_i. We say that C_j is an *ultimate input of* C_i if C_j is a direct input of C_i or a direct input of some direct input of C_i, or a direct input of some direct input of a direct input of C_i, and so on.

We now choose as a 'yardstick' some commodity-type that is *universal*, in the sense that it is an ultimate input of *every* commodity-type. For the sake of illustration, let us suppose that petrol (C_1) is a universal commodity-type—a very realistic assumption—and let us use it as our yardstick. To each commodity-type C_i we assign a positive number v_1^i called the *petrol-content* of one unit of C_i. This is equal to the number of units of C_1 (that is, the number of litres of petrol) used up as direct and indirect inputs in producing one unit of C_i. (The subscript '1' in v_1^i indicates that we are using C_1 as yardstick; the superscript 'i' indicates that we are measuring the C_1-content of a unit of C_i.)

The numbers v_1^0, v_1^1, v_1^2, ..., v_1^n must satisfy certain *consistency* conditions. To see this, consider for example v_1^2, the petrol content of one kilogram of sugar. This must equal the amount of petrol used up as a *direct* input in producing a kilo of sugar (namely a_1^2) plus the petrol-content of all the other direct inputs used up to produce the same kilo of sugar. Thus

$$v_1^2 = a_0^2 v_1^0 + a_1^2 + a_2^2 v_1^2 + a_3^2 v_1^3 + \cdots + a_n^2 v_1^n.$$

Here on the right-hand side we have, in addition to the *direct* contribution of petrol (namely a_1^2), also the *indirect* contributions of petrol through the other direct inputs of our kilo of sugar. Thus for $k \neq 1$ the amount of C_k used up directly is a_k^2 and the petrol-content of each unit of C_k is v_1^k, so the indirect contribution of petrol through C_k is $a_k^2 v_1^k$.

Of course, a similar equation must hold not only for sugar but also for any other commodity-type. We therefore have

$$v_1^i = a_0^i v_1^0 + a_1^i + a_2^i v_1^2 + a_3^i v_1^3 + \cdots + a_n^i v_1^n \qquad \text{for } i = 0, 1, 2, \ldots, n.$$

We have thus got a system of $n + 1$ linear equations which the $n + 1$ positive quantities $v_1^0, v_1^1, v_1^2, \ldots, v_1^n$ must satisfy.

If the input-output coefficients fulfil certain mathematical conditions whose economic interpretation is quite reasonable—namely, that the production system under consideration is capable of generating a physical surplus—then these $n + 1$ equations do have a solution $v_1^0, v_1^1, v_1^2, \ldots, v_1^n$ consisting of $n + 1$ positive numbers such that, moreover, the number v_1^1 is smaller than 1.

This last inequality, $v_1^1 < 1$, seems rather odd at first sight, because it asserts that the petrol-content of one litre of petrol is less than one litre. But we must remember that according to the definition of the term 'petrol content' this inequality does *not* mean that one litre of petrol has a *physical* content of less than one litre of petrol—which would indeed be absurd—but rather that the production of one litre of petrol uses up (both directly and indirectly) less than the same quantity of petrol. If it were the case that $v_1^1 = 1$, then all the petrol available at any one moment would have to be used up merely to re-produce the same amount of petrol, leaving nothing for the production of surplus of any kind. Every single product, since it has some petrol-content, would have to be used up as input in the process of production of some other product, or be consumed by workers and their families in order to re-produce labour power. If $v_1^1 > 1$, the position would be even worse: the system would produce less petrol than it uses up; and, since by assumption petrol is universal, that is, needed as an ultimate input of every commodity-type, there would be a physical deficit in all commodity-types.

It is therefore legitimate to assume that in a reasonable production system, if a given commodity-type—say petrol—is a universal commodity-type, then we can assign a positive petrol content to a unit of each commodity-type such that, moreover, the petrol-content of a unit of petrol is less than 1.

We remark that a similar assumption is legitimate not only with respect to the particular version of the input-output production model we have outlined here, which we have kept as simple as possible in order to facilitate our exposition, but also with respect to more general versions.[8]

Once we have assigned a petrol-content to a unit of each commodity-type, we have a common measure for all commodities, because each commodity consists of a definite number of units of a given type of commodity. The petrol content of c units of C_i is equal to cv_1^i; for example, the petrol-content of one and a half kilograms of sugar is $3v_1^2/2$.

Of course, petrol has been used here only for the sake of illustration. Any other universal commodity-type can be similarly used as a yardstick. Each such measure varies in time, because it depends on the current input-output coefficients which, in turn, depend on the current technological conditions as well as on social circumstances. (The latter are most directly involved in determining the coefficients a_j^0, which make up the standard real wage, or standard consumption basket.) But at any given time each measure of this kind is fixed and determinate, not a random variable.

Indeed, the great advantage common to these measures, which has made them a useful standard tool in certain economic considerations, is precisely the fact that they arise not from the market, the sphere of circulation and exchange wherein lies the essential indeterminacy of a capitalist economy, but from the conditions of production (including the re-production of labour power), which can legitimately be taken as relatively determinate at any given time.[9, 10]

For our particular purpose—that of constituting price as a random variable common to transactions involving more than one commodity-type—a measure of this kind will be particularly convenient, both technically and conceptually. Suppose that in a given transaction a commodity measuring m units (by some particular universal yardstick of the kind we have just been discussing) is sold for p units of money; then our unit-price random variable will assume, for this transaction, the numerical value p/m. In this ratio the numerator p arises in the uncertain sphere of the market, whereas the denominator m comes from the sphere of production, where determinism rules. Thus, in our unit-price random variable the two spheres—circulation and production, chaos and organization—come together, but each nevertheless retains its own distinguishable role.

Having decided to use some universal commodity-type as a yardstick to measure all commodities, it is a matter of considerable consequence which universal commodity-type is chosen for this special role. The choice makes a difference, because different universal commodity-types yield measures which, far from being identical, are not even proportional to each other. For example, if one commodity has a higher petrol-content than another commodity, it does not follow by any means that the former's pig-iron content is also higher than the latter's.

From a purely formal and abstract point of view, there is little reason to prefer any one universal commodity-type over another.[11] However, looking at the matter less abstractly, in the light of a real capitalist economy rather than that of a purely mathematical formalism, we shall argue that one special yardstick is inherently most suitable. The universal yardstick that we shall use is *labour*: we shall measure each commodity by its *labour-content*.

In using labour-content as a common measure of commodities, we shall be following in the footsteps of Marx, who in turn followed Adam Smith and David Ricardo in this respect.[12] Indeed, the labour-content of a commodity is—apart from certain minor differences, discussed in appendix II—essentially what Marx calls its *value*. Marx's use of the term 'value' to denote labour-content is of course intimately bound up with the fact that he believes equilibrium prices (Adam Smith's 'natural' prices) to be determined by the labour-content of commodities. In the first volume of *Capital* he assumes provisionally that the equilibrium prices of commodities are proportional to their 'value'. (It is argued by many that this also reflects, in Marx's view, an early historical stage in the exchange of commodities.) Later, in the third volume, he modifies this by introducing the assumption of an equilibrium uniform ('general') rate of profit. With this modification the determination of equilibrium prices ('prices of production') by values is mediated by the uniform rate of profit.[13] Nevertheless, equilibrium prices are still claimed to be *determined* by values, albeit in a mediated and 'transformed' manner.

However, since we have rejected the very notion of equilibrium prices (as well as that of a uniform equilibrium rate of profit) and since we cannot claim any *deterministic* relation between labour-content and price, it would be inappropriate for us to use the term 'value' in an unqualified form as synonymous with labour-content. Therefore we shall normally stick to the term 'labour-content'. But occasionally, in particular when we compare our own approach with the more traditional Marxist one, we shall say 'labour-value' or '*value*'.

In Marx's analysis, labour-value plays not one but two roles, which must not be conflated with each other and which, in our view, should indeed be separated from one another. On the one hand, there is labour-value as a universal measure of commodities; on the other hand, there is the specific—and deterministic—role that Marx assigns to labour-values in his theory of prices: the determination of 'prices of production' by labour-values, mediated by the 'general' rate of profit.

In our own probabilistic analysis, labour-content does not *determine* prices. We have no 'prices of production', or any other kind of ideal 'natural' price, but only actual market prices. The latter are connected to labour-content, but the connection is a *probabilistic* one.

On the other hand, we do follow Marx and the classical tradition in using labour-content as the fundamental universal measure of commodities. However, we do so not as a mere gesture of loyalty to Marx or to the classical tradition, but because we believe that there are several good and weighty arguments in favour of using labour-content in this capacity, as a measure to which prices should be related, yielding the ratio *price per unit of labour-content* as a central random variable in probabilistic economic theory. The rest of the present chapter will be devoted to detailing these arguments.

1. Labour as the Essential Substance of Economics

The decision as to which universal commodity-type is to be used as a measure is not a purely formal matter, but depends crucially on one's point of view on the nature of economics, as well as on one's purpose and interests—in both senses of 'interests', the intellectual and the material.

An economy is analogous to an organic metabolic system. (The difference is, of course, that the former is a social rather than a biological organism, and the processes whereby inputs are transformed into outputs are processes of production rather than bio-chemical ones.) Like an organic metabolic system, an economy transforms inputs into outputs, some of which are in turn used as inputs to produce other outputs, and so on. Through more or less complicated metabolic pathways, the system re-produces its inputs (often in greater quantities than the original ones) and also excretes some of the surplus products, which do not re-enter the metabolism as inputs and are therefore, from the metabolic point of view, 'waste' products. The surplus products that are not excreted are used by the organism for its growth.

To select a given universal commodity-type as a measure of all commodities is, in effect, to highlight this commodity-type as *the* essential 'substance', whose transubstantiation through the system, the pathways of its absorption as direct and indirect input into all outputs, is 'what the system is all about'.

For a given special purpose, or from a special point of view, a certain commodity-type may suggest itself as the natural choice for this central role. For example, if one is particularly interested (either intellectually or materially) in crude oil and its role in the economy, then it is reasonable to choose crude oil as the yardstick, because by measuring commodities in terms of their crude-oil-content one highlights the 'metabolism' of crude oil through the economic system. The economic system itself is then regarded primarily as an *oil economy*; and, from an oil economist's (or oil tycoon's) point of view, the two most important quantitative measures of *any* commodity are its price and its crude-oil-content.

However, we are concerned here not with any special viewpoint, but with the viewpoint of *general* economic theory. And we believe that from this general viewpoint labour is, *par excellence*, the essential substance of an economy, and should therefore be taken in economic theory as the fundamental yardstick. In making this statement we are, in effect, also expressing our opinion as to what economics is all about: *it is about the social productive activity of human beings, social labour. The science of economics, taken in the most general sense, is concerned with the study of the social processes and structures by means of which and through which social labour is organized and performed, and the output of this labour distributed and allocated to various uses.*

To be sure, this thesis about the nature of economics is not a theorem that can be proved or refuted. It is a matter of opinion, on which people may and do differ. However, one opinion may be more reasonable than another, or more consonant with one's views on other matters. For example, our own view of economics harmonizes better than others with a commitment to the labour movement.

To those who do not think that economics is concerned essentially and necessarily with human social labour—who maintain, for example, that it is a sort of game-theory, or that it is about the optimum allocation of scarce resources between competing claims—we can say little except that in our view they are missing, or mystifying, the main point. We certainly cannot convince them that labour-content, as a common measure of commodities, should play a central role in economic theory.

However, we must stress that this works both ways. A rejection of labour-content as a central economic concept is not merely a difference on a point of technical detail: it is in effect a rejection of the thesis that economics is primarily about the 'metabolism' of human social labour. For, from this point of view, a general economic theory that does not cast labour-content in a central role is like *Hamlet* without the Prince of Denmark. Certainly, prices and rates of profit are within the province of economic theory and must be accommodated within it; but if one accepts the above thesis, then they must be regarded as epiphenomena, as mediations in the distribution of the fruits of human labour. A theory that confines its attention to prices and profits *alone* merely scratches the surface of the phenomena. Those, such as Steedman, who started off from a Marxist position and then, despairing of the orthodox Marxist attempt to reduce equilibrium prices to labour-values, banished the latter concept altogether from the core of economic theory, have, in our opinion, thrown the baby out with the dirty bath water.[14]

Of course, if it were the case that prices and labour-content had no relation whatsoever to one another, then economic theory would find itself in a very awkward position; not because that would mean —why should it?—that labour-content is not of cardinal importance, but because the unity of economics as a science would be in question. One branch of economic theory would have to deal with labour-content and another, quite unrelated branch, with prices, which (epiphenomenal though they may be) are hardly a peripheral or unimportant matter.

But this is not actually the case. The failure of input-output theory to discover a relationship between labour-content and prices is due, not to the non-existence of any such relationship, but to the error of the theorists who base themselves on the fallacious assumption of a uniform equilibrium rate of profit, and who tacitly assume that a relationship, if it exists, must be deterministic. However, as we shall try to show later, a relationship does in fact exist, but it is a *probabilistic* one.

So far, our discussion of labour as the 'essential substance' of economics has referred to an economy in general, whether it is capitalist or not. Indeed, labour is the one resource that is common to all economies, capitalist or otherwise. In this universality labour is quite unique: no other economic resource is necessarily present in *every* economic system.

The yardstick of labour-content as a measure of all products can thus be applied also to a non-capitalist economy, whether or not the products in question assume the form of commodities (that is, are produced for exchange in the market rather than for direct consumption).

However, the *concept* of labour in the abstract—irrespective of the concrete work being performed—is, properly speaking, quite modern. In traditional pre-industrial societies, a labour market either did not exist or, at best, was very restricted; different trades, crafts and occupations were often sharply divided from each other by barriers of family, caste and status, with little mobility between them. In such a society it was far from self-evident that the farmer, the blacksmith, the spinner, the miller, the mason and the goldsmith were all doing 'the same thing', albeit in different concrete forms: namely, engaging in productive labour 'on behalf of society'. The differences and distinctions between the various crafts and occupations were much more evident—and, in a sense, more real—than their mutual equivalence. This equivalence could only be deduced abstractly, for example from the fact that products of different crafts could be exchanged as commodities. But given even a relatively high development of commerce, it required a great leap in abstract thinking to form the concept of abstract labour. That the great fourteenth-century Arab historian and proto-sociologist, Ibn Khaldun, was able to anticipate this concept is therefore due not

88

only to the fact that he lived in a society in which commerce played a major role but also to his extraordinary genius.[15]

It is only with the advent of industrial capitalism that the concept of abstract labour has become almost a commonplace, a concept that corresponds more or less directly to observable everyday reality. The existence of an extensive labour market, the increased mobility between occupations, the constant de-skilling of existing crafts and the unceasing creation of new skills—all these demonstrate the essential social equivalence of different types of work, so that today one speaks as a matter of course about the 'work-force', implying not only that the products of different workers are mutually exchangeable, but also that the workers themselves are, in a rather direct sense, interchangeable.

In the present work we are concerned specifically with a modern capitalist economy. In what follows we shall therefore highlight the special and unique roles that labour (as an input) and labour-power (as a commodity) play in the capitalist mode of production.

In selecting one commodity-type as a yardstick for measuring all commodities, we shall be assigning to that commodity-type a special role in theory. To this extent the theory becomes *asymmetric*, since one commodity-type is singled out as theoretically exceptional. This theoretical asymmetry will be acceptable only if it can be shown to reflect a real, factual asymmetry—that is, if that commodity-type is seen to be exceptional in reality. We shall show that this is indeed the case with labour-power.

2. Labour-power—the Essential Commodity of Capitalism

We have argued that human labour is the one resource whose presence is essentially necessary for the existence of a capitalist economy (and indeed of any economy whatsoever).

It is true that as a matter of historical fact the development of capitalism depended on the availability of certain physical resources, such as coal and iron. Similarly, the dependence of present-day capitalism on the availability of crude oil is a well-known fact. But such resources (and any other resource except labour), however important they may be, are merely contingent. They have nothing to do with the inherent logic of capitalism as a system. Whether capitalism could have developed if there were no such thing as coal or iron is a matter for idle historical speculation. But there is certainly no *logical* reason why a coal-less or iron-less capitalism should be impossible. These resources could conceivably be replaced by others. Similarly, the question as to whether capitalism will be able to outlive the predicted exhaustion of the earth's crude oil reserves is a contingent one. There is no *logical* reason why capitalism should not be able to operate with some alternative source of energy.

The case of labour is very different. Labour, as a resource, is necessary for the existence of any economic system whatsoever. Certainly capitalism could not possibly do without it. Moreover, a capitalist economy requires not only that labour should be available, but, much more specifically, that it should be generally available *as a commodity, as labour-power, separate both from the product and from the person of the direct producer*. This double separation is characteristic of capitalism.

In some pre-capitalist economies, the production of commodities is quite widespread: many, if not most, products are not consumed by their direct producers but sold on the market. However, the vast majority of direct producers do not sell their 'raw' labour-power; instead, they sell products in which their labour is already materialized. But capitalism proper can operate only if labour-power itself becomes a commodity. With the development of capitalism, a growing proportion, and eventually the majority, of direct producers have nothing to sell but their labour-power. This is not merely a contingent fact; it is an intrinsic feature of capitalism. Moreover, labour-power is absolutely unique in that its presence *as a commodity* is essential for the existence of capitalism.

The converse is also true: labour-power as a commodity, in the strict sense of the word, exists *only* under capitalism. Although hired labour existed long before capitalism came into being, labour-power became a fully fledged commodity only when it was reified into a 'thing' owned by its seller, the worker—a thing that is alienable and strictly distinct (albeit physically inseparable) from the worker's own person.

A true commodity exchange is a contractual transaction between two parties, seller and buyer, who confront each other as formally equal and free from all extra-economic coercion.[16] It is a purely impersonal economic transaction, in which the parties are otherwise indifferent to each other. Unlike an exchange of presents, for example, a commodity exchange does not involve any personal non-economic bond between the two parties and does not alter their formal mutual indifference. Thus, for labour-power to be a commodity in the strict sense of the word, its sale must be like the exchange of a thing, which does not involve a relation of servitude between seller and buyer. Such a purely instrumental relation between worker and employer—as distinct from that between servant and master—is coeval with capitalism.[17] It first became common in England during the second half of the eighteenth century, and did not get firmly established until well into the nineteenth century.

Thus capitalism is essentially and uniquely characterized by the general availability of labour-power as a commodity for sale 'on its own', so that, when it is sold, nothing else is packaged and sold with it—neither a product (in which labour is already embodied) nor the formal personal liberty of the direct producer.

And this double separation of labour-power is also the starting point of classical political economy.

3. The Peculiarity of Labour-power as a Commodity

The uniqueness of labour-power in the sense explained above—namely, that its presence as a separate commodity is both essential for capitalism and characteristic of it—is not quite an obvious fact, but one that is revealed by economic-historical analysis. However, the main peculiarity of labour-power *as* a commodity is plain and obvious: this commodity is 'produced' without capital and sold without profit.

Labour-power may be sold and bought like any other commodity, so that in the market-place there appears to be a symmetry between all commodities, including labour-power. However, when we look at the social process of production and re-production, the symmetry vanishes. The economy is inherently divided into two distinct and asymmetric sectors. One sector is made up of capitalist firms, in which capital is invested, and which are engaged in producing commodities other than labour-power; the second sector is the working population, organized in families or households, in which labour-power is generated and regenerated.

The asymmetry becomes even more pronounced when we look at the balance of costs and revenues in each sector. In the sector of capitalist firms, revenues must exceed costs. To stay in business, a firm must make a profit; this means that its yearly revenue, obtained as the total price received for its yearly output, must exceed its yearly costs, the total price that it pays for its inputs. If a positive surplus is not achieved, the firm will go out of business eventually. (In practice, firms often go bust even if they make a small positive profit, because the interest they have to pay on borrowed capital is greater than their profits.) If sufficiently many firms are in this position, the economy is in crisis. For the healthy operation of a capitalist economy, the profits made in the firm sector must be sufficient to pay not only for the individual consumption of the capitalists, but also for new investments, for the accumulation of capital.

Things are very different in the other sector, that of the working population. Here total revenue (obtained as wages) must roughly equal total costs (expended on consumption). A few workers may be able to save a sufficient amount for investment, and become capitalists. But if too many workers were able to do this, the supply of labour-power would be depleted, and the capitalist economy would run into a severe crisis.[18]

If we look at a normal capitalist economy as a whole, then the total price of all outputs generated during a given period, say a year, must exceed the total price of all inputs used up. (Of course, in this grand balance many commodities appear both as inputs and as outputs.) But the sector in which labour-power is generated is exceptional in that the total price of its output roughly equals the total price of its inputs.

All this is fairly obvious. But it has the somewhat less obvious consequence that labour-content is the most appropriate non-price measure of commodities.

To see this, let us consider the total input-output balance-sheet of the same capitalist economy, measured this time not in prices but in terms of some universal commodity-type. For the sake of illustration let us first choose petrol as a yardstick, and measure all commodities in terms of their petrol-content.

Let us make the very reasonable assumption that the economy in question is capable of generating a physical surplus. We find in this case that the total petrol-content of all the outputs of the economy during, say, one year is greater than the total petrol-content of all the inputs used up during the same period. In other words, a surplus petrol-content is generated. But if we turn to examine the economy unit by unit, in order to find out exactly *where* this surplus is generated, we find that the economy splits up into two parts, an exceptional sector and a normal sector.

The *exceptional sector* is made up of all firms that do not use petrol as a *direct* input in their process of production. Such firms do not generate any surplus petrol-content. The total petrol-content of the inputs of such a firm is simply passed on to its outputs, without any diminution or augmentation.

The *normal sector* is made up of those firms that do use petrol as a direct input in their process of production. In such firms a surplus petrol-content *is* generated. To see why this is so, recall that (in an economy capable of producing a physical surplus) the petrol-content of a litre of petrol is less than one litre. Suppose, for the sake of illustration, that the petrol-content of a litre of petrol is $\frac{1}{3}$ litre. If, during a year, a given firm uses up x litres of petrol as direct input, then in the sum total of the petrol-content of all the firm's *inputs* during that year the contribution of these x litres will be only $x/3$ litres, because the petrol-content of x litres of petrol is $x/3$ litres. But each litre of petrol used as input transmits to the output not $\frac{1}{3}$ litre but *a full litre* of petrol-content. Therefore the contribution of the x litres of petrol to the petrol-content of the total *output* of the firm will be x litres. All the inputs other than petrol simply pass on their petrol-content to the output, without change. It follows that the total petrol-content of the yearly output of this firm exceeds the total petrol-content of its yearly inputs by $2x/3$ litres (since $x - x/3 = 2x/3$).

As for the units that generate labour-power—namely, workers' households—they will belong to the normal sector if petrol is one of the items in the standard consumption basket (which is indeed the case in the advanced capitalist countries). In the contrary case, they belong to the exceptional sector.

Thus we see that our 'petrol-content accounting' splits up the economy in a completely different way from our previous price-and-profit accounting. In the former—obviously artificial—split-up, the exceptional sector is made up of those branches of production that do not use petrol as direct input, and hence do not generate a surplus petrol-content. In the latter, the exceptional sector is made up of the working population, which does not make a profit. Needless to say, this latter split-up corresponds directly to the socio-economic structure of the capitalist system.

Since we are looking for a non-price measure of commodities that can be used *alongside prices* and can be statistically related to prices, the choice of petrol-content for such a purpose would be quite inappropriate, for it would impose on us a schizophrenic double division of the economy in two completely unrelated ways.

The same stricture applies equally to all other similar yardsticks, except one: labour-content. For, under a 'labour-content accounting' the economy splits up in exactly the same way as under the price-and-profit accounting: the normal sector is made up precisely of all capitalist firms, because they all buy the commodity labour-power on the labour market and use labour as a direct input, and therefore generate a labour-content surplus in their process of production. The exceptional sector consists of the working population.

Surplus money-value and surplus labour-value are generated in parallel, in the same part of the economy. (Once we notice this fact, it is very tempting to suppose, as did Marx and his classical predecessors, that there is some deterministic relation between 'natural' money-prices and labour-values. But this supposition, however tempting, is incorrect.)

4. Labour-content as an Invariable Measure of Commodities

So far, in discussing the advantages and disadvantages of various measures of commodities, we have tacitly assumed that the different commodities being measured all belong to the same economy—which means, in practice, that they are sold-and-bought in the same country at about the same time, say within one year.

However, if economic theory is not to be completely static and localized, it ought to be able to consider simultaneously several economies separated from each other in space or time. We must be able to compare the German economy with the Japanese, and the British economy at present with the British economy of 1867. It will, therefore, be of great advantage to have a measure by means of which commodities of different economies can be compared meaningfully.

Price, by itself, is clearly not such a measure. If commodity A was sold for £2 in England in January 1980 and commodity B was sold for £4, also in England, but in June 1981, it does not follow that B was really twice as expensive as A. In order to make a realistic comparison between the two prices, we must take into account the change in the 'purchasing power' of the pound sterling between the two dates. In practice, this is done as follows. A certain sample or 'basket' of commodities, thought to be a 'representative sample', is chosen in January 1980, and its total price is noted. Then, in June 1981 the total price of an exactly similar basket of commodities is noted again. By comparing the two results one obtains a *price index*, which is supposed to reflect the change in the purchasing power of the pound. But this calculation depends on the somewhat arbitrary selection of a 'representative' sample of commodities. Moreover, the meaningfulness of the index depends on the assumption that if a given basket of commodities is a representative sample (however this term may be defined) for January 1980, then an exactly similar basket is also representative for June 1981. This assumption, in our particular example, may be fairly reasonable, since the two dates are quite close to each other. But the same assumption becomes absurd if the two dates for which the comparison is made are sufficiently far apart.

For example, suppose we want to compare the prices of two commodities sold in England, the first in 1867 and the second in 1981. To compare the two respective nominal prices would be nonsense. For a realistic comparison, we need again to take into account the change in the pound's purchasing power; in other words, we need to compute a price index for comparing 1867 prices with 1981 prices. But there is no reasonable basis for computing such an index. If a given basket of commodities were a representative sample of the commodities sold in 1867, then a similar assortment could not be found today anywhere, except possibly in a museum. The vast majority of commodity-types that were produced in 1867 have long gone out of production. Conversely, most commodity-types produced today were undreamt of in Victorian times. Between 1867 and 1981, the commodity-types produced in England have changed almost beyond recognition; moreover, consumption habits and the very structure of society have altered so much, that any comparison of prices between the two economies is virtually meaningless.

Similar difficulties are encountered if one tries to compare prices paid for commodities in two different countries, even at the same time. The rate of exchange between the two currencies is of little help. For example, at the time of writing, the rate of exchange between the pound sterling and the US dollar is $1.86 per £1. But this does not mean at all that £1 has in Britain the 'same' purchasing power as $1.86 in the USA. In order to make a realistic comparison, we would again need a price-index for translating US dollar prices into British pound prices. The computation of such an index is highly problematic, even between these two countries, whose economies are relatively similar. For two countries whose economies are very dissimilar, say Germany and India, the computation of a reasonable comparative price-index is quite impossible. Economic statisticians do try to compute such indexes, just as economic historians try to compute comparative price-indexes for different historical epochs, but the real significance of these exercises is not very great, and their results are, at best, tentative.

All this is merely a manifestation of the fact that prices are largely an economic epiphenomenon. Comparison of commodities in terms of their prices is meaningful only if the commodities being compared are located in the same economy, or at least in very similar economies, and are not too far apart in time.

Next let us consider the possibility of comparing commodities in different economies in terms of their C-content, where C is some universal commodity-type other than labour. For example, let us take petrol-content as a standard of comparison. What, of general economic significance, can we learn from the fact that commodity A in one economy has the same petrol-content as commodity B in another economy? Not very much. In any case, such a comparison is not even possible, in general. There are economies in which petrol is either not used at all, or is not a universal commodity-type; the measure of commodities in terms of their petrol-content is inapplicable in such an economy. As we have seen, the presence of any resource other than labour is merely a contingent fact as far as economics is concerned.

96

By contrast, comparison of commodities in terms of their labour-content is always quite meaningful and informative, whether the commodities in question are located in the same economy or not. The labour-content of a given commodity is a measure of its 'cost' to society—not cost in epiphenomenal money terms, but in terms of real human social effort. The statement that the labour-content of a certain commodity is, say, ten worker-hours makes sense, and has basically the same meaning, whether the commodity in question is located in the England of 1867, the Germany of 1960, or the India of 1981.[19]

5. The Importance of Labour-content as a Theoretical Concept

The price of a commodity is, in general, a plain and palpable quantity, which can be directly observed at the moment of sale.[20] In contrast, labour-content is an abstract notion, which, though it can be made sufficiently intelligible, is meaningful only within a theoretical and more or less idealized model. The labour-content of a given commodity cannot be observed directly; it can only be measured—or, better, estimated—indirectly and subject to various theoretical assumptions and idealizations of reality. Thus of the two concepts, *price* and *labour-content*, the former is relatively more empirical and the latter more theoretical.[21] On the other hand, the price of a commodity is influenced by a variety of contingent and accidental circumstances, whereas its labour-content is, as it were, made inherent in it through the process of its production.

Analogous pairs of concepts exist also in other sciences. For example, the concepts of *weight* and *mass* in mechanics. Although in everyday usage these concepts are often conflated with each other, they are in principle very different. Weight is more directly observable and measurable, but it is subject to contingent circumstances: the same body will weigh more in the polar regions than near the Equator, more on Earth than on the Moon, and it will weigh nothing in an artificial satellite. Mass, on the other hand, is a highly theoretical notion, which has meaning only with reference to a particular theoretical framework (such as classical mechanics, or relativistic mechanics). The mass of a body is not directly observable, and cannot be estimated without making fairly far-reaching theoretical assumptions. But it is inherent in the body, and independent of contingent circumstances.[22]

An even better analogy is provided by the pair of concepts *phenotype* and *genotype* in biology. The phenotype of an organism is more or less directly observable; its genotype is a highly abstract theoretical construct.[23] The phenotype is affected by a great variety of contingent and environmental circumstances, while the genotype of a given organism is, according to current theory, inherent in the organism from the moment of its generation. And the analogy with the pair of concepts *price* and *labour-content* is particularly apt, because the relation between phenotype and genotype is not deterministic, inasmuch as there is a statistical variation in phenotypic characteristics of organisms that have identical genotype, due to the large number of random environmental factors.

A scientific theory cannot confine itself to dealing with what is directly observable, to the exclusion of abstract theoretical concepts. The attempt to expunge theoretical concepts, such as labour-content, from economic theory, leaving only directly observable quantities, such as prices, is a manifestation of instrumentalism, an extreme form of empiricism, which is destructive of all science. Without the concept of labour-content, economic theory would be condemned to scratching the surface of phenomena, and would be unable to consider, let alone explain, certain basic tendencies of the capitalist mode of production.

As an example of such a tendency, which is of great economic interest but which cannot even be formulated without the concept of labour-content, consider the *law of increasing productivity of labour*, or *decreasing labour-content*. This law amounts, roughly speaking, to the seemingly commonplace observation that as a capitalist economy develops, and as techniques of production develop with it, it takes less labour-time to produce the same product. To be more precise: consider a given capitalist economy as it evolves over a period of, say, a few decades; let C be a commodity-type (other than labour-power) that is produced in the economy throughout this period; then there is virtual certainty (probability very near 1) that the labour-content of one unit of C will be lower at the end of the period than it was at the beginning.

This law is strongly suggested by common experience and

observation; indeed, most economists would take it more or less for granted. It seems quite clear that it takes less labour-time to produce one kilogram of wheat grain today than it did fifty or seventy years ago. The same applies also to other commodity-types that have retained their identity over a similar period.

But from a logical point of view the law is far from being self-evident. It is not at all obvious that it can be deduced from any other economic law.

If there were no fundamental change in the methods of production, then it would be reasonable to expect that the amount of labour required to produce one unit of output should rise in time, rather than fall, especially if there is an increase in the total volume of output. This is what is known as the law of diminishing marginal returns—the application of more labour to the same method of production may yield more output, but the ratio of output to the input of labour tends to decline.

Therefore, if the labour-content of a physical unit of output in fact tends to decline, despite the increase of total output, this must be associated with changes in the methods of production. But even so, the nature of this association is not at all obvious. Under capitalism, technological change is not aimed directly at reducing the labour-content of a physical unit of output, but at increasing profit margins, mainly by reducing unit costs. And on the face of it there is no logical reason why reduction of unit cost should in fact lead to reduction in unit labour-content.

Indeed, in formal input-output theory (with a uniform rate of profit) it is possible to obtain a model whose input-output coefficients vary in time (formally reflecting 'technological development') in such a way as *to increase both the rate of profit and the labour-content of a unit of each commodity-type*, while the real wage-basket remains unchanged. Thus, formally speaking, 'maximization of profit' does not imply a decline in unit labour-content.

Moreover, turning from formal theory to actual facts, it is certainly possible to find factual examples—admittedly, very rare, localized and rather short-lived—where increased profitability is achieved by changing the method of production in such a way as to *increase* the input of labour per unit of output. However, the *probability* of such a development is very low.

This suggests that the law of decreasing labour-content is really a probabilistic one, as indeed we have formulated it: the probability of a decline in the unit labour-content of each commodity-type (other than labour-power) is very near 1, but not quite equal to 1. Such laws are common in all probabilistic scientific theories. For example, according to probabilistic demography it is possible—though very highly unlikely—that all the babies born in China on the first of April 1996, will be female. Similarly, it is consistent with the laws of statistical mechanics for a cube of ice to form spontaneously in the middle of a hot cup of tea, but the probability of this is negligibly small.

The only major exception to the law of decreasing labour-content is the commodity-type labour power. The reason for this is not difficult to see. We have suggested above that there is a connection—albeit indirect and probabilistic—between the decline in the labour-content of a unit of output of a given type and the tendency to reduce unit costs in the process of its production, in order to increase the margin of profit. But labour-power is the one type of commodity that is not sold for profit. Here there is no distinction between selling price and cost—both are equal to the wage. Workers continually struggle to *increase* the price (which is also the cost) of their labour-power, thus leading to a gradual increase in the physical standard consumption basket. If the labour-content of consumer goods did not tend to decline, then an increase in the standard physical consumption of workers would mean an *increase* in the labour-content of a unit of labour-power. However, the labour-content of consumer goods does tend to decline.

As a matter of fact, the labour-content of the real wage has remained more or less stable for many decades (if not longer) in the main centres of capitalist production. In other words, the physical increase in the average working-class consumption basket has been more or less exactly offset by the decline in the labour-content of consumer goods.

The question now arises: is it possible to explain logically why the law of decreasing labour-content is valid under normal conditions of capitalist development? In other words, can this law be deduced from some other—perhaps more immediately recognizable and verifiable—laws of motion and development of a capitalist economy, such as the free movement of capital, the drive to reduce unit costs (in money terms), and so forth.

It is quite clear that such an explanation, if it is possible at all, can be given only within a theory that relates the notion of labour-content to those of price and profit. Thus we see that a unified theory of labour-content, price and profit is needed for an explanation of one of the simplest and seemingly obvious tendencies of the capitalist system. We shall discuss this law and some of its implications in chapter VII.

Chapter Five
Price and Wage as Random Variables

We have already remarked in chapter IV that an essential feature of the capitalist mode of production is the *combination* of the planned, rational and efficient social process of production *within* each factory, with the unplanned, haphazard and unpredictable behaviour of the market.

Viewed as a whole, from a broad social perspective, capitalism may indeed be seen as deranged, irrational and wasteful. But within the narrow, alienated context of a given process of production, and in a purely relative technical sense, rationality rules. Within each enterprise, every minute step in the production process is scrutinized, calculated and subjected to detailed cost-analysis, so as to optimize performance. The mutual cooperation of the workers and their utmost obedience to a single plan and a single authority are rigorously enforced. But the interactions between different enterprises are *in principle* chaotic and unplanned; free competition rules. This duality of order and disorder is reflected in the relationship between labour-content and price.

Labour-content makes sense as a measure of commodities precisely because within each enterprise extreme care is taken to rationalize the use of labour. The capitalist system, as a totality, is notorious for its shameless squandering of this precious human resource; but within each productive unit the greatest care is taken to economize in the use of labour, not only because labour-power is expensive, but also because it is unruly. Each capitalist strives to minimize his or her own dependence upon living labour, in order to become less vulnerable to shifts in the balance of power between the two main classes. The rationalization of labour is thus an important weapon in the arsenal of the capitalists.

On the other hand, the chaotic nature of the relations between different capitalist firms is reflected in the behaviour of quantities related to market prices. Free competition implies that each commodity fights for its survival and for its optimal price in utter disregard for all other commodities, including labour-power. If need be, it would happily push forward at the expense of other commodities.

The fluidity of the market is reflected in the behaviour of prices and even in the very shape and form of products, which are everchanging, just as the rate of profit of any given firm is subject to unpredictable change. In minding its own business, each firm tries to manipulate its prices, and varies the form and substance of its products, so as to optimize the chances of its survival and growth.

This perpetual state of flux, in which the prices of commodities of any given type, as well as the very nature of the commodity-types themselves, are subject to continual and unpredictable changes, is inherent in the system of competitive capitalism. Any island of predictability, any 'window' of information, rapidly calls forth a rush of capital seeking to take advantage of it; but such a rush of capital soon erases the former data, swamps the island of predictability—and randomness is reconstituted.

We conclude that a conceptual framework that does not take full account of this essential randomness can provide only a very limited insight into the working of the system. In particular, a mathematical analysis of prices should not postulate the existence of a *fixed* assortment of commodity-types that keep being reproduced. Rather, it should allow for the fact that the composition of the total product of the system is indeterminate, inasmuch as new commodity-types keep appearing on the market and existing types go out of production.

Yet, all current formal models of capitalist price-systems start precisely from this postulate: that there is a fixed finite set of commodity-types. This is because the only meaning that these price-theories can assign to the notion of 'price' is that of an ideal exchange ratio between two commodity-types. It is posited that to every two given commodity-types it is possible to assign an ideal exchange ratio (for example, 1 unit of commodity-type **A** = x units of commodity-type **B**), which constitutes their ideal relative price. A fixed unit of some particular commodity-type—say an ounce of gold—is then selected as a yardstick, or *numéraire*, in terms of which the ideal unit price of every commodity-type can be expressed (for example, 1 unit of commodity-type A = x ounces of gold). This ideal, or 'natural', unit-price is supposed to be the time-average around which actual market prices oscillate.

Thus, existing price-theories do not concern themselves directly with *actual* market-prices, at which commodities are in fact sold and bought on the market, but with purely theoretical ideal 'equilibrium' prices. The only way in which such theories are allegedly related to real prices is indirectly, through the supposition that the ideal unit-price of each commodity-type is the long-term time-average of its real unit-price. However—quite apart from the fact that it is in general illegitimate to postulate that in a state of equilibrium a random variable assumes its mean value—the very notion of a 'long-term average unit price' hardly makes sense for a commodity-type whose lifetime in the market is brief. It is obviously meaningful to talk about the long-term average price of a ton of granulated white sugar (measured, say, in dollars and corrected for inflation, or, better, in gold). But what meaning can one attribute to the 'long-term average' price of a given model of electronic computer, or digital wrist-watch, or car—a model that remains in production for perhaps a couple of years (if that), and is then replaced by another model, differing in design, construction and qualities? It thus appears on closer inspection that, for these ephemeral commodity-types, the only bridge between the purely theoretical ideal unit-price and the actual price paid on the market—the bridge of long-term average unit price—is itself a fictional, purely imaginary construct, without reference to reality.

It should be stressed, moreover, that in a well-developed modern capitalist economy the majority of commodity-types are of this ephemeral kind. There are relatively few commodity-types that preserve their self-identity over long periods of time.

(Among these enduring commodity-types, which do preserve their identity, the most important is labour-power, provided we understand 'labour-power' in the abstract sense explained in appendix II. Indeed, as explained in chapter IV, labour-power is unique in that its presence in the market as a major commodity-type is a *sine qua non* for the existence of a capitalist economy. The persistence of other commodity-types is merely a contingent fact.)

Because of the continual flux in the nature and identity of commodity-types—which is an essential feature of capitalism—we forgo any attempt to develop a theory concerning the distribution of the unit-price of each separate commodity-type. Rather, we lump together *all* commodity-types (except labour-power) into one aggregate type: 'commodity-in-general' or, as we shall call it, *'general commodity'*. This aggregation is possible insofar as all commodity-types can be measured by a common yardstick; and, as we have argued at length in chapter IV, an eminently reasonable common yardstick is provided by *labour-content*.

Thus for our present price-theory we postulate that each commodity of any type (other than labour-power) has a definite labour-content, equal to the total amount of labour-time that is required, both directly and indirectly, for its production by the standard method prevailing in the economy under consideration. Then, as our random variable, whose distribution reflects the price-structure in the economy, we take the variable *price per unit of labour-content*, or, as we shall call it, *specific price*, which equals the ratio between the price paid for a commodity and the labour-content of that commodity.[1] We shall denote this random variable, specific price, by Ψ. When a given commodity is sold, its labour-content λ *realizes* or *captures* a certain price π; we then say that for this transaction Ψ assumes the numerical value π/λ.

Note that our aggregate 'general commodity' (whose specific price is measured by Ψ) includes commodities of all types whatsoever, *except one: labour-power*. We single out labour-power for separate treatment, and its price (that is, *wages*) will feature as a separate random variable. The exclusion of labour-power from the general commodity, and its treatment as a separate type, is justified on the grounds that labour-power is in several ways a peculiar and exceptional commodity-type. The detailed discussion of this point (see chapter IV) need not be rehearsed here. We merely wish to note that, in the present context, the most crucial peculiarity of labour-power is that it is produced without capital, outside the framework of organized social production, and is not sold for profit.

When an ordinary commodity is sold, the price it fetches resolves itself into a sum of two terms: the costs of its production + profit. Of course, the second term, profit, can occasionally be zero or even negative, since some commodities may be sold at cost price or at a loss; but the *probability* of such an event must normally be small. The case with labour-power is markedly different: the price it fetches (wages) must normally just about cover the costs of its reproduction. It is therefore prudent to assume that the price of labour-power obeys statistical laws that may be qualitatively rather different from those governing the distribution of other prices. If we lumped labour-power together with all other commodity-types, the difference between the two kinds of law would become submerged, and valuable information might be lost.

Another advantage of treating labour-power separately is that it allows us to avoid using (explicitly or implicitly) the rather questionable notion: 'the labour-content of a unit of labour-power'. In postulating that every non-labour commodity has a definite labour-content, we assumed that for every type of commodity (other than labour-power) there is a 'standard' method of production, requiring definite amounts of inputs per unit of output. This is obviously an idealization, an oversimplification of reality. However, it is not an unreasonable one. And, in any case, it can be shown that labour-content can be defined for non-labour commodities even in an economy with several acceptable methods of production. (See note 8 to chapter IV.) However, in order to attribute a definite labour-content to a unit of labour-power, we would have to assume the existence of a 'standard real-wage basket', consisting of definite amounts of each type of consumer good, per each unit of labour-power. This assumption seems quite doubtful, since in reality consumption patterns can vary widely, both quantitatively and qualitatively, within the working population of a country at a given time.

On the other hand, since labour-power (in the abstract sense explained in appendix II) retains both its self-identity and its essential economic role throughout the era of capitalism, it is perfectly feasible to treat it separately, as a well-defined special commodity.

We therefore introduce two separate random variables, one for the wage and the other for the specific price of the general commodity, which is the aggregate of all commodity-types except labour-power.

We first fix a particular interval of time T, called the *reference period*. The exact length of the period T is of little importance, but it must be long enough so that the number of transactions performed during it is sufficiently large to allow the application of probabilistic methods; yet it must be short enough to allow us to neglect any changes in the structure of employment, wages and prices during the period T itself. Realistically, we may take T to be, say, a given month.

We now define a sample space, called the *labour-power space* as follows. Each point in the labour-power space consists of a unit of labour-power sold by a worker to a capitalist firm in the given economy during the reference period T. Let us suppose that the unit of labour-power is a *worker-hour*; then the number of points in the labour-power space is equal to the number of worker-hours sold-and-bought in the economy during the period T. All points in this space are assigned equal weights. The random variable *wage*, denoted by W, is then defined as follows: if the gross wage paid for the i-th point of the labour-power space (that is, for the i-th worker-hour) is w, then $W(i) = w$.

In order to make W well-defined, we must specify the monetary units in which wages are to be measured. If we were interested only in one single economy at one single period, then the choice of monetary unit would be of no importance. But in order to facilitate at least a rough comparison between different economies, or between different periods of one and the same economy, we follow the suggestion of Adam Smith[2] and use as our monetary unit the *average unit wage*. Thus, if during the period T the number of worker-hours bought-and-sold was 5.4 billion, and if the *total* gross wage paid for this labour-power was £13.50 billion, then we measure each $W(i)$ not in units of £1.00 but in units of £2.50 ($= 13.50/5.4$). In other words, we always measure wages in such units so as to make the average unit wage $\mathbf{E}W$ equal 1.

In this connection, several remarks should be made. First, the unit used here, the average unit wage (briefly, a.u.w.), will clearly vary in currency terms (that is, in terms of, say, pounds sterling or dollars) from economy to economy and from period to period. If Jane Brown was paid $\frac{3}{4}$ a.u.w. for an hour of her labour in April 1970 and John Smith got $1\frac{1}{2}$ a.u.w. for an hour of his labour in June 1980, this does not mean that he received twice as much money (in pounds sterling) as she had received. Still less does it mean that his wage enabled him to buy twice as much of the same goods she had been able to buy with her wage. All it means is that in the given transactions she was paid at $\frac{3}{4}$ of the average wage rate prevailing in April 1970, and he was paid at $1\frac{1}{2}$ times the average wage rate of June 1980. Thus the distribution of the random variable W tells us nothing directly about the nominal level of wages, or about the real purchasing power of wages. What it does tell us is how the *total* wage paid in the given economy during the given period T was distributed among the units of labour-power employed.

Second, we have taken the unit of labour-power to be a worker-hour rather than a larger unit such as worker-day, because the latter is less well defined: some working days are longer than others. Also, the wage-rate of one and the same worker may vary from hour to hour during a given day (for example, there is a separate rate for overtime). Of course, it would be possible to choose a *smaller* unit, such as worker-minute. This would have no effect on the c.d.f. F_W, provided the a.u.w. is also adjusted accordingly. The exact size of the unit of labour-power is of little consequence; what matters is that the unit for measuring labour-power and the unit for measuring wages are chosen *jointly* in such a way as to make $\mathbf{E}W = 1$.

Third, the c.d.f. F_W obviously depends on the choice of the particular period T, and will therefore vary in time. However, in normal times (that is, excluding rare times of drastic rapid changes in the pattern of employment and wages) the changes in F_W from month to month (for a given economy) are very slow and gradual. Thus, for a given economy, we can expect F_W to be affected very little whether we choose the period T to be May 1978 or June of the same year, or indeed the two-month period May-June of that year. Of course, if the economy is at equilibrium then—by definition—there is virtual certainty that the time dependence of F_W is altogether negligible.

We now turn to the general commodity. Referring to the same period T as before, we define a sample space called the *market space* (for the given period T). The points of this space are all the transactions performed during T, in which commodities other than labour-power were sold-and-bought.[3] Here it would obviously be inappropriate to assign equal weights to all transactions, irrespective of whether the commodity in question is, say, a box of matches or an oil tanker; the weight assigned to a given transaction must be proportional to the quantity of the commodity sold-and-bought. For reasons explained in chapter IV, the quantity of the commodity involved will be measured by its labour-content. Thus, let $\Lambda(i)$ be the labour-content of the commodity sold-and-bought in the i-th transaction; then the weight p_i assigned to this transaction is given by $\Lambda(i)/\Sigma\Lambda(j)$, where the summation is over all transactions. This means that all units of labour-content contribute equal weights. The weights p_i are clearly positive, and add up to 1. The random variable *specific price*, denoted by Ψ (pronounced 'psi'), is now defined as follows. If the price paid in the i-th transaction was $\Pi(i)$, then $\Psi(i) = \Pi(i)/\Lambda(i)$. Thus $\Psi(i)$ is the price paid in the i-th transaction *per unit of labour-content*.

Here, too, in order for Ψ to be well defined we must fix the units for measuring labour-content and prices. But these can no longer be chosen arbitrarily: if we wish our treatment of specific price and wage to be coherent, we must use the same units in both cases. Thus, if labour-power is measured in worker-hours, then $\Lambda(i)$ must also be measured in the same units. Similarly, the price $\Pi(i)$ must be measured in the same units as the price of labour-power, that is, in a.u.w. (average unit wage). Thus, whereas $\Lambda(i)$ is the total amount of human labour *embodied* in the commodity of the i-th transaction, $\Pi(i)$ is the amount of averagely-paid labour-power which the price paid for that commodity could *command* (as Adam Smith puts it). Also (again using the great Scot's term), $\Pi(i)$ is the *real* price of the commodity in question, as opposed to its *nominal* price measured in units of currency.

As to the time-dependence of the c.d.f. F_Ψ, and the relative insensitivity of F_Ψ to different choices of T (say May 1978 rather than June 1978 or May-June 1978)—the same remark applies here as in the case of F_W.

Let us now inquire into the nature of the distributions of our random variables W and Ψ. The c.d.f.'s F_W and F_Ψ are, strictly speaking, step functions. But if the period T is sufficiently long these functions can be taken, to a high degree of approximation, as smooth; so the p.d.f.'s f_W and f_Ψ may be assumed to exist. We would like to find out as much as we can about the shape of these p.d.f.'s.

We shall first deal with f_W. We shall not propose any mathematical formula for this function. Nevertheless, certain qualitative features of the graph of f_W can be stated with some confidence, based on empirical economic common sense. In this connection it is

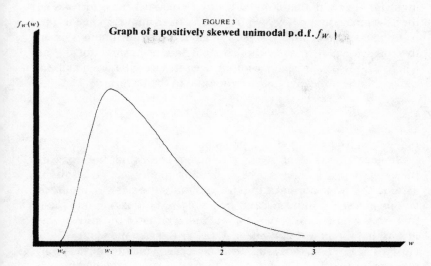

FIGURE 3
Graph of a positively skewed unimodal p.d.f. f_W

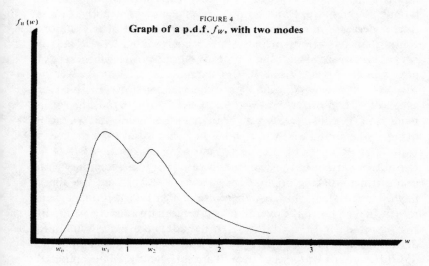

FIGURE 4
Graph of a p.d.f. f_W, with two modes

important to recall that if a and b are any real numbers, with $a < b$, then the area bounded by the graph of f_W from above, by the w-axis from below, by the line $w = a$ on the left and by the line $w = b$ on the right is equal to the proportion of labour-power, out of the whole labour-power space, whose wage rates were between a and b a.u.w. Mathematically, this area is equal to the integral

$$\int_a^b f_W(w)\mathrm{d}w.$$

(See appendix I and cf. fig. 2 in chapter II.)

On general, 'common sense' grounds, it seems that the shape of the graph of f_W is likely to be something like fig. 3. It is safe to assume that in a normal capitalist economy the pay for a unit of labour-power is bounded from below by some positive minimum unit wage w_0, perhaps equal to about one quarter of the a.u.w. This means that for all $w < w_0$ we have $f_W(w) = 0$. From the point w_0, the curve of $f_W(w)$ rises fairly rapidly and reaches a maximum at a point w_1. This w_1 is called the *modal* unit wage; wages in the neighbourhood of the modal unit wage are relatively the most common in the labour-power space. From w_1 on, $f_W(w)$ decreases steadily, but its rate of decrease (the slope of the curve on the right of w_1) is more gentle than its rate of increase had been from w_0 to w_1. This is because there are always some units of labour-power whose rate of pay is many times an a.u.w. (for example, the labour-power of workers with rare skills and great bargaining power). Thus the graph of f_W is *positively skewed* (or *skewed to the right*): its right-hand 'tail' is considerably longer than its left-hand 'tail'. Consequently, the modal unit wage w_1 is somewhat lower than the mean value $\mathbf{E}W$. Because of our choice of units, we always have $\mathbf{E}W = 1$.

Another variant of the f_W curve corresponds to an economy with two distinct working populations, between which there is a sharp pay differential. In this case there are in fact two labour markets rather than one, and the overall f_W is produced by a superposition of two separate curves, each with its own modal point. If the standard deviations of the two separate groups (that is, roughly speaking, the pay differentials *within* each group) are sufficiently small compared to the difference between the two modes, then the overall f_W curve will be *bimodal* rather than *unimodal*; in other words, it will have two 'humps' rather than one. (See fig. 4.) It seems quite likely that the South African economy has such a bimodal distribution of W, because of the sharp segregation of the 'white' and 'non-white' working populations and the extreme pay differentials between them. A somewhat similar effect may perhaps be produced in more 'normal' capitalist countries, due to the presence of a large underpaid migrant working population, or to discrimination against female workers. (Certainly, female labour is consistently underpaid in most countries, if not in all. But whether this discrimination is sharp enough to result in a bimodal f_W curve is far less certain.)

Empirical statistical investigation of the distribution of W in different economies at different periods is clearly of great value in connection with the study of a number of important socio-economic problems.

We must now turn to specific price, Ψ. Here we venture a definite hypothesis as to the mathematical law that governs the equilibrium distribution of this random variable. Namely, we conjecture that Ψ is approximately *normally distributed* ;[4] and we shall also try to estimate its mean value and standard deviation, and argue that the latter is quite small. We do not claim to have anything like a proper theoretical *proof* of our hypothesis; yet, there are plausible arguments—mostly based on very general probability-theoretical grounds, but partly also on empirically observed facts—which in our view strongly suggest it.

Before proceeding to justify our conjecture, we must specify certain simplifying assumptions. First, we shall assume that all non-labour commodities are sold by capitalist firms. An individual seller can also be regarded as a firm in which he or she is 'self-employed'.[5] In this case, however, we must assume that somehow the income of such an individual can be decomposed into self-paid wages and profits.

Second, we assume that each commodity is produced by the firm that sells it (or, more precisely, by the workers of that firm). At first sight this seems incorrect; for example, a supermarket sells sugar but does not produce it. However, economically speaking one must regard sugar-at-the-supermarket, sugar-at-the-wholesaler's and sugar-at-the-sugar-mill as three different types of commodity. The wholesaler produces sugar-at-the-wholesaler's from inputs that include sugar-at-the-sugar-mill, as well as labour, etc. Similarly, the supermarket produces sugar-at-the-supermarket from sugar-at-the-wholesaler's and other inputs (including the labour of shop-assistants etc.). Thus merchandizing is subsumed under production, and the distribution industry is regarded as part of industry.

Third, we shall assume that there are no indirect taxes. The effect of such taxes can be superimposed later on the result of our analysis. The simplest case is that of a value-added tax imposed at a flat rate on all commodities, as is done in some capitalist countries. It is easy to see (and will become even clearer from our analysis) that the effect of such a tax is to inflate all prices by a constant proportion. Other methods of indirect taxation may have a more complicated effect on the detailed structure of prices, but statistically speaking their effect on the overall distribution of Ψ is unlikely to be very different from that of a flat-rate VAT.

Fourth, we shall ignore ground rent. For a modern capitalist economy, this is not a drastic over-simplification.

Finally, we shall assume that the economy is closed (no import or export) and is at equilibrium.

We have listed these simplifying assumptions merely to facilitate reference. Naturally, not all of the theoretical considerations below depend on all of these assumptions simultaneously, or to the same extent.[6]

In order to ascertain the nature of the distribution of Ψ we shall need to decompose the price of each commodity into its constituent parts. This will enable us, among other things, to apply some basic and powerful theorems of probability theory, notably the Central Limit Theorem and the Law of Large Numbers (see appendix I). Our plan is, first, to estimate the expected (mean) value of Ψ, denoted as usual by **E**Ψ. Next, going a bit further, we shall argue that it seems reasonable to apply the Central Limit Theorem to Ψ and hence to conclude that the distribution of this random variable is quite close to normal. Finally, using certain facts about the normal distribution, we shall arrive at a rough estimate of the standard deviation of Ψ.

Consider any particular commodity, C, which is the object of some given transaction in our market space. Let the labour-content of C —measured, say, in worker-hours—be equal to λ; and let the price paid for C—measured in a.u.w., that is, in units of average hourly wage—be equal to π. Assuming (as we have agreed to do) that the effects of indirect taxation, ground rent and foreign imports can be ignored, we shall show that the price π paid for C can be represented as the sum of two quantities,

$$\pi = v + s, \tag{1}$$

where v and s are, respectively, the total share of labour-costs (wages) and the total share of profits in the price π. In other words, v is the sum total of wages paid to all workers who participated directly or indirectly in the production of C, each for his or her contribution of labour-power. Similarly, s is the sum total of profits made by all firms involved directly or indirectly in the production of C, each in respect of its workers' part in the production of this particular commodity.

To see why (1) holds, consider first the price π of C from the point of view of the firm F that has just sold C on the market. As far as firm F is concerned, the price π received for C resolves itself into three components: one component, π', goes to cover the cost of the non-labour direct inputs used up in the production of C; a second component, v', goes to cover the labour-costs incurred by F in the production of C; and the residue, s', is the profit that the firm makes on C. Thus

$$\pi = \pi' + v' + s'.$$

In common economic parlance, the sum of the last two components, $v' + s'$, is the *value added* by firm F in the production of C from its non-labour inputs.

Clearly, π, π' and v' are necessarily non-negative. The remaining term, s', can in principle be negative, although the probability of such an occurrence is quite small. In any case, the probability that the whole value added $v' + s'$ is non-positive is very small indeed and can be neglected safely. Thus we may assume with virtual certainty that $\pi' < \pi$.

Now, π' is the price paid by firm F for the non-labour inputs used up in the production of C. For simplicity of exposition, let us suppose that there is just one such input, which F bought from some other firm, F'. (The general case can be treated in a similar way.)

For firm F' the price π' splits up again into three components in a similar way as π split up for firm F:

$$\pi' = \pi'' + v'' + s'',$$

where π'', v'' and s'' are the non-labour costs, the labour costs and the profit of firm F' in respect of its transaction with firm F. Here too we may safely assume that $\pi'' < \pi'$. Substituting this last equality into the previous one, we obtain

$$\pi = \pi'' + (v' + s') + (v'' + s'').$$

If the production of C required more than one non-labour input, then the term $(v'' + s'')$ in this last equality is replaced by several terms of the same form, one term for each input. Thus the price π of C splits up into a residual non-labour cost π'' (representing the total cost of the direct non-labour inputs used up in producing the direct non-labour inputs of C) plus two or more value-added terms.

This procedure can now be iterated: the residual non-labour cost π'' can be split up again (as π and then π' were split up before), and so on repeatedly. Each time round, we get new value-added terms, while the residual non-labour cost grows successively smaller and will in fact tend to zero. Ultimately we obtain the equality

$$\pi = (v' + s') + (v'' + s'') + (v''' + s''') + \cdots \qquad (2)$$

in which the whole of π is completely resolved into a sum of value-added terms.[7]

Each of these terms, $(v' + s')$, $(v'' + s'')$, $(v''' + s''')$, $\cdots$, is a quantum of value added, a portion of the total price π of C contributed by some particular firm involved directly or indirectly in the production of C. Clearly, a given firm may contribute more than one such term, because in the overall metabolism of production there are many 'loops': some of the indirect inputs that go into a commodity produced by a given firm may well have been produced by that very firm.

We would like to rearrange (2) so as to obtain a one-to-one correspondence between value-added terms and firms. To this end, we enumerate all the firms in the economy in some arbitrary order: F_1,

$F_2, \ldots, F_m$. This ordering, albeit arbitrary, will be held fixed for the rest of this chapter. Now, let us consider the first firm in this enumeration, F_1. We add together all the value-added terms on the right-hand side of (2) that were contributed by F_1; more precisely, we add together all the wage parts of these terms and, separately, all the profit parts. We obtain a single term $(v_1 + s_1)$, which is the total contribution of F_1. Out of the price π paid by the buyer of C, a sum of v_1 goes to cover the wages paid by F_1 to its workers for their share (direct or indirect) in producing C; and s_1 goes to cover the profits made by F_1 in respect of its workers' part in producing C. If F_1 had no role (not even indirect) in the production of C, then of course we must put $v_1 = 0$ and $s_1 = 0$.

Proceeding similarly for $F_2, \ldots, F_m$, we obtain

$$\pi = (v_1 + s_1) + (v_2 + s_2) + \cdots + (v_m + s_m). \tag{3}$$

If we define v and s to be the total shares of wages and profits, respectively, in the price π, then we have

$$v = v_1 + v_2 + \cdots + v_m, \tag{4}$$
$$s = s_1 + s_2 + \cdots + s_m. \tag{5}$$

Equality (3) can now be written as: $\pi = v + s$, which is precisely our (1), whose validity is now established.

So far, in deriving equalities (1) to (5), we have considered a particular commodity C. Now let C_i be the commodity bought-and-sold in the i-th transaction (the i-th point of the market space). Then, for any i, we can take C_i to be the C in the foregoing discussion. Thus, each of the quantities occurring in (1) and in (3)-(5) can be regarded as the value, at the i-th point of the market-space, of the corresponding random variable. For example, (1) can be written as an identity

$$\Pi(i) = V(i) + S(i),$$

that holds for all i. Here Π is the price random variable defined above, such that for every i the value $\Pi(i)$ is the price paid for C_i. V and S are two new random variables, defined as follows: for each i, the values $V(i)$ and $S(i)$ are, respectively, the total share of wages and the total share of profits in the price of C_i. Since we have here an identity, which holds for all i, we obtain an equality involving these three random variables:

$$\Pi = V + S. \tag{1'}$$

Similarly, (3)-(5) yield the following equalities between random variables:

$$\Pi = (V_1 + S_1) + (V_2 + S_2) + \cdots + (V_m + S_m), \tag{3'}$$
$$V = V_1 + V_2 + \cdots + V_m, \tag{4'}$$
$$S = S_1 + S_2 + \cdots + S_m. \tag{5'}$$

Here V_j and S_j (where $j = 1, 2, \ldots, m$) are defined as follows: for each i, the value $V_j(i)$ is the total wage paid to the workers of the j-th firm F_j for their direct and indirect contributions to the production of C_i; and $S_j(i)$ is the total profit, direct and indirect, made by F_j on the commodity C_i.

Dividing (1') by the labour-content random variable Λ and recalling the definition of Ψ, we get

$$\Psi = \frac{V}{\Lambda} + \frac{S}{\Lambda}. \tag{6}$$

This equality can be used to yield a very good estimate of the mean value $\mathbf{E}\Psi$ of Ψ. By a general theorem (see appendix I), the mean of a sum of random variables is equal to the sum of their means; hence $\mathbf{E}\Psi = \mathbf{E}(V/\Lambda) + \mathbf{E}(S/\Lambda)$. We shall now try to estimate $\mathbf{E}(V/\Lambda)$ and $\mathbf{E}(S/\Lambda)$, and hence obtain an estimate for their sum, $\mathbf{E}\Psi$.

Let us start with $\mathbf{E}(V/\Lambda)$. By definition (see appendix I), $\mathbf{E}(V/\Lambda)$ $= \Sigma p_i[V(i)/\Lambda(i)]$, where the summation ranges over the whole market space—that is, over all transactions performed during the period T—and the p_i are the weights, which in this space are given by: $p_i = \Lambda(i)/\Sigma\Lambda(j)$. Using this expression for the weights we obtain,

$$\mathbf{E}\left(\frac{V}{\Lambda}\right) = \frac{\Sigma V(i)}{\Sigma\Lambda(i)}. \tag{7}$$

To understand the meaning of the right-hand side of this formula, let us denote by **C** the aggregate of all the commodities bought-and-sold during the reference period T. Then $\Sigma V(i)$ is the sum total of wages paid to workers who have contributed directly or indirectly to the production of **C**, for their respective contributions. And $\Sigma \Lambda(i)$ is the total labour-content of **C**.

If the economy were in a steady state, simply reproducing itself without expansion or structural change, then the aggregate **C'** of all commodities *produced* during the reference period T would have to be an exact replica of the aggregate **C** *sold* during the same period. Also, the sum total of wages paid during the period T, for all labour performed in producing **C'**, would equal the sum $\Sigma V(i)$ of all wages that have been paid to workers for producing **C**. And the total amount of labour performed during T (the labour-content of **C'**) would be equal to the total labour-content of **C**, which is $\Sigma \Lambda(i)$. In this case, the right-hand side of (7) would be equal to the quotient: total wages paid during T/total amount of labour performed during T. But this quotient is $\mathsf{E}W$; therefore we would have $\mathsf{E}(V/\Lambda) = \mathsf{E}W$.

In reality, the economy is never in a steady state and the aggregate **C'** produced during T is not an exact replica of **C**. The quantity $\mathsf{E}(V/\Lambda)$ is indeed a kind of average unit wage, but computed on a basis different from that on which $\mathsf{E}W$ is computed. In (7), the numerator $\Sigma V(i)$ is the sum total of wages that have been paid in respect of the labour performed to produce **C**, part of which was executed before T. But, strictly speaking, the denominator $\Sigma \Lambda(i)$ (the total labour-content of **C**) is not the total amount of labour that was *actually* performed (some of it prior to T) to produce **C**, but the total amount of labour that *would be* required to produce **C** from scratch *using methods of production that are standard in the period T itself*, rather than in the past.[8]

Nevertheless, since we are assuming that the economy is at or near dynamic equilibrium, overall economic conditions (including the methods of production and the distribution of wages) may be taken to vary relatively slowly. Therefore—noting that the labour embodied in **C** must for the most part have been performed during T or not long before[9]—the two averages $\mathsf{E}W$ and $\mathsf{E}(V/\Lambda)$ must be very nearly equal. We shall therefore use $\mathsf{E}W$ as a very good approximation for $\mathsf{E}(V/\Lambda)$.

Next, let us consider $E(S/\Lambda)$. A simple calculation, similar to that used to derive (7), yields

$$E\left(\frac{S}{\Lambda}\right) = \frac{\Sigma S(i)}{\Sigma \Lambda(i)}.$$

From this and (7) we obtain

$$E\left(\frac{S}{\Lambda}\right) = e^* E\left(\frac{V}{\Lambda}\right), \text{ where } e^* = \frac{\Sigma S(i)}{\Sigma V(i)}. \tag{8}$$

What is the meaning of the quotient e^*? We have seen above that the price of each commodity can be decomposed into a sum of value-added quanta; the total price is made up of bits of value-added, generated at various stages of its production. By definition, e^* is the ratio in which the total value-added embodied in the aggregate C of all commodities sold during T is apportioned between profits and wages.

Now recall that at the end of chapter III we observed that the ratio in which the total value-added of the economy (excluding rent, which we ignore here) is divided between gross profits and gross wages is equal to $e_0 = ER/EZ$.

It is true that e_0 and e^* are not calculated on the same basis. The ratio e_0 is defined with reference to the *firm space*; if we calculate e_0 for the period T, we obtain the ratio in which the *new* value-added *generated during this period* is being shared between capital and labour. On the other hand, e^* is defined with reference to the *market space*; it measures the ratio in which the price, which is also the total value-added embodied in C—some of which has been generated *before* the period T—was shared between capital and labour.

Nevertheless, if the economy is at or near dynamic equilibrium, the two ratios must be extremely close to each other, because the ratio between total profits and total wages cannot change rapidly. Indeed, as we observed in chapter III, empirical data show that e_0 is extremely stable over very long periods of time in developed capitalist countries. We therefore regard e_0 as an excellent approximation for e^*.

We are now ready to derive our estimate for $E\Psi$. From (6) and (8) we get

$$\mathsf{E}\Psi = \mathsf{E}\left(\frac{V}{\Lambda}\right) + \mathsf{E}\left(\frac{S}{\Lambda}\right) = (1 + e^*)\mathsf{E}\left(\frac{V}{\Lambda}\right).$$

Using e_0 and $\mathsf{E}\,W$ as good approximations for e^* and $\mathsf{E}(V/\Lambda)$, respectively, and recalling that by our choice of units $\mathsf{E}\,W$ must be 1, we get

$$\mathsf{E}\Psi = 1 + e_0, \tag{9}$$

as a good approximation.[10]

We have observed in chapter III that in Britain, the USA, and other developed capitalist countries e_0 is close to 1 and—disregarding minor short-term fluctuations—has remained close to 1 for many decades. It follows that a realistic numerical estimate for $\mathsf{E}\Psi$ is 2.

Before proceeding to discuss the form of the distribution of Ψ, we pause to make some important observations based on the Law of Large Numbers, which will yield another, independent, estimate of $\mathsf{E}\Psi$.

If we consider not *one* randomly selected commodity out of the market space, but a random sample or 'basket' **B** consisting of at least a few dozen items bought-and-sold in separate transactions, and if we compute the specific price of the *whole* basket **B**, that is, $\pi(\mathbf{B})/\lambda(\mathbf{B})$ = (total price of **B**/total labour-content of **B**), then it follows from the Law of Large Numbers (see appendix I) that, with high probability, this quantity is very close to $\mathsf{E}\Psi$. Thus, for a large random basket **B** of commodities, the formula

$$\frac{\pi(\mathbf{B})}{\lambda(\mathbf{B})} = \mathsf{E}\Psi \tag{10}$$

is, with high probability, a very good approximation; and the approximation becomes better as the size of the sample grows larger. In view of (9), we can also say that the formula

$$\frac{\pi(\mathbf{B})}{\lambda(\mathbf{B})} = 1 + e_0 \tag{11}$$

is, with high probability, a good approximation.[11]

These approximations are valid for any large representative—that is, 'fair' or unbiased—selection of commodities. The question is whether certain economically meaningful, or 'naturally occurring', aggregates of commodities—such as the monthly consumption basket of an ordinary family, or the monthly collection of non-labour inputs of a firm engaged in production—can be regarded as unbiased, or almost unbiased, samples.

We believe that today they can be so regarded. In the early days of industrial capitalism, the main goods of mass consumption were agricultural products, produced by more or less traditional methods, and a few articles made by handicraft or, later, by light industry. On the other hand, the inputs for nascent industry were drawn from mining and heavy industry; the major agricultural input of industry, cotton, was produced in a separate sector, by slaves. It was then quite possible that consumption goods on the one hand, and industrial inputs on the other, represented quite different, and therefore biased, mixes of commodities—in terms of their conditions of production and price structures.

But in the course of its development capitalism has brought about a far-reaching transformation in consumer habits and needs, and thus in the pattern of mass consumption. In a modern developed capitalist country, an ordinary family's consumption basket consists of a great variety of items, produced under the most diverse technical and economic conditions, in virtually all sectors of the economy. Some important items of consumption (mainly energy, in the form of gas, electricity and petroleum) are at the same time also major industrial inputs; other consumer goods (such as mechanical, electro-mechanical and electronic durables) are produced by modern industry under conditions broadly similar to those in which many industrial inputs are also produced, often by the same firms. Thus, for example, the automobile industry produces both motor-cars for the individual consumer and heavier vehicles for use in industry and commercial transportation. Even traditional food items are often produced by modern capitalist methods, or at any rate by techniques similar to those used also for major inputs for industry. Moreover, especially during the long growth period 1945-72, sectors and firms that traditionally manufactured only means of production (or destruction) made a massive effort to break into the booming consumer market.

At the same time, the variety and diversity of industry's inputs have also grown apace. For these reasons, we hold that (10) is a valid approximation where **B** is a collection of commodities such as a family's monthly consumption basket or a firm's monthly set of inputs.

As an application of the foregoing, we shall derive a formula connecting $\mathbf{E}\Psi$ with Marx's *rate of surplus value* (sometimes known also as the *rate of exploitation*), which we shall denote by e_M. More precisely, e_M is the *global* rate of surplus value, defined for the entire economy, as follows.

Let N be the new labour-value produced in the whole economy during a given period, say a week. Let **V** be the total physical wage, the collection of all commodities consumed by all workers and their families during the same week. Then e_M is the quotient: (N minus the labour-value of **V**)/(the labour-value of **V**).

Despite certain reservations (discussed in detail in appendix II) we feel that in the present context we are justified in identifying Marx's notion of *value* with our notion of labour-content. We then have,

$$e_M = \frac{N - \lambda(\mathbf{V})}{\lambda(\mathbf{V})}, \tag{12}$$

where $\lambda(\mathbf{V})$ is the labour-content of **V**, and N is simply the amount of labour (the number of worker-hours) performed in the whole economy during the given week.

Now, **V** is a *huge* aggregate of commodities, the entire consumption of the whole working population during one week; also, for reasons explained above, it can be regarded as an unbiased sample of all commodities. Therefore we can apply (10), with **V** as the **B**, and conclude with virtual certainty that the ratio $\pi(\mathbf{V})/\lambda(\mathbf{V})$ is as near $\mathbf{E}\Psi$ as makes no difference. So we put

$$\mathbf{E}\Psi = \frac{\pi(\mathbf{V})}{\lambda(\mathbf{V})}.$$

Here $\pi(\mathbf{V})$ is of course the total price of **V**.

To proceed, let us agree to neglect savings by workers from their wages; direct taxes on wages; and the 'social wage', which consists of goods and services provided free of charge by the state. Then the total price $\pi(\mathbf{V})$ of what the workers consume during the given week must be exactly equal to the sum total of money wages received during the same period, because this sum must exactly pay for **V**. But the total amount of labour performed during that period was assumed to be N worker-hours, and the average hourly wage is $\mathbf{E}W = 1$; hence the sum total of all wages (in units of a.u.w.) is N. Thus we have $\pi(\mathbf{V}) = N$, and our last formula for $\mathbf{E}\Psi$ assumes the form $\mathbf{E}\Psi = N/\lambda(\mathbf{V})$. In view of (12) we now have $e_{\mathrm{M}} = \mathbf{E}\Psi - 1$, or

$$\mathbf{E}\Psi = 1 + e_{\mathrm{M}}. \tag{13}$$

Comparing this result with (9), we conclude that e_0 must be equal or very nearly equal to e_{M}.[12]

The results obtained so far in this chapter can be regarded as securely established, subject to our simplifying assumptions. Turning now to the law of distribution of Ψ, we must proceed more tentatively.

Dividing both sides of (3') by Λ, we obtain

$$\Psi = \frac{V_1 + S_1}{\Lambda} + \frac{V_2 + S_2}{\Lambda} + \cdots + \frac{V_m + S_m}{\Lambda}. \tag{14}$$

Here the specific price of the general commodity is represented as the sum of m terms, where m is the number of all firms in the economy and is therefore very large. For each j, the j-th term, $(V_j + S_j)/\Lambda$, represents the specific value-added (value-added per unit of labour-content) 'contributed' by the j-th firm. Each such contribution is relatively small. In fact, the contribution of each firm is on average roughly proportional to the firm's size, as measured by its annual value-added; but even the biggest firms are quite small relative to the economy as a whole.

On the other hand, for any given point (transaction) in the market space, very many terms in (14) assume non-zero values. This is just another way of saying that, due to the highly integrated nature of modern capitalism, each commodity requires a large number of direct and indirect inputs from extremely diverse sectors of the economy, so that in reality it is the joint product of many firms, spread widely throughout the economy. The workers whose labour goes into a given product are a truly motley army of labour: women and men, some highly skilled and others not, some comparatively highly paid and some badly underpaid. Between them they represent a great number of different trades and skills; and they are employed by a great variety of firms—small, medium and large—belonging to various sectors of the highly integrated economy. (That this remarkable integration is mediated through the chaos of the market is equally true and important, but need not concern us just now.)

Also, it seems that the statistical dependence between pairs of terms in (14) is for the most part very weak if not negligible.

Now, it is a rule of thumb in statistics, that if a random variable with an unknown distribution can be represented as the sum of a large number of variables, each of which is small relative to the whole sum, such that these variables are mutually independent or nearly independent, then a very plausible hypothesis is that the unknown distribution is approximately normal. (This rule is too imprecise to be capable of proof, but a rough theoretical justification can be given, using a general form of the Central Limit Theorem; see appendix I.) In view of this, we advance the hypothesis that Ψ is approximately normally distributed.

Since we have shown that $E\Psi$ is very close to $1 + e_0$, our hypothesis is that the distribution of Ψ is given, to a very good approximation, by the law $\mathfrak{N}(1 + e_0, \sigma)$, where σ is the standard deviation of Ψ.

We shall now assume, as a working hypothesis, that Ψ does indeed have a normal distribution $\mathfrak{N}(1 + e_0, \sigma)$ and on this basis get a rough upper bound for σ.

Let us consider the probability $P(\Psi < 1)$. If for a given i we have $\Psi(i) < 1$, this means that $\Pi(i) < \Lambda(i)$. This, in turn, means that the price paid for the commodity C_i is smaller than the labour-content of C_i. In other words, the price paid for C_i would not even be sufficient to pay, at the average wage rate $EW = 1$, for the whole of the labour-power required to produce this commodity. The probability $P(\Psi < 1)$ of such an event is obviously very small; as a guesstimate, it is no more than $\frac{1}{1000}$. But if Ψ has the distribution $\mathfrak{N}(1 + e_0, \sigma)$, then in order for $P(\Psi < 1)$ to be no more than $\frac{1}{1000}$, σ must be smaller than $e_0/3$ (see appendix I). Taking e_0 to be about 1—a realistic value, judging by empirical data—it follows that the standard deviation σ is smaller than $\frac{1}{3}$.

Of course, our hypothesis that the distribution of Ψ is approximately given by $\mathfrak{N}(1 + e_0, \sigma)$, with small σ (say $\frac{1}{3}$ or less), can be tested empirically. But this is not an easy task. Recall that $\Psi = \Pi/\Lambda$; so in order to collect empirical data on the distribution of Ψ, we must take a sample of commodities C_i and for each i we must find $\Pi(i)$ and $\Lambda(i)$. The price $\Pi(i)$ is directly observable, but the labour-content $\Lambda(i)$ can only be estimated from complex data on production, involving the whole economy. At any rate, the task of finding the empirical distribution of Ψ is beyond our own competence.

If, as we believe, our hypothesis is correct, then the distribution of Ψ is quite narrow. Fig. 17 in appendix I shows how narrow the graph of a normal p.d.f. is with standard deviation of $\frac{1}{2}$; with standard deviation of $\frac{1}{3}$ or less, the graph would be narrower still. If—to take a realistic case—the distribution of Ψ is $\boldsymbol{\Omega}(2, \frac{1}{3})$, then the probability of Ψ being between $\frac{5}{3}$ and $\frac{7}{3}$ is about 0.68, or 68 per cent. This *does not* mean that the price of all, or even most, commodities is roughly proportional to their labour-content. What it does mean is that if we weigh each commodity by its labour-content, then the total weight of those commodities whose specific price deviates from the mean 2 by less than $\frac{1}{3}$ is about 68 per cent of the total weight of *all* commodities.

Chapter Six
Dissolution of the Transformation Problem

The ideas and results presented in this book are the outcome of investigations that originated in our preoccupation with the so-called transformation problem in Marxian economic theory. It is therefore fitting that we should now turn to appraise this area of the Marxian theory from our present point of view.

Clearly, the view we are advocating is opposed to any theory that takes as its point of departure the assumption that the rate of profit, in a capitalist economy at equilibrium, is uniform. Since this assumption is false, any deduction made from it is invalid; and if the assumption is made at the very beginning of a theory, then the *whole* theory must be suspect. Such is the case with the various price theories based on input-output models, as well as with theories of the neoclassical schools.

In this respect the Marxian theory is rather different. Marx does not make the uniformity assumption a point of departure for his analysis; on the contrary, the bulk of *Capital* is quite independent of it. The supposed tendency of the rate of profit towards uniformity is introduced at a late stage of his analysis, in the third volume of *Capital*, as a source of theoretical complication. For, in the context of the theory developed up to that point, the new assumption appears as an anomaly, which must be resolved by a modification of the original model. The problem of reconciling the new assumption with the original model has become known as the *transformation problem*, and a controversy around it (whether the solution proposed by Marx is correct, and whether it is capable of any solution at all) has been going on for almost a century.[1]

To understand the problem, we must outline Marx's theory of prices. All economists, both before Marx and after him down to the present, have been perfectly aware that, due to a host of contingent, accidental and random circumstances, the market price at which commodities are actually sold is not determinate, but subject to fluctuation and variation, not only in the course of time but also between transactions made in close spatial and temporal proximity. However, they have been unable to theorize directly the notion of randomly varying prices, for this would have required a probabilistic theoretical framework, contrary to the methodological determinism still prevalent in economics.[2] Their theories, therefore, are about determinate *ideal* prices, which are supposed to prevail in a hypothetical state of equilibrium, in the absence of the real-life 'noise' of contingent, accidental and random circumstances. All that such a theory can imply about market prices is that they fluctuate around, and tend towards, those ideal prices.[3]

In this respect, Marx's theory is no different from others. However, his price theory has not one but two models for ideal prices. In the first model, used almost throughout *Capital*, ideal prices of commodities are proportional to their so-called *values*. In the second, modified model, these ideal prices are *transformed* into new ideal prices, called *prices of production* (hence the 'transformation problem') so as to yield a uniform rate of profit.

Marx's notion of *value* is not quite the same as the notion of *labour-content* used in this book. However, the divergences (discussed in appendix II) are irrelevant to the present discussion. So we shall identify the *value* of any given commodity C with its labour-content $\lambda(C)$. Therefore in the first model the price $\bar{\lambda}(C)$ of any commodity C, *including the commodity-type labour-power*,[4] is connected to $\lambda(C)$ by the formula

$$\frac{\bar{\pi}(C)}{\lambda(C)} = \psi_0, \tag{1}$$

where ψ_0 is a 'universal' constant, equal for all commodities in the economy at a given time, and dependent only on the units in which prices and labour-values (labour-content) are measured. It must be stressed that the quantity $\bar{\pi}(C)$ in (1) is an *ideal* price rather than a real-life market price.

We shall calculate the rate of profit of a firm in this first model. For simplicity, let us use the same unit of time—one week—both for calculating the rate of profit and for measuring labour (and labour-power); *so the rate of profit we shall be concerned with is the rate of profit per week* (rather than per annum), *and labour will be measured in worker-weeks*.

Let us denote by $\bar{\pi}_0$ and λ_0 the (ideal) price and labour-value, respectively, of one unit of labour-power. Thus, $\bar{\pi}_0$ is the weekly wage; it equals the price of a standard weekly consumption basket that a worker (and his or her family) needs to consume, in the prevailing social conditions, in order to work for one week. And λ_0 is the labour-value of the same consumption basket, which equals the amount of labour required to produce it. As explained in chapter IV, we must assume that $\lambda_0 < 1$; otherwise there could be no surplus, because in order to work one week a worker would need to consume wage-goods that themselves take at least one worker-week to produce. Also, as a particular case of (1), we must have $\bar{\pi}_0/\lambda_0 = \psi_0$.

Now consider a firm that hires n workers for one week; in other words, the firm buys n units of labour-power. During the week, the workers produce an output **C**, and in this process non-labour inputs **I** are used up. Let **K** be the capital employed by the firm. Note that **C**, **I** and **K** are *not numbers or sums of money but physical collections of commodities*. Also note that **K** is the *whole* of the firm's capital, so that in general only part of **K** will be used up during the week. If one assumes an ideal state of equilibrium in which each commodity sells at its ideal price, then the rate of profit r of the firm is given by

$$r = \frac{\bar{\pi}(\mathbf{C}) - \bar{\pi}(\mathbf{I}) - n\bar{\pi}_0}{\bar{\pi}(\mathbf{K})} \quad \text{per week.}$$

Using (1), we can replace each of the four price terms in this formula by ψ_0 multiplied by the corresponding labour-value; but then ψ_0 cancels out and we get

$$r = \frac{\lambda(\mathbf{C}) - \lambda(\mathbf{I}) - n\lambda_0}{\lambda(\mathbf{K})} \quad \text{per week.}$$

However, the difference $\lambda(\mathbf{C}) - \lambda(\mathbf{I})$ is clearly equal to the amount of labour needed to produce the output **C** from the non-labour input **I**, which is n worker-weeks (n workers working for a week). Thus

$$r = \frac{(1 - \lambda_0)n}{\lambda(\mathbf{K})} \quad \text{per week.} \tag{2}$$

Next, let us calculate the *average* rate of profit r_G, for the whole economy, in this model. This average rate of profit can be obtained by a calculation similar to that which has led us to (2), except that now we must consider the whole economy as though it were one firm. We obtain

$$r_G = \frac{(1 - \lambda_0)N}{\lambda(\mathbf{K}_G)} \quad \text{per week,}$$

where N is the total number of workers employed by all firms and $\mathbf{K}_G$ is the entire capital employed in the economy. This formula may be re-written in a somewhat different form. Let $\mathbf{V}$ be the total physical wage of the entire work-force during a week. Then clearly $\lambda(\mathbf{V})$ is equal to $\lambda_0 N$ and hence we get

$$r_G = \frac{N - \lambda(\mathbf{V})}{\lambda(\mathbf{K}_G)} \quad \text{per week.} \tag{3}$$

Formulas (1), (2) and (3) express fundamental mathematical relations between labour-values, prices and rates of profit in Marx's first model. However, Marx regarded this model as unsatisfactory because (2) was unacceptable to him.

What does (2) say? Note that the factor $(1 - \lambda_0)$ occurring in that formula is, at any given time, constant for the whole economy; it is the same for all firms. But n and $\lambda(\mathbf{K})$—the number of workers and the quantity of capital, as measured by its labour-value—are of course different for different firms. Thus (2) says that the rate of profit of each firm is directly proportional to the number of its workers, and inversely proportional to the quantity (labour-value) of its capital. Or, in other words, the rate of profit r is inversely proportional to the amount of capital per worker, $\lambda(\mathbf{K})/n$.

This conclusion was unacceptable to Marx because he subscribed to the classical doctrine (which is still part of conventional wisdom) that, due to competition, rates of profit tend to equalize over time. Moreover, he assumed that one can and should proceed in theory *as though* rates of profit are already uniform, and that it is possible to understand the internal logic of the relations between prices, profits etc. by positing an ideal situation in which these variables are replaced by their averages.

He therefore proposed to modify his original model as follows.[5] In the new modified model, a uniform rate of profit prevails in the whole economy. This rate, called the *general* rate of profit, is the r_G given by (3). Thus, the uniform ('general') rate of profit in the modified model is equal to the *average* rate of profit of the old model. The (ideal) prices of the new model, called *prices of production*, no longer satisfy (1), but are determined in such a way as to yield the same rate of profit r_G throughout the economy.[6]

Marx was unable to carry out the modification of his model in mathematical detail and generality; he merely gave a few numerical examples, incompletely worked out. But if one attempts to carry out this programme mathematically, one encounters a grave difficulty. Since the mathematical technicalities involved have received exhaustive treatment in the literature, we shall not go into them here, but merely report the outcome of the mathematical analysis.[7]

Consider a closed economy, in which commodities of types C_0, C_1, C_2, ..., C_m are produced and re-produced. For simplicity we assume that each type is produced by one standard method, and we ignore joint production. We assume that C_0 is labour-power. The following two sets of production coefficients are assumed to be given:

Input-output coefficients. For each i and j, the coefficient a_j^i is equal to the number of units of C_j used up directly in the production of one unit of C_i. In particular, for $i = 0$, the coefficients a_j^0 constitute a 'standard real-wage basket'. (Some authors rightly point out that it is highly unrealistic to assume these coefficients a_j^0 as given.[8] Instead, one can assume a given proportion between the unit wage and the unit price of some other commodity-type. This alternative assumption does not essentially affect the result mentioned below.)

Fixed capital coefficients. For each $i \neq 0$ and each j, the fixed capital coefficient f_j^i is defined as follows. Suppose C_i is produced at the rate of x units per week, and in this process y units of C_j are used (but not necessarily used up) as capital stock, then $f_j^i = y/x$. For example, suppose C_j is a type of lathe used in the course of producing C_i;

suppose also that a factory that produces 3000 units of C_i per week needs exactly three lathes. Then $f_j^i = \frac{3}{3000} = \frac{1}{1000}$. (Here, as well as above in connection with the input-output coefficients, we are assuming constant returns to scale.)

Now, it can be proved that if these two kinds of data are given and if moreover the unit prices of all commodity-types are to be fixed so as to yield the same rate of profit r for all non-labour commodity-types, then there is at most one possible numerical value that r can have, and this numerical value can be computed from these data.[9]

Thus, the assumption of a uniform rate of profit is an extremely strong one: once it is made, then (subject to the above assumptions, which are wholly in line with the assumptions that Marx himself makes) the numerical value of the rate of profit r is completely determined by the 'technical' data of the system and the real-wage basket (or, instead of the real-wage basket, the level of wages in terms of some other commodity-type).

This numerical value of r is determined without any reference to labour-values, despite Marx's dictum that without a deduction in terms of labour-values (using, say, (2) or (3)) 'an average rate of profit (and consequently a price of production of commodities), remains a vague and senseless conception.'[10]

Worse still, the value of r imposed in this way by the data is, in general, *not* the same as r_G determined in (3). The reason for this is that only the former, r, is totally independent of the quantities of each C_i produced per unit of time, whereas r_G depends on these quantities, or, more precisely, on the proportions between these quantities. To state this more precisely, let us denote by q_i the number of units of C_i produced in the economy per week. In particular, q_0 is the number of units of labour-power reproduced per week, which is easily seen to be equal to the number N of workers employed in the economy. Let $\mathbf{q}$ be the m-dimensional vector $(q_1/q_0, q_2/q_0, \ldots, q_m/q_0)$. Then the r imposed by the data is independent of $\mathbf{q}$, while r_G of formula (3) does depend on $\mathbf{q}$. So the condition that $r = r_G$, as Marx apparently postulated, is equivalent to a particular condition on the vector $\mathbf{q}$. But this condition on $\mathbf{q}$ seems to be quite arbitrary; no one has ever been able to explain why $\mathbf{q}$ should satisfy such a condition, or to propose any mechanism whereby the economy would gravitate towards it. (It does not correspond to any reasonable state of static or dynamic equilibrium.)

We are thus faced with an anomaly in Marx's theory of prices and profits. In fact, this anomaly became known a very long time ago, although not quite in the modern formulation in which we have presented it here. The controversy around it is long-standing, and by now quite stagnant. It has divided students of Marxian economic theory into three main camps. The revisionists, greatly impressed by linear algebra, have concluded that labour-values are useless—at any rate useless for any reasonable quantitative theory of profit. The blinkered faithful have managed to ignore the whole issue, and are satisfied by repeating the word of the Master, who surely knew best. The more sophisticated orthodox Marxists—a contradiction in terms, for how can one be both orthodox and Marxist?—have tried to fudge the issue by putting far-fetched or scholastic interpretations upon what Marx actually said.[11]

All three camps have concurred in accepting as reasonable and coherent the postulate that at equilibrium the rate of profit is (or would be, if equilibrium ever existed) uniform. But, as we have argued in detail in the beginning of this book, this postulate, which gave rise to the whole problem in the first place, is fallacious. The so-called transformation problem is—as far as proper economic theory (rather than pure linear algebra) is concerned—a pseudo-problem. No solution is possible, or indeed necessary, because the terms in which the 'problem' has been posed are themselves erroneous.

But there is greater irony still. Let us suppose for one moment that Marx had not accepted the economists' story about the alleged tendency of the rate of profit towards uniformity. Presumably, he would then have stuck to the original unmodified model of the first volume of *Capital*. What does this model actually tell us about prices? Let us turn back to formula (1) and compare it with our own theory developed in chapter V. In (1) we have left the constant ψ_0 unspecified. To specify this constant, we must fix the unit in which prices are to be measured. (We have already agreed to measure labour-values in worker-weeks.)

To facilitate comparison with chapter V, let us take the (ideal) unit wage $\bar{\pi}_0$ as our price unit.

We have observed above that for the commodity-type labour-power formula (1) assumes the form $\bar{\pi}_0/\lambda_0 = \psi_0$. But we have now chosen our price unit so as to make $\bar{\pi}_0$ equal to 1; hence $\psi_0 = 1/\lambda_0$ and formula (1) can be re-written, for *all* C, in the form

$$\frac{\bar{\pi}(C)}{\lambda(C)} = \frac{1}{\lambda_0}. \tag{1'}$$

Next, let us express λ_0 in terms of Marx's rate of surplus value e_M. We turn back to formula (12) of chapter V, which defines e_M, and observe that the N and $\mathbf{V}$ occurring in that formula have there exactly the same meaning as in the present chapter. (Here we have taken N to be the number of workers employed in the economy, but if labour is measured in worker-weeks, then N is also equal to the new labour-value generated in the economy during one week.) Also recall that in the present chapter, on our way to (3), we observed that $\lambda(\mathbf{V}) = \lambda_0 N$. Using this equality, formula (12) of chapter V now reduces to $e_M = (1 - \lambda_0)/\lambda_0$. (This simply means that the rate of surplus value defined globally for the whole economy is equal, *in Marx's model*, to the rate of surplus value computed 'locally' for each unit of labour-value generated in the economy.)

Solving the equation $e_M = (1 - \lambda_0)/\lambda_0$ for λ_0, we get $\lambda_0 = 1/(1 + e_M)$, so that for every commodity C formula (1') becomes

$$\frac{\bar{\pi}(C)}{\lambda(C)} = 1 + e_M. \tag{4}$$

We have deduced this formula *within* Marx's original unmodified model. Needless to say, in this model (and, for that matter, in the modified model) taxation, liquid saving, and the social wage are ignored.

Now compare (4) with formula (13) of chapter V. The latter was deduced within our own model, neglecting direct taxes on wages, savings from wages, and the social wage. The right-hand side of (4) is identical with the expression that we have deduced for $\mathbf{E}\Psi$, the average specific price.

Furthermore, note that the term $\bar{\pi}(C)$ in (4) does *not* denote the real market-price of C but only its ideal price. Even where Marx uses this model and assumes it (provisionally) to be correct, he does not imply that commodities are actually sold at their ideal prices.

Thus the left-hand side of (4) *cannot* quite be interpreted as the specific price of C, which by definition equals the ratio between the *market* price and the labour-content of that commodity. In other words, (4) has nothing explicit to say about our random variable Ψ; this variable is simply not defined within this (or any other) deterministic model. But (4) can very reasonably be taken to *imply* something about Ψ: namely, that it 'fluctuates' around $1 + e_M$, or in other words that it is randomly distributed around this quantity and stays more or less close to it. And if we asked the statisticians to make an educated guess as to the shape of this distribution, then at least nine statisticians out of ten would say that if the fluctuations are due to a large number of independent (or almost independent) additive causes, then the distribution is very likely to be approximately normal.

In other words, the generally rejected model of the first volume of *Capital* happens to point to the same results, concerning the specific price of non-labour commodities,[12] for which we have argued in chapter V. So, from the point of view of our own theory, the model leads, *in this particular but important case*, to a broadly correct conclusion.

Now let us turn to the modified model of the third volume of *Capital*. Suppose for a moment that by some miracle of linear algebra the transformation 'problem' could be solved, so that the *mathematical* objection to Marx's modified model were removed. Or, alternatively, suppose that we forget about Marx's postulate (3) concerning r_G, and accept the uniform rate of profit r and prices of production corresponding to it, as imposed by the input-output coefficients etc., and the iron hand of linear algebra. What does such a model tell us about prices?

One thing is certain: if we now denote by $\bar{\pi}(C)$ the price of production of commodity C, then, with this new meaning of $\bar{\pi}(C)$, equation (4) is no longer generally true. Moreover, even without detailed calculation it is quite clear that if C is manufactured by a firm with a relatively high ratio $\lambda(\mathbf{K})/n$ (amount of capital per worker) then $\bar{\pi}(C)/\lambda(C)$ will be greater than $1 + e_M$; and, conversely, if the amount of capital per worker is relatively low, then $\bar{\pi}(C)/\lambda(C)$ will be smaller than $1 + e_M$. However, since this model (or, for that matter, any deterministic theory known to us) does not impose any restriction whatsoever upon the variation of $\lambda(\mathbf{K})/n$ between the various branches of production, it is quite consistent with this model to assume that this ratio is extremely widely dispersed: about half the capital of the economy may be invested in firms whose quantity of capital per worker is near 0, and the other half in firms whose quantity of capital per worker is some huge number. In that case the ratio $\bar{\pi}(C)/\lambda(C)$ will always be quite far from $1 + e_M$—either far above or far below it. In short, this model is powerless to make any definite statement about the behaviour of the ratio $\bar{\pi}(C)/\lambda(C)$, the ratio between price of production and labour-content. Since specific price—the ratio between *market* price and labour content—presumably fluctuates around $\bar{\pi}(C)/\lambda(C)$, the model cannot make any definite statement about specific price either. Unlike the original model of *Capital* Volume 1, this 'improved' model fails to make what we would regard as even a roughly correct prediction about specific price.

Thus, even if the transformation problem could be solved mathematically, the resulting model would not only rest on the fallacious assumption of the uniformity of the rate of profit, but would actually be inferior to the original unmodified model in respect of prices.

Another way of putting it is the following. In a realistic theory, both the rate of profit R and specific price Ψ should be taken as nondegenerate random variables (even at equilibrium). To replace random variables by their mean values is, in principle, wrong and can lead to grave errors, because a relation that holds between random variables may fail to hold even approximately between their respective means. For example, if X_1, X_2, and X_3 are random variables such that $X_1 X_2 = X_3$, it does not follow that $(\mathsf{E}X_1)(\mathsf{E}X_2) = \mathsf{E}X_3$, even approximately. Now, in the modified model of *Capital* Volume 3, Marx postulates, in effect, that R is degenerate—with the result that he can no longer say anything definite about specific price. In the original model of *Capital* Volume 1, it is assumed, in effect, that Ψ is degenerate—which leads (as Marx himself recognized) to an erroneous expression (2) for the rate of profit of a firm. However, in reality the distribution of R is quite wide, while (as we have argued in chapter V) that of Ψ is rather narrow;[13] so *in this sense* the assumption underlying the original model is the less unrealistic of the two.

Still, the model of *Capital* Volume 1 is unrealistic, because although Ψ has a narrow distribution, it is by no means degenerate. However, when it comes to large and 'unbiased' aggregates of commodities, the specific price of such an aggregate (total price/total labour-content) can, with high probability, be taken as very nearly constant. This is the meaning of formula (10) of chapter V, which we have justified without any recourse to 'ideal' prices, by very general economic and probabilistic arguments (the highly socialized and integrated nature of capitalist production; the Law of Large Numbers). This has a very interesting consequence regarding the model of *Capital* Volume 1. Any result deduced from (1) concerning a micro-entity, such as a particular commodity-type or a particular firm, is suspect and in general quite unrealistic. On the other hand, results deduced from (1) that concern large and varied aggregates can turn out to be, with high probability, very good approximations —not because (1) itself is valid (it isn't), but by virtue of formula (10) of chapter V.

We shall illustrate this by examining the results (2) and (3) concerning the rate of profit. Recall that (2) was deduced from (1) and gives (assuming that (1) is valid) the rate of profit r of a firm that employs n workers and capital $\mathbf{K}$. Clearly, (2) is highly unrealistic. This has nothing to do with the supposed uniformity of the rate of profit: in reality, the rate of profit does not tend to uniformity—but neither is the rate of profit of a firm inversely proportional to the quantity of its capital per worker.

Now let us turn to (3), which is nothing but the global form of (2), taken over the whole economy. We have seen that *if* the rate of profit in the economy were uniform, then this uniform rate of profit would not, in general, be equal to the r_G given by (3). This is a very nice theorem of linear algebra; but its economic significance is doubtful, since the rate of profit is *not* uniform even at equilibrium. On the other hand, in our own model we can show that r_G is, with high probability, a very good approximation to the average rate of profit $\mathbf{E}R$, provided the distorting effects of direct taxation on wages, savings from wages, and the social wage are disregarded.

To see this, recall that the N in (3) is the total number of workers employed by all firms in the economy; hence N is also the total amount of labour (measured in worker-weeks) performed by these workers in the given week. Therefore we have $N = \lambda(\mathbf{C}_G) - \lambda(\mathbf{I}_G)$, where $\mathbf{C}_G$ is the total physical output produced in the economy during the week and $\mathbf{I}_G$ is the total direct non-labour input used up in this process. (These are not quantities but physical aggregates of commodities.) Hence (3) can be written thus:

$$r_G = \frac{\lambda(\mathbf{C}_G) - \lambda(\mathbf{I}_G) - \lambda(\mathbf{V})}{\lambda(\mathbf{K}_G)} \quad \text{per week.}$$

Now, $\mathbf{C}_G$, $\mathbf{I}_G$, $\mathbf{V}$ and $\mathbf{K}_G$ are huge and extremely varied aggregates of commodities, to which formula (10) of chapter V can be applied with considerable confidence. This means that we may replace each λ term in the last formula by the corresponding π term divided by $\mathbf{E}\Psi$. Then $\mathbf{E}\Psi$ cancels out and we get the following, as a good approximation:

$$r_G = \frac{\pi(\mathbf{C}_G) - \pi(\mathbf{I}_G) - \pi(\mathbf{V})}{\pi(\mathbf{K}_G)} \quad \text{per week.} \tag{5}$$

Here π is not some ideal price but ordinary market price. Now, if we ignore direct taxation on wages etc., $\pi(\mathbf{V})$ must equal the total weekly money-wage paid by all firms in the economy. Hence the numerator in (5) is exactly the total profit of all firms for one week. Also, $\pi(\mathbf{K}_G)$ is the total price of all capital employed in the economy. Therefore the right-hand side of (5) is equal to the average rate of profit in the firm space, $\mathbf{E}R$. In other words, (5) can be re-stated as:

$$r_G = \mathbf{E}R \quad \text{approximately.} \tag{6}$$

A clear merit of (3), however, is that—just as Marx insisted—it displays the social meaning of profits, by expressing the average rate of profit (or a very good approximation to it) in terms of deep-level economic quantities, labour-values, rather than in terms of prices, which are epiphenomenal.[14]

The implication of the ideas presented in this chapter should by now be clear. The transformation 'problem' is best forgotten; but new ideas, of the kind we have attempted to develop in chapter V, ought to be marshalled to bring about a modern—and, necessarily, unorthodox—reconstruction of Marxian economic theory.

In such a reconstructed theory, Marx's notion of labour-value—or, at any rate, some notion generically similar to it, such as our own notion of labour-content—must play a central role. Otherwise, the very purpose and meaning of political economy are subverted.[15] The contradictions in the traditional theory arise not from the notion of labour-value, but from the insistence on a deterministic connection between labour-values and *individual* ideal prices and rates of profit. On the other hand, at the aggregate level, indexes defined in terms of labour-values—such as e_M and r_G—are of great importance for a deep analysis of the economic metabolism.

Chapter Seven
Elements of Dynamics

In the preceding chapters we have recast two central concepts of political economy—price and profit—in a probabilistic framework, as random variables, so as to reflect better the irreducibly chaotic nature of a capitalist economy. Our discussion so far has concentrated on the probabilistic behaviour of these variables *at a given moment of time*. We have assumed that the economy is at or near equilibrium, in the sense that macroscopic conditions—and macroscopic parameters, such as the average rate of profit or the global rate of surplus value—are constant or vary comparatively slowly. To be sure, even under such relatively stable conditions the equilibrium we are referring to is dynamic and merely statistical; it allows for rapid changes in 'microscopic' parameters—such as the rate of profit of an individual firm, or the rate of pay of an individual worker—which are inherent in a competitive market economy. The assumption of equilibrium is legitimate, inasmuch as in a real economy macroscopic parameters vary much more slowly (at least in normal times) than most microscopic ones.

Nevertheless, over periods of several years or of decades, noticeable global changes do take place. New commodity-types appear on the market and replace old ones; patterns of consumption undergo change; technical innovations are continually made and build up into so-called technological revolutions. The whole system evolves through time, and with it the macroscopic parameters—or at any rate some of them—also gradually change.[1] This gradual evolution is occasionally interrupted by periods of more or less acute crisis, during which macroscopic parameters may change rather rapidly.

The question then arises: can this dynamic be integrated into our probabilistic framework? Do the real changes reflect themselves on the theoretical level in law-like interconnected changes in the measures and variables defined in the preceding chapters, such as labour-content, specific price and rate of profit?

We are convinced that the answer is affirmative. To be sure, the elaboration of a fully fledged probabilistic economic dynamics is a major project, which will require long years of research. At present we are able to present only a few rudiments of such a dynamics. Our discussion will concentrate on two topics, which turn out to be closely interconnected.

First, *the law of decreasing labour-content* mentioned in chapter IV. To our mind this is perhaps the most basic dynamic law of capitalism, archetype of all capitalist development. Yet its position in economics is paradoxical.

Empirically, the law is non-controversial and its validity is half recognized by economists of all schools (usually under the name of 'the law of increasing productivity'). But for all non-Marxist economic schools it has remained an external observation, unintegrated into the foundations of economic theory. Indeed, the law itself cannot be properly stated, let alone explained, in the theoretical framework adopted by most of those schools, and therefore little theoretical use can be made of it. In the present chapter we shall show that the law integrates in a natural way into our probabilistic framework. We shall also explain how such a law can and must arise.

Second, we shall consider the problem of global capital accumulation (that is, accumulation of the total social capital rather than that of the individual firm). Here again, even the very concept of accumulation is problematic. What is it exactly that 'accumulates'? The answer to this is by no means obvious.

The rate at which global capital accumulates (if indeed it does) is apparently connected with the average rate of profit. Here, too, there are some puzzling questions. For example, why has the average rate of profit remained confined between stable and relatively narrow limits in most developed capitalist countries over a very long period? Of course, the average rate of profit does vary from year to year; but its magnitude is in fact bounded between about 10% and 20% per annum. Why should this be so? The input-output theorists tell us that the rate of profit (which they take to be uniform) depends crucially on the technological parameters encapsulated in their matrices. According to the neo-classical school, the rate of profit is determined by production functions. If so, why has the average rate of profit not risen to, say, 85% or fallen to 2%? What do today's input-output matrices or production functions have to do with those of fifty, seventy-five or a hundred years ago? What is the use of the unreasonably strong and unrealistic assumption that the rate of profit is uniform, if it does not help in explaining elementary features of the historical movement of the average rate of profit, such as the rather narrow limits within which it varies?

In what follows we shall try to show that some of the fundamental questions concerning the law of decreasing labour-content, the global accumulation of capital and the historical movement of the average rate of profit receive reasonable answers on the basis of the probabilistic connections that we have derived between labour-content, prices and profit.

Law of Decreasing Labour-content

Let us recall what this law says. In a given capitalist economy, consider a commodity-type **C** (other than labour-power) that continues to be produced over a long period (say several decades). Then the law says that there is virtual certainty (probability close to 1) that the labour-content of one unit of **C** at the end of the period is smaller than it was at the beginning.

The same law applies, more generally, to a commodity-type that does not remain the same but evolves in its internal constitution, provided its function (use-value) remains the same or very nearly the same. For example, a modern electronic watch does not, strictly speaking, represent the same commodity-type as an old-fashioned mechanical watch, since they are very different in their internal make-up; but they have very nearly the same function, so the law applies in this case. The same holds for various other products that were formerly made from wood, metal or glass and are now made wholly or partly from synthetic materials.

It is quite obvious that this law cannot even be formulated within an economic theory in which the very notion of labour-content is absent. This is the position of neo-classical theories, in which labour and 'capital' are regarded as separate (and to some extent alternative) 'factors of production', and which do not regard means of production as themselves being so much congealed labour, and hence reducible to labour.

In input-output theories of prices and profit the notion of labour-content can be defined, and the law can certainly be *formulated*. But it cannot be deduced or explained, because in these theories there is no general systematic connection between labour-content and price.

Let us explain this latter point. As we pointed out in chapter IV, the law of decreasing labour-content must be an outcome of the continual changes in methods of production, whereby labour is made increasingly more productive. However, the capitalists, who introduce these changes, do not consciously aim to reduce the labour-content of any commodity. The very notion of labour-content is a highly theoretical one, as explained in chapter IV. A commodity does not wear its labour-content on its sleeve. The labour-content of commodities can only be estimated by a compli-cated theoretical procedure and remains hidden from the eyes of most human protagonists in the economy. In particular, the capital-ist is, like Oscar Wilde's cynic, a person who knows the price of everything but the *value* of nothing. The capitalist's decision to implement a given technical or organizational change in production depends on a knowledge of existing *prices* and is designed to affect future *prices* so as to increase the rate of profit or the volume of profit in *money* terms. Labour-content does not enter into the calcu-lation.

The law of decreasing labour-content is a prime example of a ten-dency that operates 'behind the backs' of the social protagonists, as though it were a law of nature. The fact that it nevertheless does operate must be explained by the existence of some systematic con-nection between the visible and the invisible—between price and labour-content. Without such a 'black law' (to use Rosa Luxem-burg's apt phrase) it is quite incomprehensible why individual actions motivated by considerations of price should in the long term result in a systematic effect on labour-content.

In this regard, the traditional Marxist theory does much better than its rivals. However, here too there is a touch of irony. In the original model of the first volume of *Capital*, the (ideal) price of each commodity is proportional to its labour-content.[2] Under this assumption it is very easy to see why the capitalists' actions, designed to reduce costs of production, should result in a decrease in the labour-content per unit of product. But this model is later rejected in favour of the modified model of the third volume. Here the new (ideal) prices—the so-called prices of production—are indirectly determined by labour-content, but there is no longer a uniform ratio between price and labour-content. But without some information concerning the *distribution* of this ratio—which this model does not provide, and which must therefore be supplied extraneously—it is no longer quite so clear why the law should hold.

Explanation of the Law

We shall now show how the law of decreasing labour-content may be explained within our own probabilistic theoretical framework.

We start from the observation that each capitalist firm is strongly motivated by competition to try to reduce its unit costs (that is, cost per physical unit of output). A firm that achieves such a reduction before its competitors is able to increase its rate of profit without raising the prices of its output. Better still, it can sell its output at reduced prices—thus squeezing its competitors out of some of their market—while not reducing, or even while increasing, its rate of profit. A firm whose competitors have reduced their unit costs, or are likely to do so, must do likewise on pain of being beaten out of its own market.

There are four basic strategies for reducing unit costs:

(i) The firm may try to reduce its workers' rates of pay.

(ii) The firm may try to beat down the prices it pays to the suppliers of its non-labour direct inputs.

(iii) The firm may try to reduce the direct labour-time spent per unit of output, either by speeding up the labour process or by 'rationalizing' it so as to minimize the time 'wasted' between jobs, etc.

(iv) Finally, the firm may try to replace its existing non-labour inputs by others, which it can buy more cheaply per unit of output.

Although in practice two or more of these strategies may be used conjointly, it will be convenient to discuss each of them separately, in its pure form, so as to determine its effects. In each case we shall assume that the strategy in question has been applied not just by one firm, but has been copied and adopted by all firms producing the same commodity-type.

The first two strategies do not involve any change in the method of production; and they have no effect whatsoever on the labour-content of a unit of output. Therefore they are irrelevant to the law under consideration, and we need not discuss them any further. We merely wish to point out that the application of these two strategies is severely hindered, by the resistance of the workers in the first case, and by that of the suppliers in the second. This resistance can only be overcome in rather exceptional circumstances.

The other two strategies are much more commonly used, often combined together. Both involve changes in the method of production; in the case of strategy (iii) the changes are mainly organizational, while strategy (iv) involves technical change.[3]

The effect of strategy (iii) is clearly to reduce the labour-content of a unit of output. No probabilistic consideration is needed here, because the effect is certain; once sufficiently many firms producing a given type of commodity have reorganized their method of production so as to reduce the labour-time spent directly per unit of output, then the new method must be regarded as standard, and the labour-content of a unit of output must be considered to have decreased accordingly.

It must however be pointed out that although strategy (iii) does have this effect directly and certainly, the intention that motivates its application is not to reduce labour-content, but cost (in this case, labour-costs) per unit of output. The decrease in labour-content is merely an incidental, albeit necessary, result.

We now come to strategy (iv), which is by far the most important and most commonly used. Contrary to the other three strategies, it is in principle limitless. Indeed, its continual application is mostly responsible for the phenomenal transformation of production, and with it the whole of economic life, under capitalism. If the application of this strategy did not lead to a reduction of labour-content per unit of output, then the law would remain quite unexplained, because strategy (iii) by itself—being rather limited in scope—is incapable of accounting for it.

Yet, it is precisely the effects of this fourth strategy that present the most difficult theoretical problem, because there is no reason why an application of this strategy should *necessarily* result in any reduction of the labour-content of a unit of output; on the contrary, it may well result in its increase.

In the simplest case, an application of this strategy consists in replacing one type of non-labour input—be it a raw material, a fuel, a machine or some other input—by an alternative one, which the firm is able (or expects) to obtain more cheaply per unit of output. More generally, a whole collection of such inputs may be replaced by an alternative collection, provided again that the new collection works out cheaper (per unit of output) than the one it replaces.

From the point of view of the capitalist firm that decides to implement such a change, the thing that matters is this reduction in unit cost. A reduction in labour-content is not at all intended, *nor does it always take place*. Indeed, since specific price (the ratio of price to labour-content) is not constant but can take any positive numerical value, it is quite possible for the new alternative input (or collection of inputs) to be both cheaper *and* to have higher labour-content than the old one which it replaces.[4] The increase in the labour-content of the input will then be passed on to the output, resulting in a *rise* of the labour-content per unit of the latter.

It may be objected that a technical change, the application of strategy (iv), must be accompanied by a reorganization of the production process so as to save direct labour, since new techniques are less labour-intensive (require a lower direct input of labour) per unit of output. This argument is quite false. There is no *necessary* reason why a more profitable technique of production should require a smaller direct input of labour per unit of output than an older, less profitable one. A firm may well decide to employ *more* labour-power per unit of output, if the increased labour-costs are outweighed by saving on the cost of non-labour inputs. Such things do occasionally occur in reality. Indeed, it is quite possible for a new technique of production to require a greater direct input of labour, as well as a greater indirect labour input (by using alternative inputs with higher labour-content)—and still to result in reduced unit costs. The primary aim of a capitalist is not to save social labour but to make more money; and if more money can be made by employing (directly or indirectly or both) more labour per unit of output—as indeed it sometimes can—then the capitalist is quite happy to do so.

Despite all this, we claim that continued application of strategy (iv)—even in its 'pure' form, unaccompanied by any saving of *direct* labour input—will, *with high probability*, result in a reduction of the labour-content of a unit of output. The problem we are dealing with here (namely, the effect of strategy (iv) on the labour-content of the output) absolutely demands a probabilistic approach. A deterministic theory is quite incapable of coping with it in a realistic way.

Within a deterministic theory, the only question that can be asked in the present context is whether a reduction of unit costs achieved by strategy (iv) results in a reduction of labour-content per unit of output. The answer is that this may or may not happen (and, in reality, it sometimes does and sometimes does not)—and there the matter ends. But this question is not the right one to ask. Rather, the question to ask is *how probable* is it that repeated application of strategy (iv) would result in lowering the labour-content of a unit of output.

This latter question—which is the really important one—is considerably more subtle. But fortunately it can be answered in a reasonable way within the present theoretical framework. Not surprisingly, it turns out that the odds are better than even that an application of strategy (iv) would result in reducing the labour-content per unit of output. And with *repeated* application of strategy (iv), the probability of such a reduction grows closer and closer to certainty.

In the following few pages we shall carry out the necessary mathematical calculation. But even without this, the argument can be readily understood at an informal intuitive level.

The crux of the matter is that the basket of inputs of a firm is, in general, a rather diverse collection of commodities. For such diverse collections, the correlation between price and labour-content is very high—much higher than for *individual* commodities. (This follows from the Law of Large Numbers, discussed in appendix I.) Therefore, a development of methods of production that succeeds in reducing the money cost of the basket of inputs is very likely to achieve also a reduction in the labour-content of that basket.

Turning now to a more formal mathematical treatment, let us first consider a given particular application of strategy (iv). Suppose a firm uses up a 'basket' B_1 of non-labour inputs to produce one unit of output (that is, one physical unit of some given commodity-type). Then a technical change is made in the method of production, and the old basket B_1 is replaced by a new basket B_2 with a different composition—different raw materials, fuels, machines. Let us

146

denote by $\bar{\pi}_1$ and $\bar{\pi}_2$ the respective prices of $\mathbf{B}_1$ and $\mathbf{B}_2$, measured in a.u.w., at the time when the replacement is made. Suppose that this change represents a cheapening of the non-labour inputs by a factor c; that is,

$$\frac{\bar{\pi}_1}{\bar{\pi}_2} = c, \tag{1}$$

where the *cheapening factor c* is some given number, greater than 1.[5]

Next, let the labour-contents of $\mathbf{B}_1$ and $\mathbf{B}_2$ be $\bar{\lambda}_1$ and λ_2, respectively. We are interested in the ratio

$$h = \frac{\bar{\lambda}_1}{\bar{\lambda}_2}. \tag{2}$$

If this *labour-content ratio* (briefly, l.c.r.) is greater than 1, a reduction of labour-content (per unit of output) has taken place; if, on the other hand, the l.c.r. is smaller than 1 then the labour-content of a unit of output has gone up.

If $\bar{\psi}_1$ and $\bar{\psi}_2$ are the respective specific prices of $\mathbf{B}_1$ and $\mathbf{B}_2$, then $\bar{\lambda}_1 = \bar{\pi}_1/\bar{\psi}_1$ and $\bar{\lambda}_2 = \bar{\pi}_2/\bar{\psi}_2$. Substituting this into (2) and using (1) we obtain the following expression for the l.c.r. h:

$$h = c \cdot \frac{\bar{\psi}_2}{\bar{\psi}_1}. \tag{3}$$

Now, instead of considering one *particular* given application of strategy (iv), let us suppose that a change of inputs *is made completely at random as far as the specific prices in question are concerned*. Of course, we are not suggesting that decisions to change inputs are made at random; but as far as the specific prices are concerned they might as well be.

Technically speaking, what we are proposing to do is to replace the two particular specific prices in (3) by two random variables $\bar{\Psi}_1$ and $\bar{\Psi}_2$, which can be assumed to have the same distribution.[6] This *theoretical* assumption is the most reasonable one in the circumstances, in view of the fact that a firm that implements a change of inputs is completely in the dark as to the specific prices of the two alternative input baskets. There is no reason whatsoever to believe that the statistical behaviour of the new specific price is any different from that of the old one it replaces. (As a matter of fact, the assumption that $\bar{\Psi}_1$ and $\bar{\Psi}_2$ have the same distribution will not be fully exploited.)

The cheapening factor must also now be taken as a random variable, since it has no fixed value, but varies from case to case. We therefore replace the constant c in (3) by a random variable C, independent of $\bar{\Psi}_1$ and $\bar{\Psi}_2$. Concerning this variable itself we only make a single assumption: that its values are always greater than 1, so that $P(C \leq 1) = 0$. The justification for this assumption is obvious: the new inputs must be cheaper than the old ones. No further assumption on the distribution of C seems reasonable, and none will be needed.

The l.c.r. itself now becomes a random variable, which we denote by H, and formula (3) becomes the following equality between random variables:

$$ H = C \frac{\bar{\Psi}_2}{\bar{\Psi}_1}. \tag{4} $$

For technical reasons that will soon emerge, we are interested not so much in H itself, as in its logarithm $\log H$, which of course is also a random variable. From (4) we get:

$$ \log H = \log C + \log \bar{\Psi}_2 - \log \bar{\Psi}_1. \tag{5} $$

Let us recall that a reduction in labour-content (per unit of output) occurs if, and only if, H happens to take a value greater than 1; but the value of H is greater than 1 precisely when the value of $\log H$ is *positive*.

Our next task is to calculate the *expected* (or *mean*) *value* of $\log H$. We use the fact that the mean of a sum of random variables is equal to the sum of their means (see appendix I) and obtain from (5):

$$ \mathbf{E}(\log H) = \mathbf{E}(\log C) + \mathbf{E}(\log \bar{\Psi}_2) - \mathbf{E}(\log \bar{\Psi}_1). $$

But since $\bar{\Psi}_1$ and $\bar{\Psi}_2$ were assumed to have the same distribution, it follows that $\mathbf{E}(\log \bar{\Psi}_1) = \mathbf{E}(\log \bar{\Psi}_2)$; hence we have:

$$ \mathbf{E}(\log H) = \mathbf{E}(\log C). \tag{6} $$

Since C is always greater than 1, it follows that $\log C$ is always positive. Therefore $\mathbf{E}(\log C)$ must be a positive number; and because of (6) we conclude that $\mathbf{E}(\log H)$ *is a positive number.*

Of course, the fact that the *expected* value of $\log H$ is positive does *not* mean that $\log H$ is *always* positive; individual cases where $\log H$ is negative (and hence labour-content per unit of output is increased) may actually occur fairly frequently. However, what mainly interests us is not what may happen in an individual case, but what tends to happen as a cumulative result of a *sequence* of changes of inputs.

Let us therefore suppose that an initial basket of inputs $\mathbf{B}_1$ is replaced by a second basket $\mathbf{B}_2$; later, $\mathbf{B}_2$ is replaced by $\mathbf{B}_3$; and so on, until finally $\mathbf{B}_n$ is replaced by $\mathbf{B}_{n+1}$. Altogether, n changes have taken place.

To each successive transition, there corresponds an l.c.r., which is, of course, a random variable. Let us denote by H_i the l.c.r. corresponding to the transition from $\mathbf{B}_i$ to $\mathbf{B}_{i+1}$; thus H_i is the ratio between the labour-content of $\mathbf{B}_i$ and that of $\mathbf{B}_{i+1}$. (Here i is any number from 1 to n, inclusive.) It is reasonable to assume that the H_i are *independent of each other.* Each of these random variables is exactly like the random variable H that we have discussed above in connection with a single change of inputs. In particular, for every i the mean value $\mathbf{E}(\log H_i)$ is a positive number.

Now consider the *overall* l.c.r. of the whole sequence of changes. This random variable, which we shall denote by H_n^*, is defined as the ratio between the labour-content of the initial basket $\mathbf{B}_1$ and that of the final basket $\mathbf{B}_{n+1}$.

It is easy to see that H_n^* is equal to the *product* of all the H_i. Therefore

$$\log H_n^* = \log H_1 + \log H_2 + \cdots + \log H_n.$$

From this equality it follows that as n increases, the probability that $\log H_n^*$ *is positive approaches* 1 *(that is, approaches certainty).*

This result can be deduced easily from the Law of Large Numbers.[7] What it means is that the cumulative effect of a sequence of input substitutions—motivated solely by the drive to cheapen costs—is to push the probability of a reduction in labour-content (per unit of output) towards certainty.

Here lies the main explanation for the law of decreasing labour-content.[8] It is a probabilistic law, not a deterministic one. Technical change under capitalism does not *always* increase the productivity of labour; but its long-term cumulative effect does tend to do so, with probability increasing towards certainty.

Further Remarks on the Law

We have shown that the probability that the cumulative effect of n technical changes (changes of input-basket) will be to reduce the labour-content of a physical unit of output is given by the expression

$$\mathbf{P}(\log H_n^* > 0);\qquad(7)$$

and we have shown that, as n increases, this probability approaches 1.

But *how quickly* does this happen? If ε is some given small fraction, how large does n have to be in order to ensure that the probability (7) is greater than $1 - \varepsilon$?

It can be shown[9] that the answer to this depends on the narrowness of the distributions of the random variables $\log H_i$. The more narrowly these variables are distributed, the faster will probability (7) converge to 1. (Here 'narrowness' is measured by the standard deviation: the smaller it is, the narrower the distribution.)

Since the distributions of the variables $\log H_i$ are all similar to that of the variable $\log H$ of formula (5), we need only concern ourselves with the latter.

We know from formula (6) that the mean value of $\log H$ must be positive. If the standard deviation of $\log H$ is small, then the values of $\log H$ will, with high probability, be close to the mean, and therefore positive. In other words, the probability $\mathbf{P}(\log H > 0)$ will be high.[10] But this is the probability that a *single* change of inputs results in a reduction of labour-content.

We shall now use, for the first time, the assumption that the variable C is independent of $\tilde{\Psi}_1$ and Ψ_2. Hence $\log C$ is independent of $\log\tilde{\Psi}_1$ and $\log\Psi_2$. If the latter two variables are also *mutually* independent, then, using the rules for computing variances, (see appendix I) we obtain from formula (5):[11]

$$\mathbf{V}(\log H) = \mathbf{V}(\log C) + \mathbf{V}(\log\bar{\Psi}_1) + \mathbf{V}(\log\bar{\Psi}_2).$$

However, rather than assuming that $\log\bar{\Psi}_1$ and $\log\bar{\Psi}_2$ are independent, it is more realistic to assume that the correlation between them is non-negative, because in general the baskets $\mathbf{B}_1$ and $\mathbf{B}_2$ are not totally different but have several ingredients in common with each other. It then follows that the correlation between $\log\bar{\Psi}_1$ and $-\log\bar{\Psi}_2$ is non-positive, and a simple calculation (see appendix I) yields the *inequality*

$$\mathbf{V}(\log H) \leq \mathbf{V}(\log C) + \mathbf{V}(\log\bar{\Psi}_1) + \mathbf{V}(\log\bar{\Psi}_2).$$

The standard deviation of $\log H$ is, by definition, the square root of the variance, and is therefore less than or equal to

$$[\mathbf{V}(\log C) + \mathbf{V}(\log\bar{\Psi}_1) + \mathbf{V}(\log\bar{\Psi}_2)]^{1/2}. \tag{8}$$

Concerning the contribution of the first term, $\mathbf{V}(\log C)$, we can say nothing, because we have no information about the distribution of C. The remaining two terms are equal to each other, because, by assumption, $\bar{\Psi}_1$ and $\bar{\Psi}_2$ have the same distribution. The contribution of these two terms is small if the (common) distribution of $\bar{\Psi}_1$ and $\bar{\Psi}_2$ is narrow.[12]

Let us therefore consider the distribution of Ψ_1 and Ψ_2. It would be wrong to assume that these two variables have the same distribution as that of the specific price variable Ψ of chapter V. The variable Ψ is the specific price of a (randomly chosen) transaction in the market space, which usually involves one commodity at a time; whereas Ψ_1 and Ψ_2 are aggregate specific prices of *baskets* of inputs, usually involving a large and diverse selection of different commodities.

The most reasonable assumption to make is that the distribution of $\bar{\Psi}_1$ and $\bar{\Psi}_2$ is the same as that of the random variable $\bar{\Psi}$—whose definition is outlined below—which measures the specific price of the aggregate basket of non-labour inputs of a (randomly chosen) firm in the firm space of chapter III.

To define this new variable $\bar{\Psi}$, let us fix a particular short period of time T, say a given month. Consider first a particular firm, say the i-th firm F_i in the firm space. Suppose that in the period T the firm F_i has bought a basket of m non-labour inputs $I_1, I_2, \ldots, I_m$ of different types.[13] For each j (from 1 to m inclusive), let ψ_j and λ_j be, respectively, the specific price and labour-content of the input I_j. (Note that each I_j is a particular commodity that has actually been bought, so its price, and hence also specific price, is well defined.) If $\bar{\psi}$ is the *aggregate* specific price of this entire basket of inputs, then clearly $\bar{\psi}$ is the *weighted average* of the $\bar{\psi}_j$, with the λ_j as 'weights':

$$\bar{\psi} = \frac{\Sigma \lambda_j \psi_j}{\Sigma \lambda_j}, \qquad (9)$$

where the summations are over all j, from 1 to m.

So far we have considered one given firm F_i. But the same reasoning applies to every i. This means that we can regard the $\bar{\psi}$ of formula (9) as the i-th value $\Psi(i)$ of a random variable Ψ defined over the firm space. Similarly, each ψ_j and each λ_j can be regarded as $\Psi_j(i)$ and $\Lambda_j(i)$ respectively, where the Ψ_j are suitable specific-price variables and the Λ_j are labour-content variables, which function as 'weights'. With this understanding, formula (9), taken for *every* i in the firm space, yields the following equality between random variables:

$$\bar{\Psi} = \frac{\Sigma \Lambda_j \Psi_j}{\Sigma \Lambda_j}, \qquad (10)$$

where the summations are again over all j, from 1 to m. The number of terms m in (10) can itself be taken as a random variable, since it differs from firm to firm. However, instead of doing this, we can resort to the following simple formal device. We *fix* m as the *maximal* number of inputs bought by any firm during the period T. Now, some firms have, of course, bought less than m inputs; so, if the firm F_i considered in deriving formula (9) actually bought only k inputs, where k is smaller than the maximal number m, we simply set $\lambda_j = 0$ in (9) for all j from $k + 1$ to m.

Now, the variables $\Psi_1, \Psi_2, \ldots, \Psi_m$ represent the specific prices of m different purchases of separate commodities in the market. It is therefore highly reasonable to assume that they are independent (or at least very nearly independent) random variables, each having the same distribution as the specific-price random variable Ψ of chapter V, which was defined over the market space.

Because of the large number and great diversity of non-labour inputs usually needed for the production of most commodities under modern conditions—a point discussed in chapter V—we believe that the Central Limit Theorem (see appendix I) can be applied to the situation represented by formula (10).

If so, then the distribution of our variable $\bar{\Psi}$ is approximately normal, $\mathfrak{N}(\mu, \bar{\sigma})$. Here the mean value μ is the common mean value of the variables Ψ_j, which is also the mean value $E\Psi$ of the random variable Ψ, for which we gave two estimates in chapter V. But the standard deviation $\bar{\sigma}$ of $\bar{\Psi}$ is *not* the same as the standard deviation σ of Ψ. In fact, it is much smaller; it can be shown to be of the same order of magnitude as $\sigma/\sqrt{\bar{m}}$, where $\bar{m}$ is the average number of non-vanishing terms in (10), or in other words, the average number of non-labour inputs needed by a firm. This number is quite large— several dozen if not hundreds. Since σ itself is quite small (in chapter V we have estimated it as no larger than about $\frac{1}{3}$, which is roughly $\frac{1}{6}$ of μ) the standard deviation of $\bar{\sigma}$ must be very small indeed, say something like $\frac{1}{15}$ or less.[14]

Now let us retrace our steps. Since the standard deviation of $\bar{\Psi}$ is very small, the same applies to $\bar{\Psi}_1$ and $\bar{\Psi}_2$, which we have assumed to possess the same distribution as $\bar{\Psi}$. This, in turn, implies that the contribution of the last two terms in (8) is very small. This means that the distribution of $\log H$ is only slightly wider than that of $\log C$. Hence $P(\log H > 0)$ is quite close to 1. Also, $P(\log H_n{}^* > 0)$ converges quite rapidly to 1.

So far, we have considered strategies (i)-(iv) in their 'pure' form. However, as we have already mentioned, it is usual for two or more of these strategies to be applied conjointly. In particular, it is very common for unit costs to be reduced by a change in the method of production that entails *both* a reduction of the direct labour input (per unit of output) *and* a replacement of the old basket B_1 of non-labour inputs by a new basket B_2. In this case, it is not necessary for the price $\bar{\pi}_2$ of the new basket to be smaller than the price $\bar{\pi}_1$ of the old. But, if a reduction of unit costs is to be achieved, the difference $\bar{\pi}_2 - \bar{\pi}_1$ must be smaller than the reduction in direct labour-costs. This case can be dealt with by the same methods we have used in connection with strategy (iv). It can be shown (although we shall not do so here) that there is a high probability that the labour-content per unit of output is reduced. Although the labour content $\bar{\lambda}_2$ of $\mathbf{B}_2$ may well be greater than the labour-content $\bar{\lambda}_1$ of $\mathbf{B}_1$, the expected rise in the labour-content of the non-labour inputs is more than offset by the expected reduction in the direct labour input.

Finally, it should be pointed out that a reduction in the labour-content of a unit of one type of commodity, $\mathbf{C}_1$, causes an automatic reduction in the labour-content of a unit of any other commodity-type, $\mathbf{C}_2$, whose production requires $\mathbf{C}_1$ as input. Thus the effects of changes in the methods of production in one branch can spread to other branches as well, even if methods of production in those other branches remain unchanged.

This concludes our discussion of the law.

Accumulation of What?

The existence of accumulation—or, in vulgar parlance, of economic 'growth'—seems to be a commonplace. Surely, in normal times (excluding occasional periods of stagnation or recession) a capitalist economy 'grows'. The mechanism for this growth also seems obvious: capitalists, driven by competition, do not usually spend all their profits on consumption, but plough back part of them into their businesses; thus the capitals of firms tend to grow, and as a result the aggregate social capital also grows, or accumulates.

However, when we inquire how this aggregate accumulation is to be verified, measured and quantified, certitude is tempered with doubt.

If technical change did not take place, and the same commodity-types continued to be produced and re-produced by unchanging processes of production, then it would have been both possible and reasonable to measure the accumulation of social capital by the *physical* growth of the total amount of capital goods—machines, stocks of raw materials, etc. In the process of production, some of these capital goods are always used up; but if new goods *of exactly the same types* were produced in greater quantities than necessary simply to replace those that have been used up, and if this excess of capital goods were to be actually employed as such, then capital accumulation would consist of (and could be measured by) a purely quantitative growth in the amount of goods of these fixed types.

But this does not happen in reality. Since the advent of capitalism, new commodity-types continually appear on the market, while old ones go out of production; techniques of production continually supersede each other. Old types of means of production are *not* forever re-produced in growing quantities, but become obsolete and are eventually relegated to the museum; meanwhile, new types of means of production are introduced.

The number of spinning 'mules' (of the type invented by Samuel Crompton in 1779) in use today is certainly not greater than it was two hundred years ago; there are not more steam engines in current use in Britain than there were a hundred years ago; nor are there more hot-metal linotype machines, or more miles of telegraph wires, or more mechanical desk calculators than there were fifty years ago.

The accumulation of capital, if it takes place, does not consist in the economy having physically 'more of the same stuff', and cannot be measured in such physical terms.

Likewise, the aggregate price—in pounds, dollars or even in gold— of the total capital employed in production is far from being a reasonable index for measuring accumulation, because a comparison of prices across long periods of time is not really meaningful. This point was discussed in chapter IV, and we need not enlarge on it here.

It seems to us that in studying the problem of accumulation over long periods of time, the most reasonable measure of the amount of capital is its *labour-content*. We shall therefore concern ourselves with the variation of this quantity—the aggregate labour-content of the capital employed in production in the whole economy—over time.

Here we are presented with a technical-methodological difficulty: the accumulation of aggregate capital must be related (as we have already noted) to the average rate of profit prevailing at any given time, and this quantity, ER, is defined in *money* terms (see chapter III). Since we have just decided that, for the purpose of studying accumulation, capital is to be measured in terms of labour-content, we cannot relate accumulation to the rate of profit without a bridge between the two sets of categories—categories of labour-content on the one hand, and those of price on the other.

Fortunately, a solution to this difficulty is already at our disposal. We have seen in chapters V and VI that when it comes to very large, varied and 'representative' collections of commodities—such as the aggregate social capital, or the total weekly consumption basket of the entire working population—the ratio between total price and total labour-content is, with high probability, very close to a constant (this constant being $E\Psi$). And this correlation between price and labour-content tends to grow stronger and stronger, as the variety and number of items in each such aggregate grows, and the individual 'weight' of each item tends to decrease due to the law of decreasing labour-content.

Indeed, using these ideas, based on the Law of Large Numbers, we saw in formula (6) of chapter VI that a good approximation for the average rate of profit ER is provided by Marx's so-called general rate of profit r_G, which is defined purely in terms of categories of labour-content rather than price.

To use this approximation, we must ignore the possibly distorting effects of direct taxation on wages, saving from wages, and the so-called social wage.[15]

It will be convenient to rewrite the formula for r_G (formula (3) of chapter VI) in a simplified form. Let us denote by v the quantity that was denoted by $\lambda(V)$ in chapters V and VI—that is, the aggregate labour-content of the total consumption basket of all workers and their families during a unit of time. Also, let us denote by k the quantity denoted by $\lambda(K_G)$ in chapter VI—namely, the aggregate labour-content of the capital employed in production throughout the economy.

Then formula (3) of chapter VI assumes the form

$$r_G = \frac{N - v}{k} \quad \text{per unit of time,} \qquad (11)$$

where N is the total number of workers employed in production, which is also the amount of new labour-content created in the economy during one unit of time. In chapter VI we took the unit of time to be one week, but any other unit of time can serve just as well. Of course, whatever unit of time is chosen, it must be used *both* for the rate of profit and for labour-content; so if, for example, r_G is measured in units per annum, then labour-content must be measured in worker-years.

It must be stressed that all four quantities mentioned in (11) are functions of time; or, to put it plainly, they all vary in time. Indeed, it is precisely their variation in time that is of interest to us here.

The numerator $N - v$ in (11) is the *surplus* labour-content created in the economy per unit of time. At any given moment, it is a given determinate quantity, depending only on the global socio-economic and technical data of the entire system (the total number of workers, the aggregate consumption of these workers and their families per unit of time, and the dominant methods of production by means of which the labour-content of each commodity is determined). Through the disorderly mechanism of competition, this given quantity is carved up among all firms, and appears as their profits. On this point—to which we alluded briefly in chapter III—our own view does not differ from that of Marx.

Since r_G can be taken as a good approximation for the average rate of profit, formula (11) embodies an important constraint upon this average rate: the average rate of profit is (to a good approximation) directly proportional to the surplus $N - v$, and inversely proportional to the labour-content of the aggregate capital employed in production in the economy.

But from the same formula we can derive an important upper bound for the speed at which k can grow. In a closed economy—which is the only case we consider—the sole source for the growth of k is the re-investment of the surplus labour-content. If the *whole* of this surplus were re-invested, it would add $N - v$ units of labour-content per unit of time to the aggregate capital. Therefore, the speed at which k grows—technically, the derivative of k with respect to time t—must be smaller than $N - v$:

$$\frac{dk}{dt} < N - v. \tag{12}$$

The left-hand side of this formula is in fact smaller than the right-hand side *not only* because part of the social surplus, rather than being re-invested, is consumed by non-workers, either individually or as a class, through the state. Even if we were to ignore this consumption, the inequality would still hold. The reason for this is that the labour-content of the *already existing* aggregate capital tends to decrease with time. This has nothing to do with the fact that part of the capital is continually used up in production; we have already allowed for this in advance in formula (11), where the quantity N is the *new* labour-content, *after* deducting the labour-content of that part of the capital that has been used up.

Or, to put it in other words, *if* the whole of the surplus were re-invested, and *if* there were no change in the methods of production, and *if* moreover no capital were ever destroyed (as opposed to merely being used up in production)—then indeed we would have an equality in (12) instead of an inequality.

The point, however, is that these 'ifs' are contrary to fact. First of all, due to technical and other changes in methods of production, the labour-content of *existing* capital goods tends to decrease with time: this follows from the law of decreasing labour-content.

As explained in appendix II, the labour-content of a commodity C at time t is defined as the total amount of labour that would be required to produce C by the methods of production prevalent at time t, *not* at the time when C was actually produced. Therefore, even if C—which may be a machine, a stock of raw material or any other capital good—just stands idle, without any part of it being used up, its labour-content tends to fall, due to the operation of the law of decreasing labour-content.

This implies that the quantity k has not only a *source*—the surplus $N - v$—from which its value is augmented, but also a *sink*, through which the value of k is depleted.

In fact, in addition to the sink provided by the operation of the law of decreasing labour-content, there are other sinks—whose operation is more spasmodic—through which part of k sometimes goes down the drain. One such sink is destruction by war or by natural calamity. Another sink operates in a minor way in normal times, but in a very major way in times of economic crisis: as firms go out of business, a considerable part of their capital goes to waste.

For all these reasons, even if the consumption of non-workers is ignored, there is overwhelming probability that the left-hand side of (12) is actually smaller than the right-hand side.

As a matter of fact, dk/dt can very well be negative—so that the amount of capital (as measured by its labour-content) decreases instead of increasing—even at a moment when some of the surplus is being re-invested; for, the augmentation of k from this source may well be more than outweighed by the simultaneous depletion of k through the sinks.

Moreover, it is in principle quite possible for k to fail to grow, or even to decrease, not only momentarily but over a more or less prolonged period of time, so that at the end of such a period k may be the same as at the beginning, or even smaller.

The same holds, with still greater force, for the quantity k/N, the amount of capital per worker. This index—whose variation in time is of still greater interest than that of k itself—may decrease even while k is increasing, because N may grow faster than k.

It is fallacious simply to take it for granted that k (let alone k/N) has a long-term tendency to increase. Such a tendency, if it exists, must be demonstrated by theoretical arguments and empirical evidence.

Of course, the long-term growth of productive capacity under capitalism can hardly be disputed, and the continual rise in the productivity of labour is an inherent tendency of capitalism, as we have shown above. Thus, new and better machinery, new and more effective methods of production do embody a huge accumulation of technological knowledge and a high degree of sophistication in the organization and manipulation of labour. But this does not necessarily imply that k or k/N must grow continually. Increasing productivity may be thought to increase the source from which k is augmented; but it is certainly one of the sinks through which k is depleted.

We find, therefore, that—contrary to naive first impressions—the supposed tendency of k and, more importantly, of k/N to grow continually is not at all a foregone conclusion.

Below we shall present our own tentative analysis of the variation of k/N with time. But as a prelude to this analysis it will be useful to give some critical consideration to the famous Marxian argument concerning the supposed long-term tendency of the average rate of profit to fall. Our own conclusions will be quite different from Marx's, but his argument can serve as a useful reference for the proper understanding of our different analysis.

'The Falling Rate of Profit'

The long-term tendency of the average rate of profit is discussed by Marx in Part III (chapters XIII-XV) of the third volume of *Capital*.

We shall reconstruct some of his argument in our own framework and terminology. In particular, we shall replace his notion of *value* by our notion of labour-content. We trust, however, that in this we do no violence to Marx's reasoning.

A careful, unbiased reading of Marx's text leaves hardly any doubt that he believed it to be a firmly established *fact* that under capitalism the average rate of profit has a long-term tendency to fall. Contrary to many later Marxists, he did not regard this tendency as a mere potentiality, which may never be actualized, but as a *real* tendency, which may be temporarily checked and retarded, but which must prevail in the long run. In this he followed some of the classical economists, most notably Ricardo.

However, he points out that the classical economists were puzzled by this (to him undoubted) phenomenon, and were unable to 'discover the law' by means of which it could be explained. He then proposes his own explanation.

Marx identified—very reasonably, as we now know—the average rate of profit with his so-called general rate of profit r_G, which is given by formula (11). The task, then, is to explain why r_G has a long-term tendency to fall. To reconstruct Marx's explanation, we must recall the definition of the global rate of exploitation e_M (which he calls 'the rate of surplus value'). This quantity is given by formula (12) of chapter V, which in our present simplified notation has the form

$$e_M = \frac{N - v}{v}. \tag{13}$$

From this and formula (11) it follows at once that

$$r_G = \frac{v}{k} e_M \quad \text{per unit of time.} \tag{14}$$

Let us denote by q_G the reciprocal of the ratio v/k; thus

$$q_G = \frac{k}{v}. \tag{15}$$

In Marxian terminology, q_G is the *organic composition* of capital, computed globally for the whole economy. It is the ratio between the amount of capital invested in the whole economy, and the amount of goods consumed by all workers and their families during a unit of time, both amounts being measured in terms of labour-content.

Now, Marx firmly believed that it is an inexorable law of capitalist development that q_G tends to grow with time. Indeed, he apparently believed that this growth is not bounded, so that, given enough time, q_G will become larger than any prescribed bound. In this he sought an explanation for the supposed tendency of r_G to fall.

Indeed, from (14) it is immediately clear that if q_G keeps growing, *and if e_M remains fixed*, then r_G must fall; moreover, if q_G grows without bound, then r_G must fall towards zero.

But this explanation explains too much. Since Marx believed that q_G tends to increase rather rapidly, the question arises as to why r_G does not fall very rapidly too; indeed why has it not fallen so close to zero as to make the continued existence of capitalism impossible.

Marx deals with this question by pointing at several 'counteracting causes', which tend to check and retard the downward tendency of r_G, without suspending it altogether. The most important such counteracting cause—and the only one that need concern us here—is that e_M may not remain fixed, but can grow with time. And it is clear from (14) that a growth of e_M tends to push r_G upwards.

Here there is a logical lacuna in Marx's argument.[16] For, if one admits the possibility that e_M may grow, it must be shown that the growth of e_M is sufficient only to retard the downward tendency of r_G rather than to reverse this tendency altogether. In principle (leaving aside empirical considerations for the moment) e_M can take any numerical value from 0 to ∞. Even if the consumption of workers (in physical terms) and the length of the working day are held constant, e_M can theoretically grow to infinity as a result of an indefinitely rising productivity of labour. If e_M grows sufficiently fast, then—despite a simultaneous growth of q_G—the trend of r_G will be upwards rather than downwards.[17] Yet, Marx does not produce any convincing argument to show that e_M cannot grow so fast as to have such an effect, at least in the long run.

We shall not go here into the thorny, much discussed (and purely academic) question as to whether such a convincing argument can nevertheless be produced. Instead, we shall present an amended version of the explanation for the supposed tendency of r_G to fall. This amended version, while being slightly different from the one proposed by Marx, is nevertheless wholly consistent with his views. And it does not encounter the logical difficulty of the original version.

We start by observing that formula (13) can be used to isolate v and express it in terms of N and e_M:

$$v = \frac{N}{1 + e_M}.$$

Substituting this expression for v into (14), we obtain

$$r_G = \left(\frac{N}{k}\right) \cdot \left(\frac{e_M}{1 + e_M}\right). \tag{16}$$

Now, Marx firmly believed that not only q_G but also k/N—which is the amount of employed capital per worker—tends to grow without bound.[18] Indeed, he sometimes seems to conflate the growth of q_G with that of k/N, although strictly speaking they are not the same thing.[19] If the ratio k/N does grow beyond all bounds, then it follows from (16) that r_G must fall towards 0. A simultaneous rise of e_M can temporarily check and retard this downward tendency of r_G, but cannot prevent it in the long run, because the factor $e_M/(1 + e_M)$, which multiplies N/k in (16), is bounded: even if e_M rises towards infinity, this factor always remains smaller than 1.

This is exactly the kind of argument that Marx was looking for: from the supposedly unlimited growth of k/N it would follow that r_G must inevitably fall towards 0, and this fall can only be temporarily retarded by a growth in the rate of exploitation.

From a purely logical point of view, this amended version of the argument is impeccable. But both it and Marx's original argument suffer from crucial *factual* defects. We shall now explore these defects and some of their consequences.

Let us start by recalling that in chapter V it was shown that a very good approximation for e_M is provided by the index e_0 defined in chapter III. This approximation is valid provided we ignore the distorting effects of indirect taxation, as well as those of direct taxes on

162

wages, saving from wages, and the social wage. But even if these distorting effects are taken into consideration, e_M can only differ marginally from e_0, the former being perhaps somewhat greater than the latter.

Next, we must recall the empirical fact, which we have mentioned several times before, that the index e_0 has been remarkably stable for a very long time (at least a century—there are few reliable data going further back) in Britain, the USA and other major capitalist countries. This index displays only mild short-term fluctuations but no significant long-term trend either upwards or downwards.

It therefore follows that the rate of exploitation e_M could not have grown to any significant extent over the last few generations. Hence the boosting effect of such growth on the average rate of profit, through formula (14), can be safely discounted. The same holds, with even greater force, for the boosting effect of a growth of e_M on r_G through formula (16); because even if e_M did grow slightly, the corresponding increase of the factor $e_M/(1 + e_M)$ would be relatively much smaller. (For example, if e_M were to grow from 1 to 1.01—an increase of 1%—then the factor $e_M/(1 + e_M)$ would grow from 0.5 to 0.5025, which is an increase of only $\frac{1}{2}$%. And the gap between the two rates of growth actually widens as e_M grows larger.)

From this, in turn, it follows that any significant increase in q_G should have been reflected by a decrease of r_G in the same, or almost the same ratio. For example, if over the last hundred years the global organic composition of US capital had doubled, then the so-called general rate of profit r_G should have been halved, or nearly halved, over the same period. A doubling of the amount of capital per worker (the ratio k/N) would have a similar effect, with even greater precision.

However, there is no empirical evidence to suggest that most of the advanced capitalist countries have experienced a significant long-term decline in their average rate of profit over the last few generations. Unlike e_0, the average rate of profit ER does display considerable short-term and medium-term fluctuations, from year to year and from decade to decade. But no general, universal long-term trend, whether upwards or downwards, can be clearly discerned.

Since we know that ER is a close approximation to r_G, we can use the logic of Marx's argument—but use it *backwards*—to conclude that *in the last few generations there could not have been a marked long-term rise in global organic composition, still less in the amount of capital per worker.* [20]

It is not the logic of Marx's argument that is at fault, but his assumptions concerning the long-term behaviour of r_G, q_G and k/N. At least, these assumptions are not corroborated by the empirical evidence available since *Capital* was written.

The real theoretical problem is to explain why the average rate of profit *does not* display a marked general long-term tendency to fall (or, for that matter, to rise) but continually fluctuates between rather stable bounds. Here lies an important clue to the problem of accumulation.

Why the Average Rate of Profit is Bounded

Some Marxists think of the fall of the average rate of profit towards zero in much the same way as Christians think of the Apocalypse: an occurrence that according to the scriptures should have 'shortly come to pass', but which has been delayed to the indefinite future; and when it finally comes about, it will be a grand and violent event which will put an end to the world as we know it.

This apocalyptic view is based on two main errors. The first error is that of believing that the average rate of profit has an inherent *long-term tendency* to decline. The second error is that of believing that the average rate of profit *can* gradually creep downwards until it is so low that capitalism as a whole will have to go out of business.

The root of this second error is the assumption that the rate of profit tends to be uniform. Under this assumption it is very tempting to visualize the behaviour of an entire capitalist economy with respect to its average rate of profit in much the same way as the behaviour of a single firm with respect to its rate of profit. [21]

But in reality these two types of behaviour are quite different, because a capitalist economy, unlike a single firm, does not have, at any given time, a *single* rate of profit but *a statistical distribution* of different rates of profit among the multitude of firms in its firm space. (See chapter III.)

First let us consider a single firm. If the firm's rate of profit is 20% per annum, then the firm is in excellent health. Even a rate of profit of 15% per annum is very handsome, while 10% per annum is still quite adequate. If the rate of profit falls to something like 5% per annum then matters begin to look a bit gloomy—note that we are talking about gross profits, before deduction of tax *and of interest to the bank*—but if the firm is not too deeply in debt then it can still survive and hope to prosper in the future. When the rate of profit goes below $2\frac{1}{2}$% per annum, the smell of death is in the air: for most firms in this position it means that, after paying taxes and interest to the bank, they are making a loss. If this goes on too long, the firm will have to go out of business.

Now let us consider an entire capitalist economy, with its firm space. Here a probabilistic treatment is absolutely essential. At any given time, whatever the average rate of profit happens to be at the moment, a certain proportion of the aggregate social capital will be doing extremely well, another proportion will be doing rather well, yet another proportion will be doing indifferently, and so on down the line. Whether the economy as a whole is in good health depends not only on the average rate of profit, but on the entire distribution.

Almost everyone knows that in reality the rate of profit is never uniform; but the economic theorists, like most exponents of pure science, think by means of theoretical models, and tend to get hypnotized by them. So, if their models assume a uniform rate of profit, the theorists sometimes forget that in reality things are very different.

Thus, if it transpires that the average rate of profit in some capitalist economy has gone down from 20% to 10% per annum, this may not sound too bad to someone who, semi-consciously, tends to assume that the *average* rate of profit is enjoyed *almost uniformly by all firms*; after all, 10% per annum is not at all bad. But we must bear in mind that a decline in the *average* rate of profit is usually accompanied by a shift of capital into the low and very low rate-of-profit brackets. Thus, even if the average still seems rather high, a substantial proportion of the aggregate social capital may find itself in dire straits, because the whole distribution is squeezed to the left.

To illustrate this point, we have compiled the following table, which gives the percentage of capital (out of the social aggregate) that finds itself in the low and very low rate-of-profit brackets—under 5% and under $2\frac{1}{2}$% per annum, respectively—for four different distributions of the rate of profit. In each case, we assume a gamma distribution, in accordance with the hypothesis made in chapter III.[22] Also, we have assumed that in each case the standard deviation is half of the mean.

| | | *Percentage of total capital in:* | |
Distribution	Mean rate of profit (%)	Low bracket (under 5% p.a.)	Very low bracket (under $2\frac{1}{2}$% p.a.)
γ(4, 20)	20	1.9	0.18
γ(4, 26.67)	15	4.6	0.49
γ(4, 40)	10	14.3	1.9
γ(4, 80)	5	56.7	14.3

From this table we can see that when the average rate of profit drops from 20% to 15% per annum, nothing very remarkable happens: the proportion of capital making low profit (less than 5% per annum) is still quite small, and only a tiny percentage of the aggregate capital is in the very low profit bracket. When the average rate of profit drops to 10% per annum, signs of trouble begin to appear: 14.3% of the aggregate capital (about one-seventh) is making a low rate of profit, and 1.9% of the total is in the very low bracket. By the time the average rate of profit reaches 5%, the economy is in deep trouble: 56.7% of the total capital is making a low profit, and about one-seventh is on the verge of ruin.[23] Clearly, some time *before* this stage is reached, the economy will have entered a crisis. Not an apocalyptic final downfall of capitalism, but an ordinary common-or-garden capitalist recession. In such a recession, however severe it may be, the economy does not grind to a halt. Even if the economy were to reach the situation represented by the bottom row of our table – an extremely unlikely event—then 43.3% of the aggregate capital would still be making reasonable profits, at over 5% per annum, and some firms would be doing quite well.

The probabilistic approach thus reveals a fact that tends to be obscured by theories that assume a uniform rate of profit; namely, that a capitalist economy is very sensitive to a relatively mild and non-catastrophic decline in the average rate of profit. Long before the average rate reaches rock bottom—which, if it did, would indeed put the whole system out of business—the economy enters an 'ordinary' crisis. By the same token, the probabilistic approach forces us to realize that even in a severe recession some parts of the economy are doing quite well.

These crucial points having been made, the rest of our argument proceeds along fairly traditional lines.

When the economy is in crisis, certain corrective mechanisms are set in motion. The sinks through which k is depleted tend to flow faster than the source from which it is augmented, with the result that k and, more importantly, k/N begin to decrease.

First, many firms go out of business and a large part of their capital is written off. Among those hit, there is a particularly high proportion of less efficient firms, where the productivity of labour is relatively low. Second, the climate of crisis stimulates hectic competition and provides an unusually high incentive to the implementation of technical and organizational innovations in production, which tend to deplete k/N through the operation of the law of decreasing labour-content. As k/N declines, the average rate of profit rises, in accordance with formula (16).

Of course, these mechanisms operate in a very imperfect, chaotic, contradictory and cruel way, like capitalism itself.[24] In particular, the pace and quality of innovation is difficult to control, and its consequences are almost impossible to foresee. If innovation is not sufficiently vigorous, recovery from the crisis will be sluggish.[25]

However, the main point is that a fall in the average rate of profit tends to stimulate countervailing mechanisms that operate not so much by increasing e_M (which is in practice very inelastic) but by decreasing k/N. For this reason, a medium-term fall in the average rate of profit is soon checked, and eventually reversed.

Now let us consider what happens when the average rate of profit becomes too high. In this situation, the source from which k is augmented—the surplus—tends to flow more rapidly than usual, while the incentive to innovate is not so strong and tends to lag behind the purely quantitative expansion of production.

There is a particular mechanism that tends to push k/N upwards at times when innovations in production methods do not keep pace with a purely quantitative expansion of the economy. This mechanism, converted into an absolute, is a corner-stone of the neo-classical theory, but the idea itself goes back to Ricardo.

We are referring of course to the famous law of *falling marginal productivity*. It states that as production of a given commodity-type expands, *using a fixed method*, then the amount of labour spent on each additional unit of output tends to increase.

This law is certainly valid for some important spheres of production, notably those which make large use of limited natural resources, such as mining and agriculture. For example, as the production of coal expands, less rich mines are brought into operation, so that each additional ton of coal requires a greater expenditure of labour (both directly and indirectly)—unless methods of production are improved sufficiently fast. *Therefore the labour-content of each ton of coal tends to rise.*

The law of falling marginal productivity comes into its own in times when the average rate of profit is high and the purely quantitative expansion of the economy is so rapid that innovation cannot keep pace with it. This process obviously tends to retard the growth of the productivity of labour, and thus to push k/N upwards, so that the rise in the average rate of profit is checked and eventually reversed.

All in all, the secular movement of the average rate of profit, and the associated but opposite movement of k/N and q_G, are governed by the mutually opposing tendencies of innovation and purely quantitative expansion, the former tending to push r_G upwards and k/N and q_G downwards, and the latter working in the opposite direction. This interaction takes place behind the backs of the human protagonists, through the chaotic medium of capitalist competition.

As a result of this interaction, the three quantities r_G, k/N and q_G undergo noticeable and occasionally quite dramatic oscillations in the short and medium terms, but in the long term they remain confined between more or less steady bounds.[26] This conclusion is illustrated empirically in the following chapter.

Further Remarks on Organic Composition

We have already observed that v can be isolated from formula (13), yielding: $v = N/(1 + e_M)$. Hence it follows that k/v equals $(1 + e_M)k/N$. Since k/v is, by definition (15), equal to q_G, we have

$$q_G = (1 + e_M)\frac{k}{N}.$$

As we have argued above, the global rate of surplus value e_M must have remained nearly constant during the last few generations in Britain, the USA and other developed capitalist countries. Therefore, although in principle the global organic composition q_G and the global ratio k/N (the amount of capital per worker) are conceptually different, they can in practice be assumed to move in tandem, the ratio between them remaining nearly constant.

In our final remarks we shall confine ourselves to dealing with organic composition.

Since q_G is defined in labour-content categories, like r_G and e_M, it is a deep-level index, not *directly* observable. However, just as we were able to find close approximations expressed in price terms for both r_G and e_M—namely, ER and e_0—so we shall now derive a close approximation to q_G that will be expressed in price terms, and is therefore more directly observable.

To this end, let us return to the firm space of chapter III and recall the definition of the random variable Z. The value $Z(i)$, which this variable assumes at the i-th point of the space (the i-th firm), is equal to the ratio between the i-th firm's total payroll per unit of time, and the firm's capital (where both quantities are measured in some arbitrary monetary unit). It follows that the mean value EZ is equal to the ratio between the total payroll of all firms engaged in production, per unit of time, and the aggregate capital of all these firms— again, measured in price terms.

By exactly the same argument that was used in chapter VI to show that ER is a close approximation to r_G—and under the same simplifying assumptions—it now follows that $1/EZ$ is, with very high probability, a close approximation to q_G.

Another variable worth considering in this connection is the random variable Q, defined by the formula

$$Q = \frac{1}{Z}. \qquad (17)$$

Thus, $Q(i)$ is equal to $1/Z(i)$, which is the ratio between the capital of the i-th firm (in price terms) and its labour-costs per unit of time. Hence $Q(i)$ can be regarded as the counterpart, in price categories, of the i-th firm's organic composition. For, in Marxian economic theory, the latter quantity is defined as the ratio between the *value* (or labour-content) of the i-th firm's capital and the *value* of the total physical wage of that firm's workers per unit of time.

Moreover, since the physical capital of a firm and the aggregate weekly consumption basket of its workers are fairly large and varied collections of commodities, we may apply to them formula (10) of chapter V, and conclude that with rather high probability $Q(i)$ is a reasonable approximation to the i-th firm's organic composition.

We must point out, however, that $1/EZ$ rather than EQ is a good approximation to q_G. These two quantities, $1/EZ$ and EQ, are *not* the same: although from formula (17) it follows that $ZQ = 1$, it does *not* follow that $(EZ)(EQ) = 1$, since Z and Q are obviously not independent (see appendix I).[27] Nevertheless, as we shall soon see, $1/EZ$ and EQ are in practice of the same order of magnitude.

The distribution of Q can be calculated if the distribution of Z is known. If we assume that, as suggested in chapter III, the distribution of Z is of the form $\mathcal{G}(\alpha, \beta)$, then we can get an explicit expression for the p.d.f. of Q, and hence calculate its mean value.[28] It turns out that $EQ = \beta/(\alpha - 1)$. Thus EQ is the reciprocal *not* of EZ but of the *mode* of Z. (See appendix I for the properties of the gamma distribution, including its mean and mode.) However, in practice EQ is of the same order of magnitude as $1/EZ$, which is equal to β/α. For example, a realistic case is that in which $\alpha = 4$ and $\beta = 20$, in which case $1/EZ = 5$ and $EQ = 6.67$.

We would like to draw attention to the fact that in our theoretical framework there are definite constraints not only on the mean values EZ and EQ but also on the *whole distributions* of the variables Z and Q. This is in sharp contrast to traditional theories, Marxian and non-Marxian alike. In those theories, an unreasonably strong assumption is made concerning the distribution of the rate of profit R, namely that it tends to be degenerate (and, in an ideal state of equilibrium, *is* degenerate); but nothing at all is said about the distribution of capital intensity or organic composition, which are allowed to be completely arbitrary.

Our results suggest that, for the functioning of a capitalist economy, the distribution of Q must assume a definite general form. It will be of great interest to subject this point to further investigation, but here we shall only make a brief comment.

There are certainly good common-sense reasons to suggest that extreme values of Q—either extremely small or extremely large—are exceedingly unlikely, so that the distribution of Q cannot be too wide.

If a firm has a very small value of Q, this means that its capital is very small in comparison with its annual payroll. In this case there is little reason for the firm's existence as a capitalist business—the workers might just as well operate as freelancers or as independent producers.

On the other hand, if a firm has a very high value of Q, this means that its production process is very capital-intensive, usually because it is very highly automated. But a highly automated system tends to become a new *commodity* in its own right, which—rather than serving as a basis for the operation of a separate firm—is bought directly by those firms or consumers who need the *products* of the given process, and is used by them as a *part* of their operating capital or as a consumer durable.

For example, in the past there used to be such things as ice factories, which used to sell ice to individuals or firms for the purpose of refrigeration. But once the process of production of ice (or of low temperatures) became sufficiently automated, it was embodied in refrigeration units and domestic electric refrigerators, which are bought by firms and individuals directly for their own use.

A more recent example is what happened to certain kinds of typesetting and compositing processes. Once they had been sufficiently automated, a new commodity appeared on the market (called a 'word processor' or 'word-processing system'), which can be bought and used directly by firms who have need for its products.

A fully automated system working as a separate business is much more common in science fiction than in capitalist reality.[29]

To conclude this chapter, let us return to considering the mean value EZ. In the last few generations this value has been fluctuating, but has remained quite firmly bounded from below. This actually follows from our previous considerations. Since $1/EZ$ is a close approximation to q_G, and since the latter quantity has been bounded from *above* (global organic composition does *not* have a tendency to rise indefinitely), it follows that EZ must be bounded from below. More directly, the same result can be seen by observing that, by the definition of e_0, we have

$$\mathbf{E}Z = e_0\mathbf{E}R.$$

Since e_0 has remained remarkably stable, and since—as we have argued—the average rate of profit $\mathbf{E}R$ in a capitalist economy cannot fall below a certain threshold, it follows that $\mathbf{E}Z$ could not do so either.

If we may extrapolate from this fact to the future, we can predict that so long as capitalism continues, global direct labour-costs will remain considerable. Taking e_0 to be about 1, total annual direct labour-costs should remain about equal to total annual gross profits, and no less than about one-tenth of the current value of the total operating capital.

This, of course, will serve as a continued impetus for capitalists to reduce labour-costs per unit of output, thereby strengthening the operation of the law of decreasing labour-content.

The continued viability of capitalism itself, in a purely economic sense (which is, of course, not the only one that matters), will depend on the ability of continual innovation in the methods of production to keep pace with the merely quantitative expansion of the economy.

Chapter Eight
Empirical Data and Open Problems

In this last chapter we wish to illustrate our discussion and results by presenting some actual economic data taken from widely available sources.

The presentation of these statistical data has two purposes. First, to serve as a real-world point of reference to our theoretical discussion. This is necessary in view of the claim in earlier chapters that our probabilistic approach should help in giving a broadly realistic quantitative description of some aspects of observable economic phenomena.

Second, the empirical economic data help to raise some problems that should be answerable by economic theory. We maintain that alternative theoretical approaches should be compared and judged by their concurrence with actual numerical data, as well as by their ability to give a proper account of the socio-economic logic of capitalism today.

We must point out that the empirical data strengthen our conviction that uniform-rate theories and in particular the Sraffian input-output model cannot hope to give an adequate explanation of the living realities of a capitalist market economy. On the other hand, we shall see how several of our theoretical claims are nicely corroborated by the available numerical data on the functioning of the economy.

As we go along, we will give some details on the data themselves and on their relation to the theoretical categories used in the present work. But a general word of caution is necessary: one cannot hope to find data that correspond exactly to one's categories. This is true in all sciences. Still, one must do with what is available—adjust it if necessary to fit one's framework. The problems and puzzles are not substantially altered by these adjustments.

Since this is not mainly an empirical work, we will keep the manipulation to a minimum; this will be enough to amply illustrate our point of view.

Rates of Profit

Consider the following diagram, which gives the empirical distribution of the rates of profit in the British non-oil manufacturing industries in 1972.[1] In the same diagram, the theoretical distribution from chapter III is plotted out. (See fig. 5.)

The lengths of the vertical bars are proportional to the relative amounts of capital that yielded the corresponding rates of profit. This rate in percentage points is given in the horizontal axis. The raw data from the source were smoothed out by the standard statistical method of 'moving average'.

The corresponding theoretical distribution $\oplus$(4.72, 32.0) is superimposed on the empirical data—it is represented by the continuous skew bell-shaped curve.

It can be seen that the various rates of profit achieved by different firms are quite widely dispersed over a range from no profit (0%) to around 40% and beyond. We have ignored the small amount of capital that made losses *before* tax and interest.

The fact that the spread of the rates is wide is expressed numerically by the size of the standard deviation which, in the above case, is 6.8% or very close to about half of the expected value (= average rate), which is 14.75%. In a 'narrow' distribution the deviation is one-fifth of the average or less.

In standard input-output theories such as the Sraffian framework it is assumed that in normal times all the vertical bars in fig. 5 below should cluster very narrowly around the average. Thus the lengths of the bars would be very small everywhere except for a few, say three or four, bars that would be relatively very long.

This hypothetical situation is illustrated in fig. 6 below. Even that does not mean uniformity; and certain phenomena can be sensitive even to small dispersion. But the point is that *nowhere* and *never* does the distribution of the rate of profit for the economy look anything like fig. 6; it is *always* of the general form given in fig. 5.

In chapter III we have given a possible formula of the law

according to which the rates of profit are distributed. This law allows for quite wide distribution around the average. The continuous curve in fig. 5 represents one such law among many. Namely, the *only one* whose average and standard deviation are the same as those of the empirical data.[2] We see that the continuous curve describes the empirical phenomena rather well, despite the very crude nature of these data. For example, it predicts well the *mode*—the most 'likely' rate of profit, namely 11.5%, which is different from the average. It also predicts correctly that there will be a very small amount of capital that will yield more than 40% profit. On the other hand, the theoretical curve overestimates the amount of capital that yields profits at less than 10%. A much larger sample from the 1981 edition of the same source is summed up in fig. 7 below. Again, it describes rather well the most probable rate of profit even though the theoretical graph was not chosen to fit this particular feature. The same goes for the way in which the probability of higher rates of profit dies out.

Notice the close similarity in shape between figs. 5 and 7. Since they depict two different years with entirely different economic climates (in 1981 Britain's manufacturing industry was already in deep crisis), the similarity is surprising. The crisis was not manifested by a decline of the average—partly because of inflation. Notice that in 1981 while the nominal average is slightly *higher* than in 1972, the standard deviation is *four times* as big as the difference in the average would suggest in normal times: there is a much higher concentration of capital in the lower rates of profits.

This raises the following problem: is it possible that a crisis can be manifested not only by a fall in the average rate in real terms, but also by a considerable *rise* in the *standard deviation* compared to the average?

We must emphasize the tentative nature of the illustrations above. They are meant mostly to suggest several possibilities.

One should, of course, be very cautious with the raw data. The numbers that appear in available sources do not have the same sense used in the text: it is not easy to come by data of *gross* profits *before* deduction of numerous expenses such as executive remuneration, as well as other items such as land-rent. In theory these remunerations ought to have been included in the gross profit—in addition to taxes, interest on loans, etc. Further, since we do not treat *rent* as

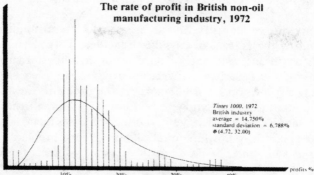

FIGURE 5
The rate of profit in British non-oil manufacturing industry, 1972

Times 1000, 1972
British industry
average = 14.750%
standard deviation = 6.788%
Φ (4.72, 32.00)

profits %

10%   20%   30%   40%

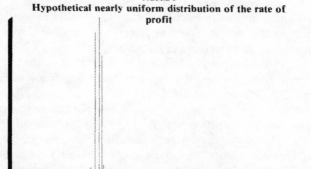

FIGURE 6
Hypothetical nearly uniform distribution of the rate of profit

profits %

10%   20%

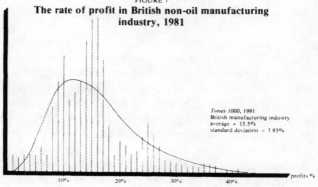

FIGURE 7
The rate of profit in British non-oil manufacturing industry, 1981

Times 1000, 1981
British manufacturing industry
average = 15.5%
standard deviation = 7.83%

profits %

10%   20%   30%   40%

such, we must turn a blind eye to certain important sectors of industry.

In fact, the oil industry, the archetype of high-rent industry, is kept out of the present discussion altogether. The question as to what is profit and what are expenses is not the only obstruction in the way of a comparison between theory and empirical data. To mention just one more hurdle, consider the problem of evaluating the amount of capital tied down or employed by a given firm. To the extent that this capital includes new direct expenses incurred during the given period—on raw materials, labour, energy, replacement of wear and tear—there is no great theoretical problem: those were bought during the production period and are used up during that period. So their prices are given empirically.

The difficult question is how to evaluate or even give a precise theoretical meaning to the amortized money-value of machinery, buildings and equipment that have been used over many periods and have not been in the market for a very long time. After all, the theoretical notion of price admitted in chapter V is the one that exists *only* at the moment of exchange: the price of a commodity used in production or consumption is indeterminate *except* at the moment of its exchange against money. We do not have a completely satisfactory answer to this problem—although it is not difficult to suggest several reasonable possibilities. In any case, the direct capital expenses incurred during the period in question and a few periods directly preceding it form the bulk of the capital employed, especially if one takes the period in question to be long enough. In addition, the existence of the stock market serves as a way of putting the entire capital of companies on the market every day, so as to attach a price-tag to it.

Beyond the questions concerning the behaviour of the rate of profit for the economy as a whole lies the problem of its behaviour for subsectors, or even for individual firms. The distribution of the rate of profit is a result of an enormous number of independent fates of individual firms. The general distribution is far from arbitrary, as can be seen from the empirical evidence and theoretical consideration. But these global considerations put very little restriction on the behaviour of the rate of profit of *individual firms* or branches. Such limitations undoubtedly exist and the problem is to discover their nature. The solution of this problem will help to describe the ways in which the present concept of rate of profit as a random variable captures the fierce competition that exists among various firms and various branches of the economy.

We saw in chapter VII that using general probabilistic considerations it can be shown that there is a strong restriction on the average rate of profit ER in terms of the fresh labour-content added and its division between the classes. But we have made no attempt to derive a *theoretical restriction* on the pattern of the *standard deviation* of R from that average: thus one can say with certainty that, on the basis of our theory, the rate of profit cannot exceed for any considerable period of time, say 60% per year, without major changes in the relative weights of the labour content of wages, and this limitation is independent of any technological development and exists under *every* technological condition. But we are unable to suggest a similar limitation on the deviation—and theoretically it could be any number, however large. We insist, however, that the deviation cannot be too small under a free market economy, as was explained in chapter I, but again we cannot suggest a theoretical restriction, say, in the form of 'The deviation is always bigger than one third of the average.' Empirical evidence, however, suggests that the deviation hovers around one half of the average—which is a relatively large deviation, statistically speaking.

Time Behaviour of Firms and Branches

From a uniform rate of profit perspective, there can be no difference, in the theoretical model of perfect competition, between various firms as far as their rate of profit is concerned. We saw that if one wants to capture the reality of chaos, one must admit transient differences as part of the theory.

However, there may be a deeper similarity between various firms in their statistical behaviour over time. To give a concrete example of such similarity, consider fig. 8 below, which is compiled out of actual profit performances of various branches in the British economy.[3]

This looks like a totally arbitrary collection of broken curves crossing each other without any order or meaning. In spite of their many intersections with each other, it is possible with some effort to

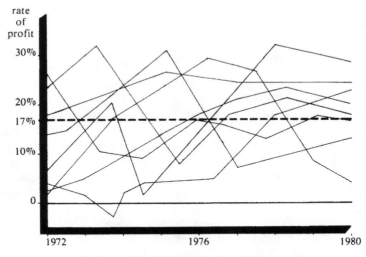

rate
of
profit

30%

20%
17%

10%

0

1972   1976   1980

SOURCE Business ratios division Inter Co. 1981
Industrial performance
movement of profit rates over time 1972-1980

follow each line separately from one end of the diagram to the
other. Each line represents a branch of British industry and traces
the evolution of the rate of profit of that branch over the time period
1972-80. We see that while there is no question of uniformity of
rates or even of average over the period, nevertheless, most curves
are similar to each other in several respects: they oscillate widely
around a rather narrow band. This band of 15%-20% is a 'centre of
gravity' to most curves. Now, it is possible that there are some regular
patterns to these oscillations which are not easily detected by the
naked eye but which can be captured by deep statistical analysis.
Under perfect competition one would expect this common band to
exist. But one would also expect some similarity among the branches
in the *pattern of deviation* from that average. Otherwise, investment
in some branches, while yielding similar rates of profit in the long
term, may be much more risky in the short and medium term. In particular, the actual period of time taken to realize a reasonable rate
should not vary greatly; otherwise competition would send capital to
those branches with lower 'risk' even if their rates were in the long
term not much different, or were even *smaller* than the average.

The elaboration of the restriction imposed by perfect competition on the deviation from average in each branch might prove very fruitful for the understanding of major problems of crisis and accumulation. Judging from similar problems in other sciences, it is an extremely difficult but deep direction of research.

Price and Labour-content

Perhaps the most striking empirical phenomenon that relates prices to labour input is the very high correlation that exists between wages and added value, and also between wages and 'surplus value' in money terms. Let us explain. Consider the collection of all firms in a given economy. For each firm consider the following two magnitudes: first, let B be the total annual wage bill paid by the firm or, in other words, the total annual labour costs of the firm—not including remuneration for the owners or directors. If we divide B by the capital employed, we get the variable Z defined in chapter III. The second variable is the annual value added in production, which is the difference between total sales and total non-labour expenses such as raw material, energy, replacement, components, etc. during one year. We denote this difference by A. It indicates in money terms how much 'value' was added to the inputs by the process of production. If we divide A by the capital employed in the given firm, we get the variable Y defined in chapter III.

A magnitude very closely related to A is that of *net output* per year. Although there are slight differences between the two, we shall use the terms interchangeably.

Consider the quotient A/B or net output per unit of wage paid. In chapter III we reported the phenomenon that this quotient *varies very little from one branch of production to the other within* (non-oil, non-rent) *manufacturing industry*. Before discussing this empirical phenomenon in some detail, let us illustrate the situation with a table taken from British industry.[4] (See fig. 9.)

Notice that the largest deviation is in the chemical industry and the food and drinks industry—this is perhaps related to the relatively high rent factor of oil and agricultural derivatives. Clearly, the low values of A/B in the shipbuilding and vehicle industries points to a deep crisis there, which is related to relatively low

FIGURE 9
Net output per £1 of wages in British industry, 1974

Industry	A/B = net output per £1 wages	Relative weight in economy %
Food, drink	2.7	17.4
Chemical industries	3.3	9.8
Metal manufacture	2.2	8.6
Mechanical engineering	1.8	9.3
Instrument engineering	1.7	1.3
Electrical engineering	1.9	7.6
Shipbuilding	1.3	1.2
Vehicles	1.4	8.3
Metal goods (others)	1.9	5.6
Textile	1.9	5.7
Leather goods	1.9	0.4
Clothing	1.7	2.5
Bricks, cement	2.1	2.7
Timber	2.1	3.4
Paper	2.1	6.5
Other	2.1	3.4
Total	**2.2**	**93.7%**

productivity. These cannot be maintained without huge state subsidies—in fact they have dramatically changed in later years. But in all other branches the value of A/B is remarkably close to the mean.

This curious phenomenon is related to another one; namely, consider the quantities A and B for the economy as a whole. It turns out that the ratio between them varies very little even over very long periods of time. For example, data taken from the US *Annual Survey of Manufacture* show that in the American economy in the period from 1880 to 1966 the correlation ϱ between total value added by manufacturing and total payroll is given by:

$$\varrho = 0.997$$

This is by any standard an amazingly high correlation and can be taken as an empirical counterpart to a theoretical correlation $\varrho = 1$, which is the highest possible correlation, corresponding to a strict linear relation between A and B.

Similar results are obtained if one considers the correlation *in any given year* between A and B in various branches of the economy. We get the following results:

FIGURE 10
**Correlation between value-added and
wage-bill**

country	year	correlation	E(A/B)
USA	1963	0.97	2.1
USA	1965	0.97	2.0
USA	1966	0.99	1.96
UK	1963	0.95	1.9
UK	1974	0.93	1.9
Holland	1960	—	2.15
S. Africa	1974	—	2.1

SOURCE: Wood; cf. footnote 4. Annual survey of manufacture 1966, US Dept. of Commerce. South Africa–Nedbank group 1977.

Thus all evidence points to the hypothesis that both the synchronic and diachronic correlation ϱ is very close to unity. This means that one may assume theoretically a linear relation between A and B. In other words, one can assume that there are some fixed numbers a and b that change only slightly over time and place, such that with very high probability the following holds:

$$A = aB + b$$

when A, B are taken from various firms.

But in our case, it turns out that b is very close to zero and a is very close to 2 as can be seen from the table above. Theoretically the assumption $b = 0$ is equivalent to the assumption that A/B as a random variable is degenerate: namely, it is distributed very closely around $a = 2$. This variable A/B is virtually the same as the quotient $(R + Z)/Z$ which equals $X + 1$, where R, Z and X are the variables discussed in chapter III.

In reality A/B is not degenerate but its standard deviation is rather low: under 20% of the expected value for both the British and American economy, and it is much smaller if the computation is restricted to industries with negligible rent factor. These relatively small deviations are illustrated by the following diagrams that give the distribution of the quotient A/B (which is very close to $(R + Z)/Z$ of chapter III) in the British economy in 1970, and the American economy in 1966.

182

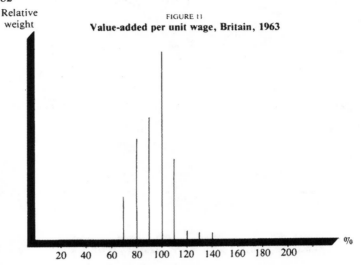

Relative
weight

FIGURE 11
Value-added per unit wage, Britain, 1963

20 40 60 80 100 120 140 160 180 200

%

Distribution of value added per unit wage in non-oil British
manufacturing 1963, given as percentage of average.
SOURCE: see footnote 4

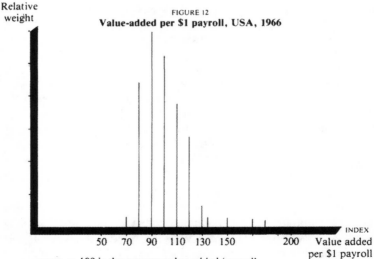

Relative
weight

FIGURE 12
Value-added per \$1 payroll, USA, 1966

50   70   90   110   130   150   200

INDEX

Value added
per \$1 payroll

INDEX = 100 is the average value added/payroll
American industrial manufacturing without oil 1966.
SOURCE: Survey, USA Dept of Commerce, 1966

What is the theoretical explanation for these striking phenomena? Our tentative answer is given at the end of chapter III. Here we would like only to emphasize that the very high correlation illustrated above and the narrow spread of the distribution of A/B is still very much an open problem.

Notice that input-output theories, whether Sraffian or not, *predict no correlation whatsoever* between wage and added-value. In fact since in an input-output model the value added of individual firms and branches depends very strongly on the 'technology' used, it can be very high even if labour inputs are tiny and wages are low. In the Sraffian model, one would expect, on the basis of the enormous technological changes over the years and the big disparities in techniques used in different branches, that there would be only a very low correlation between wages and value added. Moreover, one would expect that the ratio A/B would change considerably with technological development.

Thus input-output theory has no lever whatsoever on these phenomena. Notice also that these high correlations are entirely consistent and in fact follow immediately from a *crude labour theory of value* as presented in the first volume of *Capital—without* the assumption of uniform rate. It seems that one way to comprehend them is to use considerations of the Law of Large Numbers as we have done in chapters V-VII. We will not develop them further in the present work.

Organic Composition

In the previous section we treated an empirical phenomenon relating net output and labour costs. We remarked that their strong correlation is not at all surprising within a traditional, crude, labour theory of value, although it is utterly inexplicable from the point of view of Sraffian or other input-output theories.

In some ways those phenomena that run counter to the expectation of both input-output theories and the traditional labour theory of value are more surprising. In particular, both approaches expect no *restrictions on the variation of organic composition of capital*. They do not predict any correlation whatsoever between the labour expenses and non-labour expenses of a given firm. These two are assumed to be purely technical functions of the particular methods of producing a particular commodity. It is entirely reasonable in a Sraffian framework for half of the economy to operate perfectly normally, with high wages and high rate of profit while the total wage bill in that half represents, say, only 5% of the total expenses. In other words, no restriction on the relative weight of labour costs among all costs can be deduced from the Sraffian framework. Similarly, in the traditional Marxist framework, while the overall organic composition of capital cannot be too high without triggering a crisis, nothing can be said in that framework about the organic composition of individual branches even for a large collection of branches. The disparity of the organic composition among various branches can be arbitrarily large. In other words, there is no limitation on the *distribution* of the random variable Q = organic composition, or any other variable that relates non-labour to labour costs.

To give just one example, let us take the input-output tables from Steedman's exposition of the subject.[5] We will not recapitulate the various notations from that book since they are standard in the subject. For Steedman the following production table is as good as any other, since it can yield a positive rate of profit.

| | Inputs | | Outputs | |
	Iron	Labour	Iron	Corn
Iron industry	100	1	1000	—
Corn industry	1	1	—	20
Total	101	2	1000	20

The fact that this table is totally unrealistic in a capitalist economy, since the divergence in organic composition between the iron industry and the corn industry is huge, cannot be revealed by any uniform rate of profit theory. Thus, contrary to Steedman's remarks about logic and counter-examples, this production table cannot serve as a counter-example because it violates essential properties of capitalist production—namely properties of the standard deviation of organic compositions mentioned here and in chapter VII.

In the living realities of capitalist production, labour costs and non-labour costs are quite strongly correlated, even if not as closely as *B* and *A* discussed above.

In fig. 13 below, we have assembled data from the American economy in 1975 from Standard and Poor's reports. On average, the percentage of labour costs in the total sales of non-oil manufacturing industry is around 31 %, when the weights used in the average are total sales of the various branches. The standard deviation is relatively low —around 8 %. The standard deviation being about one quarter of the average, the scattering is much more narrow than that of the rates of profit.

In fig. 13, the length of each vertical bar is proportional to the relative weight, by sales, of all companies whose labour costs as percentage of total sales is given on the horizontal axis in percentage points. Thus for most companies labour costs represent a full 20-40% of their total sale price. In fact, in the lower brackets of under 20% one finds almost exclusively the rent-rich agricultural food products. Even in their presence, the standard deviation is quite low. Without them, in proper, non-rent manufacturing it would be much lower.

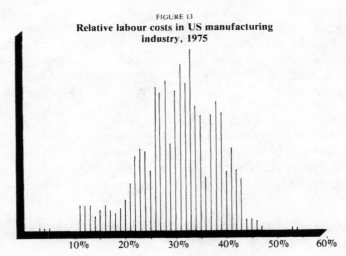

FIGURE 13
Relative labour costs in US manufacturing industry, 1975

Relative labour costs 1975 (= labour costs/total expenses)
average is 30.7% of sales
standard deviation is 7.8%

The surprise is that again in spite of greater gains in physical productivity, in spite of a tremendous technological revolution, the same
picture prevailed in the American economy of twenty-eight years earlier, in 1947. Using input-output tables for the American economy of
1947 published by Leontief (who had brought the input-output
method to the West from the Soviet Union), we get very similar
results: the share of labour costs was slightly more than 30% while the
standard deviation was again very close to 7%. Thus while labour
costs in various branches and firms may have changed dramatically
over the thirty years, the overall picture of the distribution of the relative labour costs over the economy as a whole had changed very little.
This shows once again that the precise 'technological coefficients' of
the economy have little or no influence on the general picture.

The question is what forces within the capitalist economy operate to
both narrow the distribution of *relative labour costs* and make them
so stable over the years of technological development in manufacturing industries. Is this narrow distribution related to a narrow distribution of the organic composition, or the ratio between capital costs and
labour costs either in money terms or in labour-content terms? Can a
theoretical restriction on the development of these ratios be derived?

It seems that what we see here is the operation of strong 'mixing'
forces that do not allow unduly wide disparities between various
branches to emerge—no matter how different their final products
are from the physical point of view. These mixing tendencies are
powerful consequences of free competition, and their empirical
effect is much more noticeable in the empirical economic data than
any supposed tendency of the rates of profits to equalize or to cluster narrowly around their average.

In fact, it may be that the actual mechanics by which firms influence their rates of profit and bring them closer to the optimum is not
only via an appropriate *pricing* policy, as tradition has it, but rather
by taking care that their organic composition and labour costs will
not be out of line.

Capital Accumulation in Post-war USA

In September 1982—after the draft manuscript of the present book
had been completed—the well-known monthly *Scientific American*

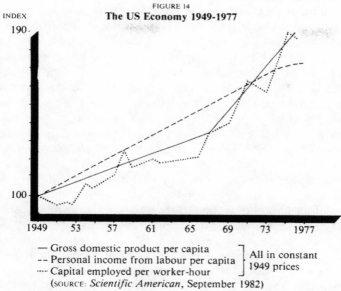

FIGURE 14
The US Economy 1949-1977

INDEX

— Gross domestic product per capita
-- Personal income from labour per capita ⎤ All in constant
···· Capital employed per worker-hour   ⎦ 1949 prices
(SOURCE: *Scientific American*, September 1982)

published an issue wholly devoted to 'two hundred years of industrial revolution' and the 'mechanization of work'. One article in this issue, in particular, contains data about post-war accumulation in the USA, which can be used to test the theoretical analysis presented by us in chapter VII. The article in question, 'The distribution of work and income', is by the celebrated economist Professor W.W. Leontief—the very man who had introduced input-output theory into Western *academia*.

A central thesis put forward by Leontief is that the amount of capital employed per worker-hour in American manufacturing industry has a *long-term* tendency to grow. He presents a graph of the evolution of this quantity (capital stock employed per worker-hour) in the USA from 1949 to 1977, which shows that it has almost doubled during those three decades. This graph is reproduced here as the dotted line in fig. 14.

At first sight, these data seem to be in complete agreement with Marx's prediction that the amount of capital per worker and global organic composition—denoted in chapter VII by k/N and q_G respectively—have an inexorable long-term tendency to grow; and they seem to refute our own thesis that these quantities may have short-term oscillations but change very little in the long term.

However, upon closer examination it transpires that the opposite is actually true. Not only are Leontief's data consistent with our findings in chapter VII, they can actually be *derived* as necessary consequences of those findings. Of course, one cannot predict theoretically the exact shape of the curves depicted in fig. 14, but one can certainly expect them to display a tendency to rise in the long run. Let us see why.

In interpreting Leontief's data, it is important to notice that he measures the 'amount' of capital in *constant 1949 prices*, whereas we measure k in *labour-content* (and Marx measures it in *labour-value*, which in the present context may be identified with labour-content). These two measures produce very different results when dealing with evolution over time. If we consider a large representative basket of commodities, then its price in *constant 1949 dollars* will, by definition, remain unchanged over time. But its labour-content will keep falling as the productivity of labour increases. Thus, if we want to use Leontief's data to test our theoretical analysis of the evolution of k/N and q_G, we must correct his data for the effect of the law of decreasing labour-content.

In fig. 14 we have included another graph—taken from the same issue of *Scientific American*—which shows the evolution of the productivity of labour (gross domestic product per capita) over the same period. If we compare the evolution of these two quantities—capital per worker-hour and product per capita, both measured in constant prices—we see that from 1949 to 1977 they have grown more or less in tandem; the *ratio* between them underwent fluctuations, but in the *long* term remained remarkably stable.

This implies that the growth in the 'amount' of capital employed per worker-hour was apparent rather than real. The growth in constant-price terms reflects a merely *physical* increase (more machines per worker); but the *labour-content k/N* of the capital employed per worker hardly changed at all over the three decades, apart from short-term fluctuations.

This is no mere quibble. Economically speaking, what is of real significance—the physical amount of capital per worker, or the *social cost* of the capital employed per worker? The former is represented by Leontief's index (the amount of capital, measured in constant prices, per worker-hour); the latter is represented by k/N, the labour-content of the capital employed per worker. The former has almost doubled over about three decades, while the latter has changed little over that period (apart from short-term fluctuations).

We believe that in comparing 'amounts' of capital at different times the correct measure to use is not constant prices, but labour-content. In practice, due to the empirical fact that the ratio e_0 is extremely stable over time, the labour-content of large representative collections of commodities varies in tandem with their prices *as measured in terms of the average unit wage*, not in constant prices.

Now let us turn to the global organic composition q_G in the American economy, and see how this quantity has evolved over the period 1949-77 in the light of Leontief's data.

As explained in chapter VII, a very good approximation to q_G is given by the quantity $1/EZ$. This latter quantity is equal to the ratio: (price of capital per worker-hour)/(average hourly wage). In this ratio, the price of capital and the wage may be measured by any monetary unit, provided, of course, that the *same* unit is used for both.

In fig. 14 we have included a graph (also taken from Professor Leontief's article) showing the evolution of the average wage, measured in constant 1949 prices. If we compare this graph with the graph showing the evolution of the 'amount' of capital per worker-hour (also measured in constant 1949 prices) we can see that the ratio between these two has indeed fluctuated over the three decades, but if short-term fluctuations are ignored the ratio has remained broadly stable. It is, however, worth pointing out an interesting short-term phenomenon: in the latter half of the 1970s the average wage was markedly lagging behind the amount of capital per worker as well as the productivity of labour. This phenomenon seems to be quite typical of the onset of a serious recession or crisis. Exactly the same thing happened in the late 1920s and early 1930s.

We summarise our findings in the table overleaf.

To conclude: contrary to first impressions and to Leontief's own claim, his data are in complete agreement with the thesis presented in chapter VII and do not display any *long-term* tendency of q_G and k/N to rise. The 'amount' of capital per worker has a long-term

Twenty-eight years of economic development in the USA; indexes of four economic parameters; each index taken to be = 100 in 1967

	I 1949	II 1977	ratio II/I
Capital employed per worker-hour	73	140	1.9
Personal income per capita	64	120	1.9
Average hourly wage of production worker	64	115	1.8
Gross product per capita	75	142	1.9

(Source: W.W. Leontief, *Scientific American*, September 1982)

tendency to rise only if this 'amount' is measured in monetary units (such as current prices or even constant prices) that do not take into account the rising productivity of labour. But if this amount is measured in terms of labour-content or in terms of the average unit wage (Adam Smith's 'real price'!) it has no long-term tendency to increase or, for that matter, to decrease.

When the full spectrum of global economic parameters move more or less in tandem in terms of 'constant prices', then in fact the *ratios* between them do not change significantly.

The only thing that has definitely changed in an extremely significant way is the *labour-content* of a fixed representative sample of commodities. In fact, it has been almost halved over less than thirty years. This is in accordance with the law of decreasing labour-content, and reflects the continually rising productivity of labour. The fall in price measured in 'constant dollars' is, of course, zero, on the average, because this is how 'constant prices' are *defined*.

Thus the fall in the *real* value (or real social cost) of commodities is masked when commodities are measured in 'constant prices'. The real *cheapening* of commodities (other than labour-power) as a result of technological change (and, more generally, changes in methods of production) is measured accurately in terms of their labour-content. For large and varied collections of commodities this cheapening is quite accurately reflected by their price measured in terms of the average unit wage.

Of course, the a.u.w. is by no means an absolute measure—no monetary unit can be that. But so long as e_0 remains nearly constant, prices measured in a.u.w. are highly correlated with labour-content.

Leontief's data go hand in hand with those compiled by Joseph Gillman for the American economy in the period 1849-1952.[6] His results concerning the evolution of global organic composition are summed up in the following figure.

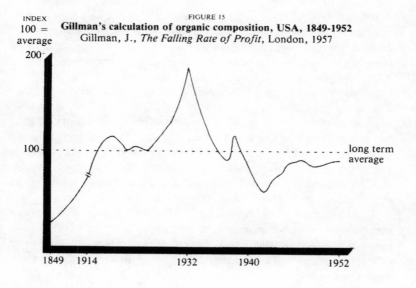

INDEX
100 = average
200-

FIGURE 15

Gillman's calculation of organic composition, USA, 1849-1952
Gillman, J., *The Falling Rate of Profit*, London, 1957

100- · long term average

1849   1914   1932   1940   1952

It can be seen that the long-term behaviour suggested by these findings—strong oscillations around a stable axis—is very similar to the picture that emerges from Leontief's data of 1982, which were obtained by a very different method.

Final Remarks

The empirical questions concerning long- and short-term tendencies in the overall organic composition and rate of surplus value have been the subject of fierce debates. In these debates various schools have produced conflicting empirical evidence. An illuminating example of such a discussion is in *Late Capitalism* by Ernest Mandel.[7] There one can find tables arranged in various ways to yield different results. Works of various authors are cited. From our point of view, the crucial observation is that no matter who is closer to the truth in these debates, the variations shown by those tables are rather small even over a long time period. For example, Mandel cites the ratio of surplus value to wages.[8] His numbers vary around 110%: namely, surplus value is greater by around 10% than wages. Now these are basically the same magnitudes taken realistically by Marx a century earlier to represent the rate of surplus value; and they are entirely in line with the numerical data presented above. Thus even if the rate of surplus value has changed by 10-20% over a hundred years or so, the real problem is *why has it changed so little*. The same goes for the surprisingly slight variations in the global organic composition. We have tried to explain these phenomena, but much work remains to be done. Observe, for example, that the most modern and 'futuristic' branch of industry, namely electronics and computer manufacturing, has a relatively low organic composition of capital: it requires huge outlays on labour-power both in research and development and in physical production.

All these phenomena of relative stability in the empirical data are inexplicable from the uniform rate of profit point of view. We believe that a non-deterministic, flexible approach based on a probabilistic labour theory of value can provide a closer understanding of the phenomena.

Appendix I
Probability Theory

In this appendix we present concepts and results from probability theory that are used throughout this work. We make no attempt at complete mathematical generality and rigour.

Sample space

A *sample space* is a set or 'population' of objects at which a probabilistic inquiry is directed. All sample spaces studied by us are finite, so their members can be labelled by numbers $1, 2, \ldots, n$. The members of a sample space are often referred to as *points*. To the i-th point we attach a positive *weight* p_i such that the sum of all weights is 1: $p_1 + p_2 + \cdots + p_n = 1$. Intuitively, p_i is thought of as the probability that when a point is selected at random out of the sample space, it will turn out to be the i-th point.

In the sample spaces considered by us, the number n (the number of points) is assumed to be very large, and each p_i separately is taken to be negligibly small.

Random Variable

Given a sample space as above, a *random variable* X is a mapping (that is, an assignment) that assigns to each i a real number $X(i)$. If A is a set of real numbers, then $\mathbf{P}(X \text{ in A})$ is the *probability that X is in* A and, by definition, it is equal to the sum of the weights of all points i for which $X(i)$ belongs to A.

It is sometimes convenient to think about $\mathbf{P}(X \text{ in A})$ in terms of betting odds. Suppose some *i* is selected at random out of the sample space. Before you know which *i* has been selected, you are asked to lay odds that $X(i)$ will turn out to be in the set A. If $\mathbf{P}(X$ in A$) = p$, then *p* to $(1 - p)$ are *fair* odds that $X(i)$ is in A—fair in the sense of not being biased either for or against you. (In a betting establishment the odds are, of course, biased against the client.)

If A consists of all real numbers less than or equal to a given number *r*, we write $\mathbf{P}(X$ in A$)$ as $\mathbf{P}(X \leq r)$. A similar notational convention is used in other cases where A is defined by means of inequalities or equalities. In particular, $\mathbf{P}(X = r)$ is the same as $\mathbf{P}(X$ in A$)$, where in this case A consists of just one number, *r*.

A random variable *X* is said to be *degenerate* if for some number *r* the probability $\mathbf{P}(X = r)$ is equal to 1 or is so near 1 that the difference $1 - \mathbf{P}(X = r)$ is negligibly small. All the economic random variables considered in this book (such as the rate of profit, price, etc.) can be safely assumed to be non-degenerate.

A constant number *c* can be regarded as a degenerate random variable: we can think of it as an *X* such that $X(i) = c$ for all *i*.

If *g* is a real-valued function of one real variable and *X* is a random variable, then $g(X)$ is the random variable *U* defined by

$$U(i) = g[X(i)] \quad \text{for all } i.$$

This may also be written as

$$[g(X)](i) = g[X(i)] \quad \text{for all } i.$$

For example, X^2 is the random variable defined by

$$X^2(i) = [X(i)]^2 \quad \text{for all } i.$$

Similarly, we can combine several random variables to form a new random variable. For example, $X + Y$ is, by definition, the random variable *Z* such that $Z(i) = X(i) + Y(i)$ for all *i*; and *XY* is, by definition, the random variable *W* such that $W(i) = X(i)Y(i)$.

Mean, variance, standard deviation

The *mean* value (also called *average* or *expected* value) of a random variable *X* is denoted by $\mathbf{E}X$ and defined by

$$\mathbf{E}X = p_1 X(1) + p_2 X(2) + \cdots + p_n \mathbf{X}(n).$$

It is not difficult to prove that if c and d are real numbers then

$$\mathbf{E}(cX + d) = c\mathbf{E}X + d.$$

In other words, if $Y = cX + d$ (which means that $Y(i) = cX(i) + d$ for all i) then $\mathbf{E}Y = c\mathbf{E}X + d$. Also, for any two random variables X and Y (defined over the same space) it is easy to show that

$$\mathbf{E}(X + Y) = \mathbf{E}X + \mathbf{E}Y.$$

However, note that in general $\mathbf{E}(XY)$ is *not* equal to $(\mathbf{E}X)(\mathbf{E}Y)$. In particular, $\mathbf{E}(X^2)$ (which is often written simply as $\mathbf{E}X^2$) is in general different from $(\mathbf{E}X)^2$. (In other words: the mean of the square is in general different from the square of the mean.)

The *variance* of a random variable X, denoted by $\mathbf{V}X$, is defined as

$$\mathbf{V}X = \mathbf{E}(X - \mathbf{E}X)^2,$$

and is always non-negative. It can be shown that

$$\mathbf{V}X = \mathbf{E}X^2 - (\mathbf{E}X)^2.$$

The variance $\mathbf{V}X$ is negligibly small if, and only if, X is a degenerate random variable. Indeed, $\mathbf{V}X$ can be taken as a measure of the 'degree of non-degeneracy' of X. A better measure is provided by the (non-negative) square root of the variance, $(\mathbf{V}X)^{1/2}$, which is called the *standard deviation* of X.

It can be shown that, for any real numbers c and d,

$$\mathbf{V}(cX + d) = c^2 \mathbf{V}X.$$

Note that $\mathbf{V}(X + Y)$ equals $\mathbf{V}X + \mathbf{V}Y$ if, and ony if, $\mathbf{E}(XY)$ equals $(\mathbf{E}X)(\mathbf{E}Y)$, which is *not* generally the case. However, if the two variables are *uncorrelated (see below) then the equality does hold*.

Correlation

We say that there is a *linear relation* between the random variables X and Y if there are constants c and d, not both equal to 0, such that the variable $cX + dY$ is degenerate. If X and Y themselves are non-degenerate, their *correlation coefficient* $\varrho(X, Y)$ is defined by

$$\varrho(X, Y) = \frac{\mathbf{E}(XY) - (\mathbf{E}X)(\mathbf{E}Y)}{(\mathbf{V}X)^{\frac{1}{2}}(\mathbf{V}Y)^{\frac{1}{2}}},$$

and is a measure of how close X and Y are to being linearly related. It can be shown that $\varrho(X, Y)$ is always between -1 and 1, and it equals one of its extreme values (-1 or 1) if, and only if, there is a linear relation between X and Y. If $\varrho(X, Y) = 0$, then X and Y are said to be *uncorrelated*. This means, roughly speaking, that they are 'as far as possible' from being linearly related.

An easy calculation yields the equality

$$\mathbf{V}(X + Y) = \mathbf{V}X + \mathbf{V}Y + 2[\mathbf{E}(XY) - (\mathbf{E}X)(\mathbf{E}Y)]$$

The third term on the right-hand side has the same sign as the correlation $\varrho(X, Y)$. Hence, if this correlation is positive, $\mathbf{V}(X + Y)$ is greater than $\mathbf{V}X + \mathbf{V}Y$; the opposite inequality holds if the correlation is negative. If X and Y are uncorrelated, then

$$\mathbf{V}(X + Y) = \mathbf{V}X + \mathbf{V}Y.$$

This equality holds, *a fortiori*, if X and Y are independent (see below).

Independence[1]

Let C be a condition satisfied by some (but not necessarily all) of the points in the sample space. *The probability of* C, denoted by $\mathbf{P}(C)$, is defined as the sum of the weights of all points that do satisfy C. We assume here that $\mathbf{P}(C) \neq 0$.

If X is a random variable and A is a set of real numbers, then the probability $\mathbf{P}(C \ \& \ X \text{ in } A)$ is the sum of the weights of those among the points satisfying C for which, in addition, $X(i)$ is in A.

For example, suppose that our sample space is an ordinary deck of cards (labelled 1, 2, ..., 52) and that each card is given the same weight, $\frac{1}{52}$. Suppose that C is the condition of being a red card. Clearly, **P**(red card) $= \frac{1}{2}$, because there are 26 red cards and $\frac{26}{52} = \frac{1}{2}$. Similarly, if we consider the condition of being a court card (jack, queen or king) then clearly **P**(court card) $= \frac{3}{13}$. If for each i we define $X(i)$ as the face value of the i-th card (taking ace, jack, queen and king to have values 1, 11, 12 and 13 respectively) then **P**(red card & $X \geq 12$) $= \frac{1}{13}$, because there are four red cards whose face value is ≥ 12 (namely the red queens and kings) with a total weight of $\frac{4}{52} = \frac{1}{13}$. Similarly, **P**(court card & $X \leq 12$) $= \frac{2}{13}$, because there are eight court cards whose value is ≤ 12.

Returning to the general case, we define the quantity **P**(x in A $|$ C) by

$$\mathbf{P}(X \text{ in A} \mid C) = \frac{\mathbf{P}(C \,\&\, X \text{ in A})}{\mathbf{P}(C)}$$

P(X in A $|$ C) is called *the conditional probability that X is in* A, *given that* C. *By definition, it equals the proportion, out of the whole of* **P**(C), of that part of it which is contributed by points for which $X(i)$ belongs to A. Its meaning is most easily understood in terms of betting odds. We have remarked above that if a point, say the i-th, is selected at random out of the sample space and, without being told what i is, you are asked to bet that $X(i)$ is in A, then fair odds for such a bet are p to $(1 - p)$, where $p = $ **P**(X in A). But now suppose that you are reliably informed that the point chosen satisfies condition C (but know nothing else about it). In the light of this information, fair odds for betting that $X(i)$ is in A are q to $(1 - q)$, where $q = $ **P**(X in A $|$ C).

For example, if a card is drawn at random from our deck of cards (which we assume to be well shuffled) and, without being told anything about that card, you are asked to bet that its face value is at most 12, then you can calculate the odds as follows: **P**($X \leq 12$) $= \frac{12}{13}$, because 48 cards out of 52 have value ≤ 12, and $\frac{48}{52} = \frac{12}{13}$. Therefore the right odds are $\frac{12}{13}$ to $\frac{1}{13}$, or 12 to 1. However, if you know that the card selected is a court card (but know nothing else about it) then you can calculate the odds as follows: **P**($X \leq 12 \mid$ court card) $= $ **P**(court card & $X \leq 12$)/**P**(court card) $= \frac{2}{13}/\frac{3}{13} = \frac{2}{3}$. So the odds now are $\frac{2}{3}$ to $\frac{1}{3}$, or 2 to 1. Of course, in such simple cases you can calculate the odds in your head much more quickly: you simply have to note that 12 out of every 13 cards in the whole deck have value $\leq$ 12, while only 2 out of every 3 *court* cards have such value, so the odds are 12 to 1 and 2 to 1 respectively. But the method used above is completely general, and can be applied even when the result is not quite so obvious.

If, for some set A of real numbers, the conditional probability $\mathbf{P}(X$ in A $\mid$ C) differs from the (unconditional) probability $\mathbf{P}(X$ in A), then the random variable X is said to *depend* on C. In the opposite case, that is if $\mathbf{P}(X$ in A $\mid$ C) = $\mathbf{P}(X$ in A) for every A, we say that X is *independent* of C.

Thus, to say that X is independent of C means that, for any A, the aggregate contribution to $\mathbf{P}$(C) of points for which $X(i)$ is in A is proportional to the total weight of such points in the entire sample space. Or, in terms of betting odds: if a point, say the i-th, is selected at random out of the sample space, then in any bet concerning the value $X(i)$ the odds are unaffected by the tip that the point selected satisfies C.

In our card-deck example, it is clear that the random variable X (the face value) depends on the condition of being a court card. But the same X is independent of the condition of being a red card, because the relative weight of cards with a given value among the red cards is the same as in the whole deck. Knowing that the card selected at random is red does not alter the odds in any bet about the face value of that card.

To take an economic example, consider the firm space and random variable R (the rate of profit) introduced in chapter III. Suppose that each firm has one managing director, and let C be the condition that the managing director has a cat. It seems highly realistic to assume that R is independent of C. (If asked to make a bet concerning the rate of profit of a firm selected at random, would the odds you were prepared to lay be influenced by the knowledge that the managing director of the firm selected has a cat?) It appears reasonable to assume that the condition in question has no connection whatsoever with R. Of course, this assumption may be wrong, and statistical investigation may reveal, to most people's surprise, that there is some connection after all.

Let X and Y be two random variables defined over the same space. We say that X is *independent* of Y if X is independent of every condition concerning the values of Y. In other words, X is independent of Y if for any two sets A and B of real numbers such that $P(Y$ in B$) \neq 0$ we have

$$P(X \text{ in A} \mid Y \text{ in B}) = P(X \text{ in A}).$$

In terms of betting odds, this means that if a point, say the i-th, is selected at random out of the sample space, then no information concerning $Y(i)$ can make any difference to the odds in a bet regarding $X(i)$. It is quite easy to prove the (unsurprising) result that if X is independent of Y then Y is also independent of X; so we can simply say that X *and Y are independent*.

In our card-deck example, let $Y(i)$ be 1, 2, 3, or 4 according as the i-th card is a heart, a spade, a diamond or a club. Then X (the face value) and Y are independent, because if a card is drawn at random, no information concerning its suit can have any bearing on the odds in a bet concerning its face value (and vice versa). Or, returning to our firm space, assuming that every firm has one managing director, who has one private telephone number, let $T(i)$ be the second digit in the private telephone number of the managing director of the i-th firm. Then it is highly realistic to assume that R (the rate of profit) and T are independent. Again, this can be tested statistically.

It can be shown that if X and Y are independent then $E(XY) = (EX)(EY)$ and therefore the correlation coefficient $\varrho(X, Y)$ is 0. (Here we are assuming that X and Y are both non-degenerate, because the correlation coefficient is defined only in this case.) Thus any statistical evidence that $\varrho(X, Y) \neq 0$ is automatically also evidence against the independence of X and Y. But if $\varrho(X, Y) = 0$ it does not necessarily follow that X and Y are independent: there are counter-examples of uncorrelated variables that are not independent. Nevertheless, since these examples are somewhat artificial, evidence that $\varrho(X, Y) = 0$ is often regarded by statisticians as tending to corroborate the hypothesis that X and Y are independent.

Note that if X and Y are independent, then $V(X + Y) = VX + VY$.

Distribution and density

The *cumulative distribution function* (c.d.f.) of a random variable X is the function F_X defined by

$$F_X(r) = \mathbf{P}(X \leq r) \quad \text{for every real number } r.$$

It is not difficult to show that F_X is always non-decreasing: if $r \leq s$ then $F_X(r) \leq F_X(s)$. Also as r tends to $-\infty$, $F_X(r)$ tends to 0; and as r tends to $+\infty$, $F_X(r)$ tends to 1.

If F_X is everywhere continuous and has a derivative f_X which is defined and continuous everywhere, except possibly at a finite number of points—briefly, if F_X is 'smooth'—then the derivative f_X is called the *probability density function* (p.d.f.) of X.

If f_X is given, F_X is uniquely determined by the facts that f_X is the derivative of F_X and that $F_X(r)$ must always be between 0 and 1 inclusive. Also, if a and b are real numbers such that $a \leq b$, then

$$\mathbf{P}(a \leq X \leq b) = \int_a^b f_X(r)\,\mathrm{d}r. \quad \text{(see fig. 2, p.47)}$$

Next, if f_X is given and $Y = g(X)$ then

$$\mathbf{E}Y = \int_{-\infty}^{\infty} g(r)f_X(r)\,\mathrm{d}r.$$

In particular, the mean and variance of X itself are given by the formula

$$\mathbf{E}Y = \int_{-\infty}^{\infty} rf(r)\,\mathrm{d}r, \quad \mathbf{V}X = \int_{-\infty}^{\infty} r^2 f_X(r)\,\mathrm{d}r - (\mathbf{E}X)^2.$$

Because of these and other useful properties of the p.d.f., it is convenient, whenever possible, to convey the law of distribution of a random variable by means of its p.d.f. f_X.

The sample spaces considered by us in this book are finite and therefore the c.d.f.'s of our random variables are step functions rather than being smooth. Nevertheless, if the length of each step of the c.d.f. F_X is negligibly small, and if also each jump between successive steps is negligibly small, then F_X can be regarded as smooth to a high degree of approximation. This amounts, in effect, to replacing the random variable X by another random variable whose c.d.f. is smooth and is very close to F_X. The same procedure is used in statistical mechanics and other statistical studies of large but finite populations. Whenever such a procedure is used, it must be assumed that for any real r the probability $P(X = r)$ is negligibly small, because in the contrary case F_X has a non-negligible jump at r.

The Gamma Distribution[2]

Let α and β be positive real numbers. A random variable X is said to have the *gamma distribution with parameters α and β* – briefly, $\mathcal{G}(\alpha, \beta)$ – if X has a p.d.f. f_X given by the formula

$$f_X(r) = \begin{cases} Cr^{\alpha-1}e^{-\beta r} & \text{for } r > 0, \\ 0 & \text{for } r \leq 0. \end{cases}$$

Here C is a constant [3] that depends on α and β.

The mean and variance of X are then given by

$$\mathsf{E}X = \frac{\alpha}{\beta}, \quad \mathsf{V}X = \frac{\alpha}{\beta^2}.$$

Conversely, α and β can be expressed in terms of $\mathsf{E}X$ and $\mathsf{V}X$:

$$\beta = \frac{\mathsf{E}X}{\mathsf{V}X}, \quad \alpha = \frac{(\mathsf{E}X)^2}{\mathsf{V}X}$$

Some special cases belonging to the gamma family are particularly well known. Thus the distribution $\mathcal{G}(n/2, \frac{1}{2})$, where n is a positive integer, is the so-called *chi-square distribution with n degrees of freedom*, used in many statistical tests. The distribution $\mathcal{G}(1, \beta)$ is called an *exponential* distribution.

The gamma family has the following useful closure property: if X and Y are independent random variables over the same space and have the gamma distributions $\mathcal{G}(\alpha_1, \beta)$ and $\mathcal{G}(\alpha_2, \beta)$ respectively, then their sum $X + Y$ has the gamma distribution $\mathcal{G}(\alpha_1 + \alpha_2, \beta)$.

The shape of the curve f_X depends on the values of the parameters α and β, most crucially on the former.

If $\alpha \leq 1$, then f_X is monotone decreasing; as r tends to ∞, $f_X(r)$ rapidly tends to 0. When r tends to 0, $f_X(r)$ tends to ∞ (if $\alpha < 1$) or to β (if $\alpha = 1$; this is the case of the exponential distribution). This general form of the curve with $\alpha \leq 1$ makes it an unlikely candidate for the p.d.f. of the random variables R and Z of chapter III.

The likely candidates are provided by the case $\alpha > 1$. In this case the curve has the shape of a skew bell (see fig. 16). At $r = 0, f_X(r)$ is also 0; it then increases quickly with r, reaching a maximum at $r = (\alpha - 1)/\beta$. This value of r, at which $f_X(r)$ is maximal, is known as the *mode* of X. As r increases beyond the mode, $f_X(r)$ begins to decrease fairly rapidly, tending to 0 as r tends to ∞. As mentioned above, $\mathbf{E}X = \alpha/\beta$, which is clearly greater than the mode. The *median* of X, defined as that r for which $F_X(r) = \mathbf{P}(X \leq r) = \frac{1}{2}$, lies between the mode and the mean value $\mathbf{E}X$.

Thus, if the rate of profit R has a gamma distribution as suggested in chapter III, and if (as seems reasonable) the parameter α is greater than 1, it follows that the average rate of profit (the total annual profit of the economy divided by the total capital of the economy) is greater than the median rate of profit (that is, the rate of profit that is surpassed by exactly half of the total capital); and the median is in turn greater than the mode (that is, the rate-of-profit bracket in which there is more capital than in any other bracket of the same width). For example, if R has distribution $\mathcal{G}(4, 20)$ then (see fig. 16) the average rate of profit is 20% (that is, 0.20) per annum, but half of the total capital in the economy achieves no more than 18.4%, and the most common rate of profit (the one around which there is the highest crowding of capital) is only 15% per annum. These figures are quite realistic; in fact, $\mathcal{G}(4, 20)$ provides a good fit to the empirical statistical data on the rate of profit of British private manufacturing industry for 1979.[4] Note that in this particular distribution the standard deviation is 0.1, which is 10%. This is quite high —half of the mean!—and is a good illustration of the general fact that the rate of profit has a fairly wide dispersion, and cannot in any way be taken as uniform.

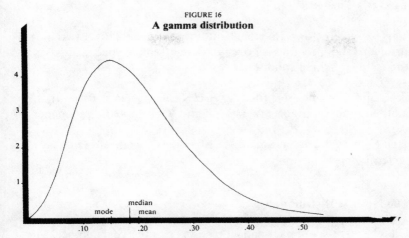

FIGURE 16
A gamma distribution

Graph of the probability density of a random variable with gamma distribution
⏿ (4, 20). The mode is 0.15, the median is 0.184 and the mean is 0.20. The
variance is 0.01 and the standard deviation is 0.1

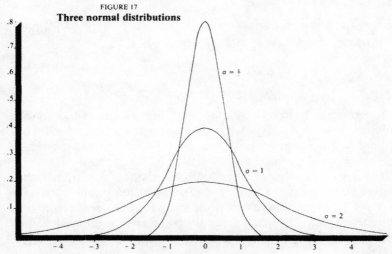

FIGURE 17
Three normal distributions

Graphs of normal probability densities with common mean 0 and standard
deviation ½, 1 and 2

Lukacs's Theorem[5]

This extremely powerful result states that if U and V are two independent random variables over the same sample space, satisfying the following three conditions:
1. U and V are non-degenerate,
2. U and V are positive (that is, $\mathbf{P}(U \leq 0) = \mathbf{P}(V \leq 0) = 0$),
3. the random variables $X = U/V$ and $Y = U + V$ are independent,

then both U and V have gamma distributions, with the same parameter β.

The Normal Distribution

Let μ be any real number and let σ be any positive real number. The random variable X is said to have a *normal* (or *Gaussian*) distribution with parameters μ and σ, briefly: $\textit{N}(\mu, \sigma)$, if X has a p.d.f. given by the formula

$$f_X(r) = \frac{1}{\sigma\sqrt{(2\pi)}} \exp\left[-\tfrac{1}{2}\left(\frac{r - \mu}{\sigma}\right)^2\right] \quad \text{for all } r,$$

where $\exp x$ stands for e^x.

The mean and variance of X are then

$$\mathbf{E}X = \mu, \qquad \mathbf{V}X = \sigma^2,$$

so that the standard deviation is σ.

The graph of f_X has the famous 'bell' shape; it has a single maximum (mode) at $r = \mu$ and decreases symmetrically on both sides of this point. The height of the 'bell' is proportional to σ and the width is inversely proportional to it. (See fig. 17.)

The normal family of distributions has the following important closure property. Let X_1 and X_2 be independent random variables over the same space, with distributions $\textit{N}(\mu_1, \sigma_1)$ and $\textit{N}(\mu_2, \sigma_2)$ respectively. Then, if a_1 and a_2 are any real numbers (not both 0) the random variable $a_1 X_1 + a_2 X_2$ has the normal distribution

$$\textit{N}\left(a_1\mu_1 + a_2\mu_2, (a_1^2\sigma_1^2 + a_2^2\sigma_2^2)^{1/2}\right).$$

A degenerate random variable, whose value equals a with probability 1 can be regarded as a limiting case of a normal variable, with distribution $\mathfrak{N}(a, 0)$.

If X has a normal distribution $\mathfrak{N}(\mu, \sigma)$, then the c.d.f. F_X is positive everywhere:

$$F_X(r) = \mathbf{P}(X \leq r) > 0 \quad \text{for all } r.$$

However, although $F_X(r)$ is always positive, it approaches 0 very rapidly when r grows smaller and smaller than μ. in this connection, the distance between r and μ is measured in units of σ rather than in absolute terms; so that, for example, if $r = \mu - 2\sigma$ we say that r is two units smaller than μ. Now, if $r = \mu - a\sigma$, where a is a positive number, then the cumulative probability $\mathbf{P}(X \leq r)$—which equals $F_X(r)$—becomes very small even for moderate values of a. This probability is quite small even for $a = 3$, and becomes negligibly small when a is about 4. The following table gives the probability $\mathbf{P}(X \leq r)$, where $r = \mu - a\sigma$, for selected values of a

a	2.3	3.1	3.7	4.3
$\mathbf{P}(X \leq r)$	$\dfrac{1}{100}$	$\dfrac{1}{1000}$	$\dfrac{1}{10,000}$	$\dfrac{1}{100,000}$

For this reason, if Y is a positive random variable (that is, $\mathbf{P}(Y \leq 0) = 0$) it may still be possible for the distribution of Y to be very nearly normal, provided the standard deviation of Y is small compared to $\mathbf{E}\,Y$ (say, not more than about one-quarter or one-fifth of $\mathbf{E}\,Y$).

In fact, normal distributions are ubiquitous; a normal law of distribution is very often an excellent approximation to the empirical distribution of a quantitative characteristic of individuals belonging to a natural or 'quasi-natural' population.

For example, in a (naturally occurring or artificially raised) interbreeding population of a given biological species, the linear size (the length) of individuals of the same sex and similar age is usually very nearly normally distributed.

The same is true of a 'population' of objects manufactured by a given industrial process. For example, consider the mass-production of steel balls for a particular type of ball bearing. Ideally, all these balls should have the same radius. But, no matter how hard one tries, this cannot be achieved, due to various perturbations in the process. In practice, it is usually found that the radii of the balls are very nearly normally distributed, and the best one can do is to reduce the standard deviation of this distribution, so as to make the balls as nearly uniform as possible.

A similar phenomenon arises in connection with the measurement of a given fixed physical linear quantity. Suppose one wants to measure, as precisely as possible, the length of a metal rod. Each act of measurement always involves a certain amount of error, due to various objective and subjective conditions, which are partly random and which accumulate and add to one another. If the measurement is repeated many times, the results are usually found to have a distribution that is very nearly normal.

Indeed, when statisticians are faced with a problem where they have to make an educated guess as to the distribution of a random variable of this type (a linear characteristic of individuals belonging to a natural or 'quasi-natural' population, or the results of repeated measurements of a fixed physical linear magnitude) then—unless there are special reasons to the contrary—the first hypothesis they consider is that the distribution is normal.

This rule of thumb is based not only on past experience of such cases. A theoretical justification is found in the Central Limit Theorem of probability theory (see below).

Note. When comparing the distribution of a random variable Y with a normal distribution, it is usual to 'standardize' Y first; that is, instead of Y itself, one considers the random variable

$$Y^* = \frac{Y - \mu}{\sigma},$$

where μ and σ are, respectively, the mean and standard deviation of Y. The new variable Y^* is *standard*, in the sense that its mean and standard deviation are equal to 0 and 1, respectively. If X itself has a normal distribution, then X^* has the *standard* normal distribution $\mathcal{N}(0, 1)$. When we say that Y has an approximately normal distribution, what we mean is that the c.d.f. of Y^* is approximated by that of the standard normal variable X^*. The extent to which the distribution of Y approaches normality is measured by the extent to which the c.d.f. of Y^* approaches that of the standard normal variable X^*.

The Central Limit Theorem

This is not a single theorem, but a whole corpus of results, which together constitute an important part of probability theory. These results share the following general form. A random variable X_n is assumed to be equal to the sum of n random variables,

$$\ddot{X}_n = Z_1 + Z_2 + \cdots + Z_n,$$

where the random variables Z_i are assumed to satisfy certain conditions which, roughly speaking, guarantee that the contribution of each Z_i to the whole sum is relatively small and that, for $i \neq j$, the variables Z_i and Z_j are independent or at least 'almost' independent. It is then proved that as n tends to infinity, the distribution of $\ddot{X}_n$ approaches normality; that is, the distribution of the standardized variable $\ddot{X}_n^*$ approaches $\mathfrak{N}(0, 1)$. When n is sufficiently large, the distribution of $\ddot{X}_n$ is very nearly normal.

For a general and rigorous treatment of this topic the reader is referred to the specialized literature.[6] Here we shall discuss briefly an important paradigmatic case of the Central Limit Theorem.

Consider a given sample space with a given random variable X defined over it. Let X have mean and standard deviation equal to μ and σ respectively. It will be convenient to visualize the sample space as a large urn full of marbles (the marbles being the 'points' of the space). For each marble, the random variable X assumes a definite numerical value; we can imagine each marble to be marked with the appropriate value of X.

Now suppose that a marble is drawn at random out of the urn, and the number on it is read out, as in the game of 'bingo'. This simple experiment is called a *single observation* on the variable X. The outcome of such an observation (the number read out) is distributed according to the c.d.f. F_X. This means that (for any real number r) the probability that the outcome of the observation will be at most r is equal to $F_X(r)$.

So far, there is nothing new; we have merely recalled the definition of F_X. But now consider an experiment consisting of *two* independent observations: as before, we draw a marble at random out of the urn and read out the number on it; then we replace the marble in the urn and (after shaking the urn thoroughly) draw out a second marble and read out the number on it. This time, the result of the experiment is given not by the single variable X, but by two independent random variables, X_1 and X_2. It is not correct to say that these two variables are the same, because the second number read out is in general not the same as the first. However, each of the variables X_1 and X_2, considered separately, has the same *distribution* as the original variable X. Therefore, each of these two variables also has the same mean and variance as X.

This two-stage experiment is described as *drawing a sample of size* 2, *with replacement*. ('Size 2', because two marbles are drawn; 'with replacement', because the first marble is replaced before the second is drawn.)

Now suppose that we add a final stage to this experiment: we compute the ordinary (arithmetical) average of the two numbers read out. The result is given by a new random variable, called the *sample-average* and denoted by $\bar{X}_2$. Clearly,

$$\bar{X}_2 = \tfrac{1}{2}(X_1 + X_2).$$

This formula can be used to compute the mean and standard deviation of $\bar{X}_2$. First, the mean: $\mathbf{E}\bar{X}_2 = \tfrac{1}{2}\mathbf{E}(X_1 + X_2) = \tfrac{1}{2}(\mathbf{E}X_1 + \mathbf{E}X_2) = \tfrac{1}{2}(\mathbf{E}X + \mathbf{E}X) = \tfrac{1}{2}(\mu + \mu) = \mu$. So the mean value of the sample-average is the same as the 'population mean' $\mathbf{E}X = \mu$.

The variance of $\bar{X}_2$ can be calculated, using the fact that X_1 and X_2 are *independent*, so that $\mathbf{V}(X_1 + X_2) = \mathbf{V}X_1 + \mathbf{V}X_2$:

$$\mathbf{V}\bar{X}_2 = (\tfrac{1}{2})^2\mathbf{V}(X_1 + X_2) = (\tfrac{1}{2})^2(\mathbf{V}X_1 + \mathbf{V}X_2) = 2(\tfrac{1}{2})^2\mathbf{V}X = \tfrac{1}{2}\mathbf{V}X.$$

So the variance of the sample-mean is only one-half of the 'population variance'. Taking square roots, we find that the standard deviation of X_2 is equal to $\sigma/\sqrt{2}$ (that is, to the population standard deviation divided by the square root of 2).

All this can be easily generalized to the case of a *sample of size n, with replacement*. Here we have *n* independent observations, given by *n* independent random variables $X_1, X_2, \ldots, X_n$. Each of these variables, considered separately, has the same distribution as the original population-variable, X. The *sample-average* $\bar{X}_n$ is defined as follows:

$$\bar{X}_n = \frac{X_1 + X_2 + \cdots + X_n}{n}.$$

A simple calculation (similar to the one performed above for the case $n = 2$) shows that the mean value of the sample-average is still μ (the same as the population mean) but the standard deviation of the sample-mean is equal to $\sigma/\sqrt{n}$ (the population standard deviation, divided by the square root of n). Thus, for a large sample size, the standard deviation of the sample-average becomes quite small. (Intuitively speaking, this means that in taking the sample-average, the individual variations of the *n* separate observations tend to get 'averaged-out'.)

What can be said about the distribution of the sample average X_n? The precise form of this distribution obviously depends on the 'population distribution', that is, on the distribution of X. However, it can be proved that, *irrespective of the distribution of X, as n grows larger, the distribution of $\bar{X}_n$ approaches* closer and closer to normal.

This is one of the simplest, most basic cases of the Central Limit Theorem. It can be generalized in several directions, which we shall now outline, without, however, stating the precise conditions under which each generalization holds.

1. The requirement that the observations X_i are mutually independent can be relaxed, so long as the dependence between the observations is not too strong. This, in particular, applies to sampling *without* replacement (where a marble drawn out of the urn is not replaced before the next marble is drawn; or, simply, a 'handful' of *n* marbles is drawn simultaneously out of the urn). In such sampling the *n* observations are not completely independent, but the Central Limit Theorem still applies to the sample-average.

2. The observations X_i need not have the same distribution. Thus, instead of all the marbles being drawn from the *same* urn, we can

210

assume that each marble is drawn from a different urn, that is, from a different 'population'. Under suitable conditions (involving the variances $\mathbf{V}X_i$) the Central Limit Theorem still applies.

3. Instead of taking $\bar{X}_n$ as the ordinary arithmetical average of the observations $X_1, X_2, \ldots, X_n$, we can take it as their *weighted* average,

$$\bar{X}_n = \frac{a_1X_1 + a_2X_2 + \cdots + a_nX_n}{a_1 + a_2 + \cdots + a_n},$$

where the 'weights' a_i are non-negative. If all the weights are the same, then $\bar{X}_n$ is again the ordinary mathematical average. But the Central Limit Theorem still holds even when the weights are not all the same, provided that the disparity between them is not too large.

4. Under certain conditions, the weights a_n may be taken not as constants, but as being themselves random variables.

5. Similarly, the size of the sample, n, may be taken as itself being random, subject to suitable conditions.

The Law of Large Numbers

Again, this is not a single theorem, but a whole corpus of results. Many versions of the Law of Large Numbers can be deduced from appropriate versions of the Central Limit Theorem; but there are cases where the former holds, while the latter fails to hold. Here we shall just state one simple version of the Law, which is sufficient for our purpose.

Again, as in connection with the Central Limit Theorem, we consider a given random variable X over a given sample space. (Here too, we can visualize the sample space as a large urn full of marbles, each marble being marked with the appropriate numerical value of X.)

As before, we consider a random sample of size n, consisting of n observations, given by n random variables $X_1, X_2, \ldots, X_n$. Each of these n variables has the same distribution as X. In the present context it does not matter whether the sampling is done with or without replacement. Again, we define $\bar{X}_n$ as the (ordinary, unweighted) sample-average:

$$\bar{X}_n = \frac{X_1 + X_2 + \cdots + X_n}{n}.$$

In our discussion of the Central Limit Theorem, we noted that the mean value of $\bar{X}_n$ is the same as the mean value of X, which we denote by μ. This result holds equally for sampling with or without replacement. But if the standard deviation of X is σ, then the standard deviation of $\bar{X}_n$ is not σ but smaller than that: in sampling with replacement (where the observations are mutually independent) it equals $\sigma/\sqrt{n}$, and in sampling without replacement it turns out to be even smaller. This suggests that the values of the sample-average tend to cluster closer to μ than do the population values (that is, the values of X). The Law of Large Numbers expresses this 'tendency' still more sharply, as follows.

Let δ be any given positive number, no matter how small; then as n grows larger, the probability

$$\mathbf{P}(\mu - \delta \leq \bar{X}_n \leq \mu + \delta)$$

tends to 1.

This means, roughly speaking, that if you want to be nearly certain that the sample-average is nearly equal to μ, then all you need to do is to make the sample size n sufficiently large. (*How large* will depend, of course, on *how nearly certain* you want to be, and *how near* μ you want the sample-average to be.)

A simple but important consequence of the Law of Large Numbers is the following. Consider a random sample of size n, *without replacement*. If the size of the whole space is N, then our sample can be regarded as a selection of n points out of the N. Let **B** be the set of those n points which happened to have been selected. Recall that, for each i, the i-th point of the space has weight p_i such that, for each single act of selection, the probability that the i-th point will be the one selected is equal to p_i.

Now consider the variable Y defined by the equality

$$Y = \frac{\sum X(i)p_i}{\sum p_i},$$

where the summation is not over the whole space, but only over those i which happen to fall in **B**. *Then it can be proved that for any positive* δ, *no matter how small, the probability*

$$\mathbf{P}(\mu - \delta \leq Y \leq \mu + \delta)$$

tends to 1 *as n grows larger*. (This probability will actually equal 1 when $n = N$, that is, when the whole space is taken as the 'sample'.)

This result is used to derive the approximate formula (10) of chapter V. There the role of X is played by the variable $\Psi = \Pi/\Lambda$ and the weights p_i are proportional to $\Lambda(i)$. In this case it is easy to see that Y has the form

$$Y = \frac{\Sigma\Pi(i)}{\Sigma\Lambda(i)},$$

where the summation is, again, over those i that fall in the sample **B**.

Appendix II
The Determination of
Labour-content

In the main text, particularly in chapters IV and V, we have treated the notion of *labour-content* as though it were relatively unproblematic, thus glossing over certain conceptual difficulties concerning its precise definition. These matters are not very crucial to the purely theoretical development of our model, and could therefore be temporarily brushed aside. But they must nevertheless be elucidated at some stage, in order to render the theoretical model empirically testable. Before the theoretical propositions of chapter V can be put to the empirical test of reality, we must be clear as to how the labour-content of a commodity might be measured, and this requires a scrutiny of the conceptual problems relating to the definition of that notion.

These conceptual problems have been quite widely discussed in connection with the Marxian notion of *value*;[1] and since our notion of labour-content is generically similar to Marx's *value*, similar problems arise for us as well. However, this does not mean that the significance of these problems for our theory is the same as for the traditional Marxian theory, or that their resolution must be the same in both cases.

Indeed, we shall try to show that the problems alluded to assume a particularly acute form for the traditional Marxian theory precisely because of the latter's deterministic character. Our own theory, being probabilistic, is not only less sensitive to these problems, but actually allows—and in a sense even requires—them to be resolved in a radically simple way. This radical solution is, we believe, in greater harmony with Marx's own concept of *abstract labour*, which is one of his deepest insights into the relations underlying a commodity-producing economy.

As is well known, in the opening pages of *Capital* Marx draws a conceptual distinction between the *use-value* and *value* embodied in any given commodity. Considered as use-value, a commodity (or indeed any object, whether or not it is exchanged as a commodity) is something functional, capable of satisfying some known human want, whether in consumption or as means of production. Use-values are not primarily quantitative; two different use-values cannot, in general, be compared numerically. Two loaves of bread may, in some sense, be twice as useful as one loaf; but it certainly makes no sense to draw a quantitative comparison between a loaf of bread and a screwdriver as use-values.

Value, on the other hand, is the common social substance—albeit an abstract 'insubstantial' substance—crystallized in all commodities as products of human labour. The outward phenomenal form in which *value* manifests itself is that of *exchange value*, the numerical ratio in which commodities of different types are exchanged. But the substance *value* itself is not a ratio. It can, however, be measured numerically: the *value* embodied in a given commodity is measured by the total quantity of (abstract) human labour socially necessary for its production. Thus *value* is a homogeneous social substance, measurable by a universal common yardstick applicable to all commodities.

To this duality of the commodity, a duality between use-value and *value*, there corresponds a duality in the character of labour, as *concrete* and *abstract* labour, respectively. In its concrete aspect, labour is a purposive human activity designed to produce some specific use-value. Different kinds of concrete labour cannot be compared numerically; baking and tool-making are qualitatively different, just as a loaf of bread and a screwdriver are qualitatively different and numerically incomparable as use-values. A commodity-producing economy presupposes a social division of labour, whereby each producer specializes in some particular species of concrete labour.

Abstract labour, on the other hand, is labour in its value-generating capacity. It is homogeneous, uniform and qualitatively undifferentiated. Viewed concretely, the baker's labour is different from that of the tool-maker; they do different kinds of work. But in the abstract sense they do the same thing: they perform socially useful work in producing part of the total social product. As such, their activities are interchangeable, just as their products are exchangeable.

The question now arises: in measuring the *value* of a commodity, ought the contributions of different types of labour to count on an equal basis, so that, for instance, a baker-hour should count as equal to a tool-maker-hour? Such an egalitarian solution is not only attractively simple, but seems most consonant with the very notion of abstract labour.

Marx, however, rejects this simple egalitarian solution. He does so, we believe, because he is aware that such a solution would be blatantly incompatible with the deterministic relation that he posits between *value* and price. Even if we discount the 'distorting effect' of the supposed tendency of the rate of profit to equalize,[2] it is not in general true that different commodities that require equal durations of labour-time, but labours of different types, are sold—or even tend to sell—at equal prices.

Differences in price between identical products, made in the same factory by the same workers, may be explained away in a deterministic theory as inessential fluctuations from some 'ideal' price. But such an explanation is of no avail here. Persistent disproportionalities between the price of commodities of different types and the total duration of labour-time required to produce them cannot be dismissed as mere 'fluctuations'. The product of an hour's work done by a computer designer will *normally* sell at a higher price than the product of an hour's work done by an ordinary mechanic.

Since Marx posits a deterministic connection between the *values* and prices (albeit ideal prices) of commodities, he is compelled to accept that equal amounts of labour of different types may generate different amounts of *value*. Hence the doctrine of 'skilled' versus 'simple' labour, which is briefly sketched in Section 2 of chapter 1 of *Capital*.

Simple labour is the expenditure of *simple* labour-power, 'which, on an average, exists in the organism of every ordinary individual' in the given society. Each type of *skilled* labour is to be considered as some numerical multiple (presumably depending on the particular type of skill) of simple labour. In other words, to each type of labour there corresponds some numerical coefficient, which we may call the *skill coefficient*; and the amount of *value* created by an input of, say, one worker-hour of labour of a given type is proportional to the skill coefficient belonging to this type of labour. We can always assume that the skill coefficient belonging to simple labour is 1. Then, if a given type of skilled labour has skill coefficient c, a worker-week of this type of labour is reducible—as far as *value*-creation is concerned—to c worker-weeks of simple labour.

At this point Marx comments that in reality 'this reduction is constantly being made. A commodity may be the product of the most skilled labour, but its value, by equating it to the product of simple unskilled labour, represents a definite quantity of the latter labour alone. The different proportions in which different sorts of labour are reduced to unskilled labour as their standard are established by a social process that goes on behind the backs of the producers and, consequently, appear to be fixed by custom.' The social process just referred to is clearly the process of commodity exchange, whereby the products of different types of labour are exchanged for each other. (In a footnote to the passage just quoted, Marx makes it clear that he is not referring to the wage-rates paid for different types of labour-power, but to the values of the *products* of different types of labour.)

Presumably, the implication of Marx's rather cryptic statement is that the skill coefficients can be worked out from the relative prices of commodities. If so, the prices that must be used for such a computation are not actual market prices (which are affected by all sorts of random factors) but ideal prices; and due allowance must be made for the 'distorting effect' of the supposed tendency of the rate of profit to equalize. In any case, Marx does not suggest in *Capital* any other method, independent of any prior knowledge of the prices of commodities, for determining the skill coefficients, nor do we know of any plausible method of this kind.

Some critics of Marx have claimed that if—as indeed seems to be the case—there is no independent way for determining the skill coefficients, and they can only be calculated as it were retrospectively, from the (ideal) prices of commodities, then this alone is sufficient to render Marx's theory of value circular: prices are supposed to be determined by *values*, but *values* are defined in terms of prices. And this circularity makes the theory devoid of any testable empirical content.[3]

This particular criticism of the Marxian theory seems to us to be unjustified. The proposition that the (ideal) prices of commodities are proportional to their respective *values* would be viciously circular only if the existence of skill coefficients making this proposition true were a mathematical tautology. If that were the case, then any conceivable set of prices could be made proportional to the respective *values*, simply by picking the appropriate skill coefficients. But in fact the existence of such skill coefficients is *not* a mathematical tautology; it is a non-vacuous consistency condition.[4]

We need not go any further into the discussion of the problem of skill coefficients within the framework of the orthodox Marxian theory. Instead, let us turn to the analogous problem in the context of our own probabilistic theory. Here the question is whether, in the definition (and empirical measurement) of the labour-content of a commodity, all types of labour should be counted on an equal basis, or the contribution of each type should be multiplied by a different skill coefficient; and if the latter, then how are these coefficients to be determined?

In the main text (chapters IV and V) we have tacitly assumed the 'egalitarian' answer to this question; all types of labour are to be counted as equal in their aspect as abstract labour. The labour-content of a commodity is measured by the total amount of labour —irrespective of type—required for its production according to the standard methods prevailing in the given society. This quantity is measured in worker-hours or worker-weeks, or by some unit of the same kind. A baker-hour, as abstract labour, counts as equal to a tool-maker-hour.[5] No skill coefficients are required (or, to be somewhat pedantic, all skill coefficients are put equal to 1).

Before proceeding to justify this approach, let us pause to consider how an opposite approach would affect the theoretical considerations of chapter V. Suppose that a system of skill coefficients could be determined by some theoretically plausible and empirically meaningful method. Suppose that the notion *labour-content* were re-defined, so that if a given type of labour has skill coefficient c, then one worker-hour of such labour would count as c worker-hours of 'simple' labour. What alterations should then be made in the theory of chapter V? The answer is: very few indeed.

The only significant qualitative change would be to make the distribution of the random variable W (wage) less skew. The skewness of the distribution suggested in chapter V results from the fact that a small, but by no means negligible, proportion of workers are relatively very highly paid. Now, if skill coefficients are introduced by some plausible method, then there should be a fairly high positive correlation (though by no means a deterministic connection) between the rates of pay for various types of labour-power and the corresponding skill coefficients. If a worker receives a wage of w units per hour for a type of labour whose skill coefficient is c, then this hour of labour now counts as c hours of 'simple' labour, and the wage counts as w/c per 'simple' hour. If w is relatively high, then c will tend to be high as well, so that w/c is considerably lower than w. Thus the introduction of skill coefficients should tend to diminish the effect of the existence of high rates of pay. For example, computed on an egalitarian basis, an air-pilot's salary is very high. But if skill coefficients are introduced, we may expect the skill coefficient of this type of labour to be quite high, so that an air-pilot-hour will count as many hours of 'simple' labour, and the pilot's salary per 'simple' hour will no longer be so high.

The introduction of a reasonable set of skill coefficients should thus be expected to make the distribution of W more like a normal distribution, with a smaller right-hand 'tail' and, incidentally, a smaller standard deviation than in the absence of skill coefficients. In fact, it can be argued that a necessary (but not sufficient) condition for a set of skill coefficients to be considered 'plausible' is that they should have the effect just described.

It can be shown also that a probable consequence of this alteration in the distribution of W is to make the standard deviation of the random variable Ψ (specific price) somewhat smaller. But the general form of the distribution of specific price would not be noticeably altered; it would still be approximately normal.

Of course, the introduction of skill coefficients would certainly change the basis on which labour-content is computed. As a result, the labour-content—and hence also the specific price—of *individual* commodities may be somewhat altered. But the general form of the *statistical* distribution of specific price would hardly be affected, because the arguments put forward in chapter V in favour of the normality of Ψ are just as valid in the presence of skill coefficients (so long as they are reasonable) as in their absence. The underlying reason for this is the highly socialized and integrated character of capitalist production, discussed in chapter V. Due to this, a randomly selected commodity will, with high probability, embody something approaching a random mix of contributions of different types of labour, with widely different skills. Hence the effect of skill coefficients will tend to 'come out in the (statistical) wash'.

We therefore conclude that our probabilistic theoretical framework is rather insensitive to the presence or absence of skill coefficients.

Nevertheless, a decision must be made, one way or another, if only in order to make the notion of labour-content well defined. We cannot avoid the question as to whether skill coefficients should be introduced, and if so, how they are to be determined.

Let us first address ourselves to the second part of this question. One thing is quite clear: we, unlike Marx, do not have the option of determining skill coefficients retrospectively, from the ideal prices of commodities—not because such a procedure would be circular, but because we do not admit the notion of ideal price in the first place. As we have already remarked, even for the classical Marxian theory it makes no sense to determine skill coefficients from the market prices of commodities, but only from ideal prices. By rejecting the notion of ideal price as theoretically erroneous and empirically suspect, we have blocked this way to defining skill coefficients. If skill coefficients are to be introduced into our theory, this must be done in some other way, independent of prior knowledge of prices. Does such a procedure exist? Perhaps; but we do not know one. We fail to see any method, theoretically convincing or even plausible and empirically meaningful, for determining skill coefficients. We must therefore do without them.

But do we really need them? Does our probabilistic theory require them in the first place? The answer is negative. Whatever some Marxist commentators may say, we believe that the main (if not the only) reason why Marx had to admit those elusive coefficients is because without them a deterministic relation between *value* and ideal price would be untenable—whereas Marx, like virtually all economic theorists to date, posited the existence of determinate ideal prices.

Within our probabilistic theory, on the contrary, there is no rigid relation between labour-content and price. The ratio between price and labour-content is a *random variable*, which can assume, for a given individual transaction, any positive numerical value whatsoever. From this point of view, the fact that equal individual quantities of labour-content may and do capture widely different

220

prices is not only perfectly acceptable but is in the very nature of things in a capitalist economy. Determinate 'ideal' prices of individual commodity-types do not exist. What the theory deals with is the *statistical distribution* of random variables such as specific price of a whole range of commodities.

The fact that equal quantities of labour-content capture different prices may or may not have something to do with the 'degree of skill' of the labour-power concerned. This comes about as follows.

Certain groups of workers find themselves in a relatively favourable bargaining position, whether by possessing rare skills,[6] or by forming a particularly strong union, or by virtue of a host of other circumstances, such as the prevalence of certain social customs and norms sedimented by past social realities. These groups are thus able to demand and receive relatively high rates of pay from their capitalist employers. For the latter, these higher rates of pay mean higher costs of production than would otherwise be the case. The capitalists are therefore impelled to demand higher prices—higher than would otherwise be the case—for commodities produced by such expensive labour-power. They do not always succeed in actually exacting these higher prices, but quite often they do. The route from higher rates of pay to higher prices is, of course, not a deterministic causal process but a probabilistic one.

The converse probabilistic causal process is at least equally real. Certain capitalist firms are able, for a variety of well-known reasons, which need not be mentioned here, to exact a relatively high price for the produce of their workers, and thus obtain a relatively high rate of profit. These workers—especially if they have rare skills, are well-organized or have some other relative advantage—find themselves in a relatively good bargaining position and are often able to extract wage concessions from their employers, because a firm whose profits are large can more easily be persuaded to incur a large total wage-bill.

These facts are well known to anyone familiar with the tug-and-pull of price bargaining on the commodity market and wage bargaining between workers and employers. What results is a certain *statistical* balance between wages, prices and profits.[7]

It is an obvious fact that the produce of certain groups of workers is sold for a relatively high price and that often—though by no means always—these workers are also relatively highly paid.

However, the proposition that such higher prices and wages are somehow necessarily connected with 'higher degrees of skill' (however this elusive concept may be defined) is neither obvious nor generally true, although it is ardently proclaimed (and probably even believed) *both* by the capitalists and by the workers concerned.

To sum up: skill coefficients are not required by our probabilistic theory, nor can we see any reasonable way of determining them. We therefore opt for the egalitarian solution of the problem.

For our probabilistic approach to prices, all we need is a consistent way of measuring the labour-content of commodities produced by a typical capitalist process of production. We claim that—no matter how odd it may seem at first sight—an egalitarian accounting, which treats the contributions of all types of labour on an equal basis, does yield such a measure which is both consistent and reasonable.[8]

Before we leave this subject, we wish to point out one consequence of our egalitarian solution, which is perhaps of some social and political interest.

According to traditional Marxist economic theory, it is highly unlikely (though perhaps not absolutely impossible) that the *value* of a worker's physical wage, consumed by the worker and his or her family—should exceed the *value* created by that worker's labour. Although in *Capital* Marx disclaims any necessary direct connection between the level of wages and the skill coefficient of a given type of labour,[9] it is nevertheless clear, as we have mentioned, that there must be a high positive correlation between the two. Therefore, generally speaking, a highly paid worker also creates more *value*. Thus the *value* consumed through the wage of even a very highly paid worker may not exceed the *value* created by him or her. In fact, throughout *Capital* Marx assumes the same rate of surplus value for all workers, which implies a uniform ratio between *value* created and consumed.

In our theory matters are different in this respect. Consider a worker whose weekly wage is w (measured in a.u.w.). For simplicity, let us ignore the distorting effect of direct taxation, and assume that the whole wage is used on consumption by the worker's family. The weekly consumption basket of a family can reasonably be taken as a fairly large and 'unbiased' sample of commodities, to which formula (10) of chapter V can be applied. Hence, if λ is the labour-content of this consumption basket (measured in worker-weeks) then the ratio w/λ is, with high probability, very near $\mathbf{E}\Psi$. Using formula (13) of chapter V, we therefore have, with high probability,

$$\lambda = \frac{w}{1 + e_M} \quad \text{approximately.}$$

On the other hand, the labour-content created by our worker in one week is just one worker-week. Hence, if w is considerably larger than $1 + e_M$, the labour-content consumed by this worker and his or her family will almost certainly exceed the value created, which equals 1.

Wages of this order of magnitude are by no means uncommon. As we know, a realistic estimate for e_0 is 1, and e_M is close to e_0 (we believe that in fact e_M is somewhat greater than e_0). Therefore, a worker whose wages are considerably higher than twice or two and a half times the average wage almost certainly consumes more labour-content than he or she creates.

This conclusion seems to add a new economic meaning to the term 'aristocracy of the working class', which Lenin and other Marxists have used in a mainly socio-political sense.

A second problem discussed in the Marxist literature regarding the Marxian notion of *value* is the following: are *values* of commodities determined solely in the sphere of production, or jointly in the spheres of production and exchange? [10]

To say that *value* is determined solely in the sphere of production does *not* mean—as some authors mistakenly believe—that it is a 'purely technical' concept. [11] What it does mean is that the *values* of commodities are determined by the methods of production dominant in the given economy, and that a commodity therefore has a definite *value* irrespective of the price at which this commodity is eventually sold, and indeed irrespective of whether it manages to get sold at all. (This does not make *value* a 'purely technical' concept, because the question as to how commodities are produced and which methods of production come to be dominant at a given place and time is itself not purely technical. In reality it is affected by a variety of economic and social factors.)

Marx's own views on this question are not always unambiguous, and may even be inconsistent. A plain reading of his definition of *value* in the beginning of the first volume of *Capital* seems to be that *values* are determined in the sphere of production alone. But in the third volume he seems to say (or at least can be interpreted as saying) that a commodity does not possess a definite *value* independent of whether it actually gets sold, or of the price for which it gets sold.

We do not wish to go into the controversy regarding the correct interpretation of Marx's statements on the subject.[12] We merely wish to point out that the proposition that *values* are determined jointly in the spheres of production and exchange (whether or not Marx actually harboured it) gains much of its attractiveness from the posited deterministic relation between *value* and ideal price.

Market prices—as the term itself correctly suggests—are determined in the sphere of exchange. A commodity that is still 'in the shop window' may have a price tag attached to it but its actual price becomes determinate only in the very act of exchange. What the price tag says is one thing, but the actual price paid (if any) is quite another. Of course, ideal price is not the same thing as market price. But if the former is to have any empirical meaning, it is as the time-average of the latter. (Marx explicitly claims that 'prices of production'—the ideal prices of his modified model—are 'the centre around which the daily market-prices revolve, and at which they are balanced out in definite periods.'[13]) In this sense, ideal prices are also determined, at least partly, in the sphere of exchange. But if *values* are rigidly (deterministically) connected to ideal prices, then one is at least tempted to conclude that *values* cannot be determined solely in the sphere of production.

In our own probabilistic theory, however, matters are rather different in this respect. For us, the disjuncture between labour-content and price is a positive virtue, reflecting the disjuncture between the two—interacting but distinct—spheres of production and exchange; the domain of discipline and determinism and the province of chaos and chance. Therefore we must state without any ambiguity: labour-content is determined solely in the sphere of production. This, of course, does not make it a 'purely technical' notion, any more than production itself is a 'purely technical' affair. What it does mean is, simply, that the labour-content of a commodity is determined solely by the socially prevalent conditions and methods of production, and does not depend on the price at which the commodity is sold, or indeed on whether it is sold at all.

Our answer to the first problem raised in this appendix—the problem of skill coefficients—clearly differs from Marx's: his notion of *value* requires such coefficients while our notion of labour-content does not. As for the second problem, Marx's own attitude is somewhat ambiguous; but if we accept the view of some interpreters, that *value* is determined jointly in the spheres of production and exchange, then our notion of labour-content differs also in this respect, because it is determined solely in the sphere of production.

We now come to the third and final problem, to which we shall give the same answer as Marx, although not quite for the same reason. The question, as posed by Marx, is whether the *value* of a commodity should be determined by the amount of labour *actually* spent on it, or by the amount of labour *socially necessary* to produce it. As is well known, Marx opts for the latter definition. In this context he explains that: 'The labour-time socially necessary is that required to produce an article under the normal conditions of production, and with the average degree of skill and intensity prevalent at the time.' Thus, strictly speaking, *value* is to be attributed to an individual commodity not by itself, but only as a generic representative of a commodity-type: 'Each individual commodity, in this connexion, is to be considered as an average sample of its class.' [14]
    Indeed, Marx had no other option. For, if *value* were to be determined by the *actual* amount of labour-time spent in producing the given individual commodity, then two identical commodities could have different *values*, simply because one of them was produced by particularly slow workers or by an antiquated technique. But if ideal price is determined by *value*, then identical commodities could have different ideal prices—which negates the very essence of ideal price. [15]
    We, on the other hand, are not bound by the same reasoning, because in our theory there is no such thing as ideal price, and the connection between real market-price and labour-content is merely probabilistic. So we could, if we wished, define the notion of labour-content in the actual-individual sense (the amount of labour *actually* spent on the *individual* commodity) rather than the potential-generic.

Moreover, the difference between the two possible definitions is not crucial as far as our main theoretical results are concerned. True, they would clearly yield different numerical values for the labour-content of individual commodities, but the general form of the distribution of Ψ (as well as other global results) would hardly be affected, because the individual differences would tend to 'come out in the (statistical) wash'.

Nevertheless, we prefer to opt for the potential-generic definition of labour-content.

The main reason for this is that—as we have stressed more than once—we conceptualize the capitalist system as a complex duality in which the chaos of the market interacts with the regimentation of production. Since we conceive of the sphere of production as the domain of determinism, and since labour-content arises in this sphere, we ought to make the definition of this concept independent of individual accidental circumstances.

It might be objected that this is an idealized view of production, because in reality not only exchange but also production is affected by many contingent, uncertain and accidental circumstances. This is indeed true, as far as it goes. But it is no reproach to a theory to say that it idealizes some aspects of reality; every theory has to do this. What must be avoided is not idealization as such, but idealization that does violence to the object of study by idealizing away its vital and distinctive attributes. In this respect the role of chance in the sphere of exchange is quite different from its role in production. In the former, it is an essential and irreducible feature of capitalism. But the logic of capitalist production, on the contrary, constantly drives towards the elimination of accidental chance factors.

The paradigm of capitalist production is assembly-line mass production, in which innumerably many identical products are churned out at a fixed 'scientifically' determined rate. In the case of mass production it is hardly meaningful to inquire how much labour is spent specifically on an *individual* product, because the product is not produced individually but as one of a large batch. In this connection it is indeed 'to be considered as an average sample of its class'.

True, not all production under capitalism is quite like this. But we believe that we do no violence to the logic of the system if we gear our theoretical notion of labour-content to this paradigm.

We therefore define the labour-content $\lambda(C)$ of a commodity C not as the amount of labour actually spent in producing C, but as the amount of labour that *would be* required to *reproduce* a commodity identical to C under existing standard conditions of production.

In what follows, we shall spell out some of the consequences of this definition.

First, it is clear that λ(C) is a function of time. But it depends on the time at which λ(C) is evaluated rather than on the time at which C itself, let alone any of its inputs, was actually produced. Thus, if after the production of C had been completed new methods of production became prevalent, the numerical value of λ(C) after this change might be different from what it was before.

Second, the notion of labour-content does not properly apply to artefacts that are essentially irreproducible, such as works of art and antiques. A masterpiece may be copied, but a copy, however good, is not equivalent to the original.

The failure of the notion of labour-content to apply to such artefacts is not really a drawback. It is true that under capitalism these things—and many others, such as honour, love and principles—are sold and bought as commodities, and may even have a 'market' of their own, but they are not produced by a typically capitalist method. Their role as commodities is merely formal, and they may properly be set aside in our economic analysis of capitalist production and exchange.

On the other hand, it is worth pointing out that the notion of labour-content does apply to an artefact produced by a typical capitalist method, but which, for purely contingent reasons, may be unique—such as a bridge, a dam or a ship built to a special design. It makes perfect sense to ask, for example, 'If this bridge were to be completely destroyed, how much labour would be required to construct one to exactly the same specifications?'

Finally, it should be noted that according to our definition the exact numerical value of λ(C) depends on the way in which the world of commodities is carved up into commodity-types, in which there is an inevitable element of arbitrariness. Since C possesses labour-content not, directly, as an individual commodity but as an average representative of a commodity-type, the way in which we conceptualize the type to which C is supposed to belong may well affect λ(C). For example, if C is a passenger motor-car, and we consider all passenger cars as one commodity-type, then λ(C) must be taken as the average amount of labour needed to produce a passenger car. But if we subdivide all cars into several types, say according to engine capacity, then λ(C) may come out somewhat different. The question is, how far do we go in such subdivision? Do we class two models of car as different types merely because they have different shapes of bonnet or grille? Do different brands of washing-powder constitute different commodity-types?

The answer to such a question is always partly—though by no means wholly—arbitrary. But in assuming, as we do, that every commodity has a definite labour-content, we are presupposing some particular aggregation of all commodities into types. In doing so, our theory imports a certain arbitrary element into the real world. This is comparable to what theoretical physics does when it imposes on the physical universe a more or less arbitrary coordinate system (frame of reference).

The presence of such an arbitrary element does not, in itself, invalidate a theory, provided the results of the theory remain essentially unchanged under different reasonable choices of the arbitrary element. Results that heavily depend on such choice are of no real significance, but a pure figment of the theory.

Therefore, just as physics rejects any final concept or physical law that depends essentially on the choice of a coordinate system, so economic theory should reject, as economically meaningless, any proposed 'law' that is sensitive to the way one chooses to aggregate commodities into types (provided that only reasonable alternative aggregations are considered).[16]

Incidentally, exactly the same caveat also applies to the subdivision of the economy into 'branches', 'sectors' and even 'firms', since all such aggregates are partly arbitrary.

Our theoretical results, being statistical in nature, are not sensitive in this sense. Although the labour-content of a particular commodity may be somewhat different under different aggregations of commodities into types, such differences tend to 'come out in the (statistical) wash', so that the global results are not significantly affected.

Appendix III
The Value Controversy

Steedman, Hodgson, Wright and Lippi

It would be an illuminating exercise to discuss in some detail the position of various authors on the foundations of political economy in the light of the present framework. A collection of some of these positions was issued by NLB under the title of *The Value Controversy* in 1981.[1] Lack of space prevents us from carrying out such a discussion here. We only wish to make a few preliminary remarks, which will concern a very short list of authors who have taken part in the so-called value controversy. This controversy concerns the relations between value magnitudes and ideal price magnitudes, and, more generally, the relevance, or the lack of it, of value magnitudes to political economy. The present remarks are restricted to modern writers because while the uniformity assumption is of considerable importance in classical political economy, Marxist or otherwise, it is not nearly as crucial for the development of those systems as in the case of the modern algebraic treatment of prices and profits, say, in the spirit of Sraffa. One cannot overemphasize the importance of this assumption and the central place it occupies in all mathematical treatments of prices and profits, especially in all arguments around the value debate. Not only is it used heavily in the equations, but mathematically and economically it can be shown that the whole development of Sraffian prices and profits will be shattered by the slightest weakening of this assumption: say, if we assume that the rates of profit deviate from uniformity by one per cent. This may be the chief reason why almost no discussion of any sort and no modern justification is given for this assumption: there is simply no room to manoeuvre with the assumption of strict uniformity. Most authors simply quote the classical texts as their only basis for the inclusion of this assumption; no serious attempt is ever made in the hundreds of articles and dozens of books in this vein to examine carefully the mathematical implications of dropping it, or even weakening it. Steedman[2] makes a very brief attempt, but withdraws quickly to the safe haven of uniformity: '...If profit rates, even though unequal, exhibit a stable structure in relative terms...then [the relevant equation] becomes formally equivalent to [that of]...uniform profit rates...'. Unfortunately, he never demonstrates the stability in a real sense, namely, the insensitivity of his model to small perturbations of the assumption of uniformity. That this assumption is extremely unstable was demonstrated by Farjoun.[3] The fatal weaknesses of this hypothesis are discussed elsewhere in the present work.

When considering the positions of adherents of the uniformity assumption one should be aware of its merits too. The chief merit, beyond the mathematical simplicity and elegance introduced by it, is the non-existence of any alternative deterministic framework. In one form or another the uniformity hypothesis seems to be the only conceivable way to capture the reality of competition in a deterministic framework that leads one to assign an ideal price to each and every commodity. The theoretical basis of this framework was formulated by Steedman with his habitual precision as follows: 'The prices considered throughout this work are always prices of production, for market prices are never considered. It should, perhaps, be remarked that, by definition, prices of production are the prices which would obtain in the (hypothetical) presence of a uniform rate of profit: the concepts of a uniform rate of profit and of prices of production are indissolubly related. It is for that reason and *not* because the determination of prices of production is a major theoretical concern in its own right, that prices of production will appear frequently in the sequel.'[4] This statement is the cornerstone of the Sraffian school: it stands and falls with it. As is evident from this passage Steedman feels quite uncomfortable with the empirical or theoretical meaning of prices of production. He realizes that their very meaning is called here into question. In a footnote he then raises the query: 'Who is interested in prices?' To which he answers, 'Anyone concerned to provide a serious theory of the rate of profit, in particular, and the laws of motion of capitalism in general.'[5]

But Steedman shies away from raising the really interesting questions: 'Why should anyone be interested in a hypothetical uniform rate of profit?' Further, 'Why does the assumption of uniform rate advance us one inch in the understanding of rate of profit as a real phenomenon, and can it serve as the *sole* basis for a serious theory of capitalism?'

We see that Steedman justifies his interest in prices of production by his interest in the level of the hypothetical uniform rate of profit. But he fails completely to give any justification to his interest in the latter. Can Steedman (or anyone else) show with his characteristic precision that a theory based on a patently false hypothesis such as uniform rate can tell us anything of interest about the true story of the 'laws of motion of capitalism'? Can they describe precisely what properties of the real rate of profit can be understood by assuming uniformity? Such questions are not treated even in a footnote.

Steedman is certainly right in saying that the assumption of a uniform rate of profit and the notion of production prices are indissolubly related. He gives a nice exposition of the Sraffa-von-Neumann theory based on these dual concepts. Steedman has done an important service in squeezing some of the most far-reaching conclusions out of this hypothesis. This is usually the best way to expose the internal difficulties of a theoretical model. It is true that the algebra of uniform rate is so powerful that, as Steedman and others claim, it makes redundant every concept other than ideal price and hypothetical uniform rate. But, as we saw, the algebra has its own weaknesses; and most importantly it rests on a wrong hypothesis and leads to wrong conclusions. For example, we have pointed out that in Sraffian theory it is certainly possible to imagine a capitalist economy developing technologically and improving wages and profits while the labour-content of most commodities goes up. Thus, confinement to a deterministic model leads to a dead end. This happened many times in other sciences—and it seems that the only way out is to abandon determinism.

If one is willing to consider non-deterministic prices and profit, then the road is open to many alternative hypotheses, which are far more realistic and reasonable than uniform rate, and which reflect competition even more faithfully.

Steedman concludes his book by stating very firmly that nothing can be gained by measuring commodities by their 'additive labour values'. (By *value* he means something very close to our notion of labour-content.) He claims, moreover, that this conclusion is a logical consequence of the assumptions he made in his book:[6]

'there are only three possible ways to respond [to my conclusions]:

'(a) to accept the proposition;

'(b) to reject *explicitly* one or more of the assumptions from which it is logically deduced;

'(c) to descend into obscurantism.'

We will not discuss here the validity of this stark statement—but we have responded to the underlying challenge by choosing option (b) —'reject explicitly one or more of the assumptions'. We have rejected in fact almost all of them—but the most important one is the assumption of uniform rate of profit. Since, as Steedman writes, prices of production are unthinkable without uniformity—it is only natural that in the present work concepts of prices of production, or any other notion of natural price, ideal price, equilibrium price and so on, are not used.

This allows us to make use of a reasonable notion of embodied labour time—not because of any dogmatic adherence to labour values—but because of the concrete and weighty reasons explained in chapter IV. We then show that some basic laws of capitalist development cannot even be conceived without some notion of labour-content, most notably the law of increasing productivity of labour (law of decreasing labour-content—see chapter VII).

An extensive discussion of Steedman's position is provided elsewhere.[7] There, the issues of joint production and the mathematical properties of price, profit and value are examined in some detail. Both Sraffa's and Steedman's treatment of these matters are shown to be mathematically incomplete and their internal difficulties are explained.

We have remarked above how very few authors attempt to demonstrate the relevance of the uniform rate hypothesis to real economic situations. One of the few exceptions to this unhappy rule is Geoff Hodgson.[8] Hodgson writes, 'It is not for the sake of convenience or uniformity that Sraffa like many other value theorists (including Marx) assumes an equalized rate of profit . . . [it is] because there are real forces in a capitalist economy that tend to bring the rates of profit in different industries into line . . . ' Then comes a long quotation from Karl Marx. Hodgson admits though that there is no reason to believe that actual uniformity is ever established. But he seems to think that a deviation from it is a deviation from 'general equilibrium' and he approvingly quotes Marx in calling such deviation 'incidental'. Now comes the typical leap: since there are pressures towards equalization, he argues, it is legitimate to assume that the rates have become equalized *in fact*. After considering several alternatives to the relevance of this assumption, with which he is clearly uncomfortable, he ends up with the following interpretation:

'Let us assume that in a certain capitalist economy, at a certain time, the forces of competition have succeeded in bringing about an equalization of the rate of profit . . . '. In *that* case, he concludes, one can catch that moment, apply Sraffa's algebraic equations, and get some interesting implications.

Hodgson is certainly right: *if* one can find an economy and a year in which the prices of all commodities at the beginning of that year are the same as those at the end, and profit rates are equal in all industries for that year, *then* one can apply uniform profit input-output algebra. But this 'if' is a very big one. We argue that this assumption is not only contrary to fact—there has never been such a year or a month or a week and there will never be one—but also contrary to the very *logic* of capitalism. This we have tried to explain in chapter I. In chapters I and II we argued that Hodgson's methodological jump is fatal. Even if it is assumed that forces of equalization are at work, this does not imply that it is realistic or even logically consistent to suppose that they will ever succeed in bringing about an equalization. To recall our analogy: in any gas there are powerful forces acting towards an equalization of the speeds of the molecules —but to assume that they will ever succeed in equalizing all the speeds contradicts a basic law of nature. From such an assumption one could draw conclusions that are contrary to our present scientific knowledge. For example, one could deduce the possibility of perpetual motion (of the second kind).

Our second objection is: Suppose that, by some miracle, in a given economy there is something like uniformity of rates once every fifty years. What does one do to examine the development of profits, price and labour productivity in between those miracle years? Does one develop a theory only for the exceptional twice-in-a-century years? If, as Hodgson argues, it is not for convenience that uniformity is assumed—then why has no one used the same algebra *without uniformity*—in order to deal with the ninety-eight years in which the said economy and the forces of competition have not 'succeeded in bringing about equalization'?

The sad mathematical fact is that it is precisely for the sake of mathematical simplicity and convenience that everyone assumes uniformity—that without this assumption Sraffa's equations will say nothing at all about prices and profits. There would be too many unknowns, too few equations. Sraffa himself warns his readers:
'It is perhaps as well to be reminded here that we are all the time concerned merely with implications of the assumption of a uniform price for all units of a commodity and a uniform rate of profit on all the means of production ...'.[9]
Nothing beyond the third page of Sraffa's book would have any meaning, nor could it be salvaged by wise algebra, without these assumptions. Likewise, Hodgson's whole argument against E.O. Wright's paper 'The value controversy and social research'[10] is based on his uncritical acceptance of the classical positions regarding uniformity, which is not at all central to Wright's position. If one is not willing to accept Sraffa's assumption quoted above, very little can be salvaged from the rest of Hodgson's position.

In fact, E.O. Wright's framework is vindicated to a large extent by the probabilistic approach. The concept of 'structural limitation' fits that model nicely. One needs to modify the former so as to recast it in probabilistic terms. Consider, for example, fig. 4 in his piece. If we take the same figure and consider his region of 'impossible profits' as a region of 'highly improbable profits', while dividing his region of the 'possible profits' into various sub-regions according to the probability of a given point occurring there, then his figure can be considered as depicting the probabilistic limitations on the profit of a firm given its surplus value. (Compare chapter VI.)
Of course, Wright only outlines a general logical approach to economic and social parameters. This approach can be realized in different ways. We claim that classical tools will not help much in making good sense of his approach—but probabilistic ones could do it very well. In the above example, given an amount of surplus

labour—there is no limit to the profit that it can realize (positive or negative!). The probabilities that this profit lies outside a given region are determined by the structure of the economy. Further, there is a wide region for which these probabilities are very small and can be ignored for most practical purposes. It is the random nature of the market and the multitude of competing influences that enforce these probabilistic limitations.

Unfortunately, Wright accepts the uniform rate hypothesis as one of the 'selecting factors' that operate within the said structural limitations. In actual fact hypothetical uniformity imposes no restriction whatsoever on the real profits of a given firm or branch—because uniformity exists only in the imagination of political economists, not in reality. The selection of real profits for each and every firm (or branch, or sector) out of all possible ones, is influenced by a huge number of factors. These factors 'select', in Wright's language, the precise profit of this or that firm. They include so many factors that some of them must be lumped together under the heading of 'chance', but others, such as the ingenuity of the managers, or the workers, the precise conditions of the 'work process' in that firm etc., must be considered carefully and weighed by economists and social scientists. What is certain, again, is that uniformity of rates and invariability of prices are not such factors. One can certainly look for the influence of the *forces* of equalization on rates of profits and prices, on the process of movement of capital from one branch to another, on the long term oscillations of the profit rates around a certain 'central band' of highly probable profits. All these are real phenomena. But these are all phenomena of non-uniformity (other branches have got more . . .) rather than uniformity.

To conclude, Wright's two models of determination involve two radically different sets of assumptions. His own 'structural limitations' require few unrestrictive and reasonable assumptions, while the model of 'selection' taken over from Sraffa depends on very restrictive and unrealistic assumptions of fixed sets of commodities, fixed prices and uniformity. It is always better to proceed as far as possible with the weakest axioms that entail an interesting conclusion.

Finally, let us turn briefly to another author, only because he uses the same analogy for economic parameters as we do, namely, that of many moving bodies bouncing against each other. Marco Lippi considers the relation between the total amount of surplus value and the total amount of profit, assuming that prices are so scaled as to be equal in their totality to the total amount of value. This question has been considered over and over again in the literature and we have explained our position on the matter in chapter VI. Lippi uses the analogy of moving bodies in order to clarify his position: 'Consider ... a system in which n spherical bodies move in a gravitational field inside an airless box.... Once the positions and velocities of the bodies at a particular time are known, the evolution of the system can be predicted ... '.[11]

If we take Lippi's n, the number of bodies, to be fairly large, then his system of many balls moving and bouncing in a box becomes exactly the usual system of monatomic gas where spherical bodies are realized by atoms: and his analogy is the same one used by Steindl and ourselves. But there is one crucial difference. He attempts to analyse the future behaviour of the system by *deterministic mechanics*: 'The evolution of the system can be predicted', by which he means, of course, that the exact position and velocity of each ball at any time in the future can be predicted. This is true: it is possible to calculate them at least in theory. Marco Lippi goes on to ask, in analogy to profit and surplus value, whether the ratio between total energy and kinetic energy is preserved through the evolution of this system of many bodies, which continue their frantic movement and collisions. He claims that: 'In general, this [preservation of ratio] does not hold for the system of spherical bodies ... [it] holds only under certain conditions, which implies a reduction in the "degree of freedom" of the system.' Lippi is right again, well almost. The equality of ratios does not always hold. But in some precise sense it *almost holds almost always*: it holds very nearly and with probability very close to one! And this near-equality-almost-always is sufficiently strong for a whole science to be built on it. It is a fact derived from probabilistic mechanics and not a deterministic one. It is an elementary truth of statistical mechanics that the proportions of the various forms of energy, under equilibrium, are virtually stable over time. Theoretically it is true that the ratios may differ by a considerable amount—but it is highly unlikely, and this unlikelihood will increase with the number of balls that are forced to dash around a box of a given size. Computer experiments made on this very problem indicate that, given the usual gas density, if there are more than fifty balls—the usual laws of thermodynamics will hold to a very high degree of accuracy.

In order to ask the really relevant question in Lippi's system—how *likely* is it for a large divergence of the ratio to develop and hold for a given period of time—one has to address the system in probabilistic terms. This is exactly the task of statistical mechanics. No physicist would be interested in the precise evolution of Lippi's system for, say, $n > 1,000$. It is uninteresting for most purposes and in fact impossible to do in practice.

This whole passage in Lippi's book is an example of how a deterministic frame of mind can lead one astray in a situation that naturally calls for the employment of statistical methods.

Also notice that Lippi's conclusion that the behaviour of the system can be completely predicted is true only under very stringent conditions—assuming we know everything there is to know about it, that it is completely deterministic and that the equations governing its motion are of a particularly simple type that can be solved accurately. On the other hand, as we pointed out in chapter II, the conclusion about the very stable nature of the ratio, does not depend on anything except the existence of a large number of balls, relative to the size of the box. Further, the laws that govern their motion can be either deterministic or probabilistic, and the shape of the balls can be arbitrary and so on.

As was explained in chapter II this analogy is used because it is clear that in real market situations there are no deterministic microeconomic laws that will allow us to make any deterministic predictions or calculations.

The questions brought out by Lippi about the stability of the ratios between the two forms of energy are exactly the relevant ones. But his answer is simply wrong: one can show that for most systems most of the time the ratio changes very little—this is a surprising but true consequence of the way in which nature operates. On such ideas the science of statistical thermodynamics rests. We think the time is ripe to use similar considerations in the foundation of political economy.

Notes

Foreword

1. E. Farjoun, 'The Production of Commodities by Means of What', in a forthcoming collection of articles on the labour theory of value, edited by Ernest Mandel.
2. I. Steedman, *Marx After Sraffa*, London 1977.
3. R.H. Langston, in Mandel (ed.).
4. J. Steindl, *Random Processes and the Growth of Firms, a Study of the Pareto Law*, London 1965.
5. E. Farjoun in Mandel (ed.).
6. The concluding sentence of Steedman is: 'It can hardly be overemphasized that the project of providing a materialist account of capitalist societies is dependent on Marx's value magnitude analysis only in the negative sense that continued adherence to the latter is a major fetter on the development of the former.'
7. The orthodox Marxists, who (rightly, in our view) find Steedman's conclusion repugnant, have yet been unable to meet his challenge convincingly by specifying explicitly which of his hypotheses should be discarded. This is hardly surprising, since they share these hypotheses.

Introduction

1. Karl Marx, *Capital*, Volume 3, Harmondsworth 1981, p. 252.
2. Ibid., p. 297. A couple of pages later, Marx points out that what he calls *price of production* '...is, as a matter of fact, the same thing which Adam Smith calls *natural price*, Ricardo *price of production* or *cost of production*, and the physiocrats *prix nécessaire*...'.
3. J.T. Schwartz, *Lectures on the Mathematical Method in Analytical Economics*, New York 1961, p. 9.
4. J.T. Schwartz, 'Mathematics as a Tool for Economic Understanding', in L.A. Steen (ed.), *Mathematics Today: Twelve Informal Essays*, New York 1978, p. 287.
5. Marx, ibid., p.280.

6. J. Robinson, *Further Contributions to Modern Economics*, Oxford 1981, p. 190. J. Robinson repeatedly points out that in reality rates of profit do not tend to uniformity. From this she does not conclude, however, that the assumption of uniformity at equilibrium is theoretically fallacious, but that equilibrium itself is rather unrealistic.

7. The free mobility of capital 'implies completely free trade within the society in question and the abolition of all monopolies *other than natural ones, i.e. those arising from the capitalist mode of production itself'*. Marx, ibid., p. 298, (our emphasis).

8. 'In theory, we assume that the laws of the capitalist mode of production develop in their pure form.' Marx, ibid., p. 275.

9. Thus, for example, if the rate of profit is 10% per annum, then $R = \frac{1}{10}$.

10. See text to notes 1 and 2.

11. The concept of *commodity-type* is defined in greater detail in chapter IV (see text to notes 2 and 3 in that chapter). For a further discussion see end of appendix II.

12. The difficulties of aggregation in such a context are well known and discussed at length in the literature. See, for example, Michio Morishima, *Marx's Economics*, Cambridge 1973. In Morishima's book, pp. 87 ff., there is an extensive discussion of the aggregation problem, which he formulates as follows: 'Under what conditions do the results obtained from a disaggregated value-determining system coincide with the corresponding results for the aggregated value-determining system?' He then formulates the analogous question for the price/profit equations. One of his conclusions with which we agree is that '[Labour] values are more solid and firmly founded aggregators than market wage and price—this is the most important analytical rationale for the labour theory of value.' (His notion of market price is not the same as ours, but his *value* is very similar to our notion of labour-content.) Morishima also notes (p. 53) that the necessary relations between surplus value and profit (which he attributes to Okishio) is convincing precisely because it can be established without using the uniformity assumption. The result is generalized by Morishima himself, again without invoking the uniformity assumption.

As far as we know, no one has found a method of aggregating the economy into a small number of branches or sectors, that allows a theoretical computation of the average rate of profit, and that is based *only* on the soft version of the uniformity assumption. There is good reason to believe that such a method cannot exist. For if it did, it would allow a theoretical computation of the average rate of profit by aggregating the whole economy into three, two or even one single sector. But in a one-sector economy all the known methods of input-output analysis collapse into empty tautologies.

13. For details concerning the full form of the price/profit equations see literature quoted in note 7 of chapter VI.

14. See text to notes 3 and 4 above.

15. In addition to these assumptions, which are common to him and the input-output theorists, Marx also postulates that the numerical magnitude

of the uniform rate of profit (his 'general' rate of profit) is equal to the ratio between the total annual *surplus value* and the labour-value of the total capital invested in the economy. The question as to whether this added postulate is consistent with the other assumptions lies at the bottom of the so-called transformation problem, discussed in chapter VI.

16. Marx does claim that the price of production of a given type of commodity is equal to the time-average of the actual market-prices at which commodities of that type are sold, taken over a period of time. (See text to note 5 above). However, this cannot be taken as a *definition* of the concept of price of production, but as a statement connecting this theoretical concept with observable phenomena. The definition is a theoretical one: the price of production of a commodity is the price that it would be sold at in a (hypothetical) state in which the sale of commodities of each and every type would yield the same 'general' rate of profit.

17. For a brief outline of this kind of application of probabilistic methods to economics, see Lawrence R. Klein, 'The Role of Mathematics in Economics', pp. 170-71. This article is included in *The Mathematical Sciences*, a collection of essays published for the US National Academy of Sciences and National Research Council, by MIT Press in 1969.

18. For a brief outline, see L.R. Klein, p. 172. It is not surprising that this approach has been favoured particularly by econometricians; concerned as they are with the measurement of real economic quantities, they often find the deterministic models of pure economic theory rather useless.

19. Josef Steindl, *Random Processes and the Growth of Firms*, London 1965.

20. Ibid., p. 5.

21. After completing the draft of our manuscript we came across a brief unpublished discussion paper by E.T. Jaynes, a noted researcher in statistical mechanics. (*How Should we use Entropy in Economics?*, October 1982.) This paper contains ideas (admittedly, 'half-baked' and 'in need of criticism') which, if they can be implemented, would considerably advance the programme undertaken in this book. Jaynes proposes a probabilistic treatment of economics, based on the concept of entropy. The paradigm for this is a well-known approach to statistical mechanics, which deduces the equilibrium states of a system from the *principle of maximum entropy*, and, more generally, characterizes the motion of a system when not at equilibrium as a *climb along the steepest entropy gradient* compatible with the constraints of the system. In this context, the notion of entropy itself is defined in a probabilistic manner. We ourselves have wondered about the feasibility of such an approach to economics, but the technical and conceptual difficulties of implementing it seem to us too great, for the time being. Rather than jump in at the deep end, we are content to start in a more cautious and piecemeal manner. But the possibility of an approach based on an 'entropy principle' should be kept in mind as a subject for further research.

While we are on the topic of entropy, let us mention the book by Nicholas Georgescu-Roegen, *The Entropy Law and the Economic Process*, Harvard University Press 1971. This is a wide-ranging philosophical discussion about

240

Life, the Universe and Everything, including economics. What it has to say about economics has (despite what the title might suggest) little to do with the programme of applying the probabilistic method to the foundations of economics. Indeed, given the author's hostility to statistical mechanics, he cannot be expected to welcome this programme. His project is to apply directly to economics the concept of entropy as defined not in statistical mechanics but in phenomenological thermodynamics (namely, entropy as a measure of the energy irretrievably dissipated in a given system). This is an intriguing idea, but we should not like to pass judgement on his success in implementing it.

Chapter One

1. Consider three variable quantities, X, Y and Z, connected by the mathematical relation $XY = Z$. (for example, suppose we have a collection of rectangles, with varying length X, width Y and area Z.) Suppose that each of the three variables has just two values, as follows:

	1st value	2nd value	average of 1st & 2nd values
X	10	2	$\frac{1}{2}(10 + 2) = 6$
Y	2	20	$\frac{1}{2}(2 + 20) = 11$
Z	20	40	$\frac{1}{2}(20 + 40) = 30$

We see that although for each of the two values of the three variables the relation $XY = Z$ holds (see first and second columns in the table), the same relation *fails* to hold for the average values: the average values of X, Y and Z are 6, 11 and 30, respectively, whereas 6 times 11 equals 66, not 30.

2. In the above discussion we have glossed over the ambiguity of the very notion of 'average'. In fact, there are many different kinds of average, and a proper mathematical framework is required in order to specify which kind of average is called for. Such a framework is presented in appendix I, in connection with the notion of random variable.

3. We have assumed this hypothesis for the sake of argument, but its empirical status is at best doubtful. For example, G. Deleplace ('Biens à double destination et polarisation des taux de profit', *Cahiers d'économie politique*, vol. 2, Amiens, 1975) presents ample statistical evidence that even when aggregating the French economy into 26 'natural' branches, the rates of profit are very diverse. They move slowly, over a period of ten years, between 5% and 26% per annum; and even the average rates over the whole period are almost as widely scattered, between 5% and 22%, among the different branches. A similar picture will emerge, no doubt, for any other modern capitalist economy, even over longer periods. In fact, Deleplace claims to discern real trends in the long-term average rate of profit away from equalization. See also the paper by O. Weinstein in the same volume.

4. See *Annual Survey of Manufacture* published by US Department of Commerce; or the corresponding statistics of other major capitalist countries. See also E.G. Wood (ed.), *British Industries—a Comparison of Performance*, London 1976. See also chapter VIII below.

5. A partial exception is the theoretical model introduced by Marx in the first volume of *Capital*. In this model, prices of all commodities (including labour-power) are proportional to their respective *values* (in Marx's sense of this term), and the ratio between annual profits and annual labour costs is indeed the same for all firms. (It equals what Marx calls the *rate of surplus value*.) However, in this model the rate of profit is *not* uniform, and—precisely because of this—Marx discards it in the third volume of *Capital* in favour of a modified model, in which the rate of profit is uniform, prices are no longer proportional to *values*, and the ratio of profits to labour-costs is no longer uniform. These matters are discussed in detail in chapter VI, in connection with the so-called transformation problem.

6. Which forces count as internal and which as external depends on the way the system is conceptualized. But the distinction is not arbitrary, inasmuch as one conceptualization is more appropriate than another. In any case, a given force cannot count simultaneously as both internal and external.

7. Here the pull of gravity is taken to be an internal force, so that the system in question is more accurately described as 'a pendulum-in-the-Earth's-field-of-gravity'.

8. Compare the following observation by Joan Robinson: 'The rate of profit is always ex post while the search for profit is ex ante. Price policy and investment plans are guided by the *rate of return* to be expected on a given outlay of finance. It is true that high current profits attract investment but then it is liable to overshoot so that continual fluctuation in profit rates ex post, rather than a gradual approach to a dead level, is the normal rule.' (Introduction to her *Further Contributions to Modern Economics*, Oxford 1980, p. xi; the same idea is repeated *passim* in that volume.) This extremely pertinent observation does not, however, go far enough; for it leaves unchallenged the uniformity assumption for an ideal state of equilibrium, around which the real economy supposedly fluctuates. After all, an oscillating pendulum also keeps 'overshooting' its equilibrium position.

9. Ibid., p. 130: 'In equilibrium, the terms rate of interest and rate of profit are interchangeable.'

Chapter Two

1. The discrepancy is particularly striking in Marx: he, more than anyone else, stresses the chaotic and uncoordinated nature of the capitalist mode of production, but his quantitative treatment is absolutely deterministic.

2. In reality, the molecules of any gas do have smaller constituent parts. By assuming away this internal structure, we are saying in effect that we are going to ignore the motion of the constituent parts of a molecule relative to each other, so that each molecule can be treated as a material point. This idealization nevertheless provides a very good approximation for the behaviour of some gases within certain limits.

3. This is, in fact, an additional assumption of this model. Later on we

shall have to deal with sample spaces for which this assumption is not made, so that different members of the sample space may have different 'weights'.

4. This assumption is tantamount to saying that the structure of the gas may be taken as approximately continuous rather than particulate. For certain *macroscopic* purposes this is indeed correct. Our assumption is therefore legitimate so long as we use it to derive certain macroscopic results, and refrain from using it at a microscopic level.

5. However, in view of note 4 it is clear that h must not be taken as too minute. If h is too small, of the same order as the distance between the particles, then the assumption that F_z is smooth and has a derivative f_z is illegitimate.

6. For the same reason as before, a and b must not be taken too near each other; the difference between them can be small, but not microscopic.

7. For a good approximation it is enough to take a period of time of moderate length by ordinary everyday standards, but long by microscopic standards, say a few seconds.

8. The whole subject of ergodic principles, their precise formulation and the justification for using them in statistical mechanics is an extremely complex and controversial one, both mathematically and methodologically. The intricate details need not concern us here, however. The interested reader is referred to A.I. Khinchin, *Mathematical Foundations of Statistical Mechanics*, New York 1949; and to R. Jancel, *Foundations of Classical and Quantum Statistical Mechanics*, Oxford 1969.

9. This principle has been modified by post-classical physics, but our model of an ideal gas is perfectly classical, and must therefore respect the classical laws. Mathematically, all the particles could be in one place if they were dimensionless points; but clearly no real gas can behave in this way.

10. Our present model of an ideal gas actually incorporates several such assumptions, for example concerning the nature of the particles.

11. In technical jargon, the equality asserts that E and g, regarded as operators on a random variable, *commute* with each other. This is the kind of assumption that a non-mathematician would tend to take for granted, but is in fact not generally correct. For example, if Z is the random variable whose c.d.f. is shown in fig. 1, then an easy calculation shows that $(EZ)^2 = (1.075)^2 = 1.156$; but $E(Z^2) = 1.723$.

12. The speed of a body is an ordinary numerical quantity. The velocity, on the other hand, is a *vector*. The speed of a travelling car is what is measured by the speedometer. The velocity of the car is a vector whose *length* is equal to the speed and whose *direction* is the one in which the car is moving at the given moment.

13. In fact, it is enough to assume that the three components of the velocity in every Cartesian coordinate system are statistically independent.

14. For details see W. Feller, *Introduction to Probability Theory and its Applications*, vol. 2, New York 1966, p. 77 ff. See also Khinchin and Jancel.

15. Cf. Khinchin p. 9.

Chapter Three

1. A.I. Khinchin, *Mathematical Foundations of Statistical Mechanics*, New York 1949, p. 9.

2. The experience of the USSR and countries with a similar economic system shows, however, that attempts to impose such a plan on a national scale by bureaucratic coercion (rather than having it adopted by consensus) are on the whole quite unsuccessful. The plan is simply not implemented in a sufficiently conscientious way by the reluctant population. The resulting behaviour of the economic system is partly planned and partly chaotic, but the chaos is quite different from the disorderliness of a capitalist market system.

3. The following quotations are from Rosa Luxemburg, 'What is Economics?', in *Rosa Luxemburg Speaks*, New York 1970, pp. 235-39.

4. One of the most important motives for the formation of such composite firms is precisely the wish to minimize the 'risk' or uncertainty in the extraction and realization of profits. By the laws of probability, the fluctuations over time of the aggregate rate of profit of several operational units taken together tend to be smaller than the fluctuations for each unit separately. (This is a particular case of the so-called *Law of Large Numbers*.)

5. Here h must be so small, that the variation of $K(i)$ and $R(i)$ during the period from t to $t + h$ can be neglected at a first approximation.

6. In the *long* term, say over several years or decades, the graph may be seen to oscillate slowly around some definite equilibrium position, or shift slowly in one direction. If the latter is the case, it indicates that as the economy evolves, its state of equilibrium also shifts. This is analogous to the behaviour of a gas whose chemical composition (unlike the simple model of the previous chapter) undergoes a gradual change.

7. It is by no means uncommon for holding companies and other conglomerates to 'cook' the accounts of one of their firms, by claiming, for example, unrealistically high costs or amortization so as to show a 'loss' that can be set off against profits made elsewhere, for the purpose of tax avoidance.

8. Note that our assumption that R is positive is very much weaker than the assumption made by those who take the rate of profit to be uniform. They assume not only that R is positive but that it takes *the same* positive value everywhere.

9. For the definition of the gamma family of distributions and its properties, see appendix I.

10. See note 21 to Introduction.

11. However, Marx is not quite consistent in his use of this term. Occasionally he uses it as if it referred to the ratio between invested capital and the *number* of workers (rather than the value of their total annual wage). These two ratios, far from being equal, are not even proportional, because the average wage per worker cannot be taken as equal for all firms.

12. For data on the British and American economies, see sources cited in note 4 of chapter I. For illustration of the narrow distribution of X, and a discussion of some apparent exceptions, see chapter VIII.

244

13. The tendency of X to have a narrow distribution can be made somewhat less puzzling as follows. Let us define a random variable L, such that for each i the value $L(i)$ is equal to the number of workers employed by the i-th firm at time t, and let the random variable M be defined by the equality

$$M = \frac{ZK}{L}.$$

Then it is easy to see that $M(i)$ is the average wage-rate in the i-th firm (that is, the wage that the i-th firm pays per worker per unit of time). Since X is, by definition, equal to R/Z, it follows that

$$X = \frac{R(K/L)}{M}.$$

The narrow distribution of X therefore means that, other things being equal, firms with high rates of profit tend to pay better wages; and also, other things again being equal, firms with high K/L (amount of capital per worker) tend to pay better wages. These phenomena are familiar and clearly observable in the real world. (At the limit, if M were directly proportional to both R and K/L, then X would be degenerate.) An interesting question, which we shall not discuss here, is the nature of the *causal* interconnection between high values of R and K/L on the one hand, and high values of M on the other.

14. Some data illustrating the remarkable behaviour of e_0 will be presented in chapter VIII.

15. See Joan Robinson, *An Essay on Marxian Economics*, 2nd edn, London 1966, p. 80. Also Marie-Thérèse Boyer, 'Salaire réel, part relative des salaires et pauperisation', *Cahiers d'économie politique*, vol. 2, Amiens 1975.

16. From a theoretical point of view, it would be highly desirable to deduce our hypothesis concerning the distributions of R and Z from some more elementary or more fundamental assumptions. The kind of thing we have in mind is the following. If one assumes that X is independent of Y and, moreover, that R is independent of Z, then it follows from Lukacs's Theorem (see appendix I) that R and Z must indeed have gamma distributions with the same second parameter β. Unfortunately, this particular deduction is inapplicable: although the mutual independence of X and Y is very plausible both theoretically and empirically, the other pair of variables, R and Z, are certainly not independent. In fact, as we have seen, there is ample empirical evidence for a strong positive correlation between R and Z. But it is quite possible that a valid deduction, using a broadly similar method, may be found.

In this connection it is worth pointing out that the strong dependence between R and Z, which is highly corroborated by empirical evidence, is completely unaccounted for by traditional economic theories, which assume that R is degenerate or tends to degeneracy and which have nothing to say about the distribution of Z. In particular, in traditional Marxian theory, the whole so-called transformation problem arises from the supposition that the rate of profit of a firm cannot have anything to do with its organic composition. By the very same logic, R and Z ought to be independent.

Chapter Four

1. For the definition of a *degenerate* random variable, see appendix I.

2. This distinction, though logically necessary, is rarely made by the conventional theories, which use the term 'commodity' in both senses. Indeed, from their point of view the distinction is not crucial, because they assume that different commodities belonging to the same type must have the same unit price. But for us the distinction is vital, because we refer unit price to a particular commodity, and commodities of the same type may have different unit prices.

3. The concept of commodity-type is indeed an abstract one—and, as we shall argue in appendix II, the demarcation between different types is to some extent arbitrary. This, however, does not mean that the concept is unreal. It attains its full reality in the era of mass production, when many, if not most, products 'naturally' belong to a large species of similar products. But even in classical times there were a few real commodity-types, notably corn, olive oil and wine.

4. Similar considerations apply to the random variable R of chapter III. This variable is unaffected by the choice of money unit (because $R(i)$ is the *ratio* of two sums of money: the profit of the i-th firm per unit of time and the capital of that firm) but it *is* affected by the choice of time unit. If we were to measure time in months instead of years, we would get a new variable R' such that $R' = R/12$. The same applies to the variables Z and Y of chapter III. The variable $X = R/Z$, however, is purely numerical ('dimensionless') and does not depend on the choice of money units or time units.

5. We do not wish to claim that the use of some common unit of measure for all commodities is the *only* possible way to tackle the problem, but merely that it proves to be interesting, fruitful and economically significant.

An alternative approach that is mathematically reasonable is to measure money in the same units, say £s, for all transactions, but to measure each commodity in such physical units that the *average* unit price for each commodity-type (taken separately) is £1. Thus, if on a given day the *average* price at which petrol was sold was £0.40 per litre, we measure petrol *on that particular day* in units of two and a half litres, making the average price £1 per unit. Treating each commodity-type in a similar way, we can then define a sample space of *all* transactions (occurring on the given day) in which commodities were sold-and-bought, irrespective of which type they belong to. A unit-price random variable can be defined over this space just as we did for a single commodity-type (sugar). A serious defect of this variable is that its distribution reflects only the variation of unit price of commodities *within*

246

each type, but obliterates the variation in unit price *between different* types. For example, suppose that on a given day the c.d.f. of this random variable is *F*. Suppose that on the following day exactly the same transactions take place as on the first day, except that in the case of one commodity-type, say petrol, the quantity sold in each transaction is half that of the corresponding transaction on the previous day, but for the same total price. (For example, if in some transaction on the first day two litres of petrol were sold for £0.83, then in the corresponding transaction on the second day one litre was sold for the same price, £0.83, and similarly for each transaction involving petrol.) Then it is not difficult to see that on the second day the random variable in question has the *same* c.d.f. as on the first day, namely *F*, although in fact the prices per litre in all sales of petrol have actually doubled, whereas other commodities have not changed their prices. Despite the anomaly we have just pointed out, this random variable is of some interest; but we shall not study it here.

Yet another approach would be to forgo any attempt at aggregation of different commodity-types into one totality, and to consider each type separately, with its own separate unit-price random variable. This approach too involves certain grave difficulties, quite apart from the fact that it does not allow us to make any statement about the aggregate variation and movement of prices. For one thing, it depends in a very crucial way on the often quite arbitrary demarcation of one commodity-type from another. (Do different brands of washing powder constitute different types?) A second difficulty arises from the fact that commodity-types themselves (and not just prices) constantly change: new types keep appearing on the market and old ones disappear. Very few types retain their identities for long (what car produced today can be classed as belonging to the same type as a car produced twenty years ago?). Thus, at each moment of time we would have not merely different distributions but a completely different set of sample spaces. Yet another difficulty is due to the existence of important commodities that are not mass produced and belong to very small types; in some cases a single commodity by itself constitutes a whole type. (How many oil super-tankers belong to the same type, and how many similar super-tankers are sold in the same country on a given day?) But the applicability of probabilistic methods to such small collections—separately to each collection—is rather dubious.

6. While we reject the fallacious treatment of 'equilibrium' prices and 'the' rate of profit in input-output theory, we have no fundamental objection to its conceptualization of production, at least as a first approximation.

7. See also a critical discussion of the model in Jacob T. Schwartz, *Lectures on the Mathematical Method in Analytical Economics*, New York 1961, pp. 11-14. The existence of a 'standard real-wage basket' is particularly questionable, and we shall not assume it in our price theory developed in the next chapter.

8. For a critique of this assumption in connection with more general models, in view of the difficulties that seem to be presented by joint production of several types of commodity by the same process of production

or by several alternative processes, see I. Steedman, *Marx after Sraffa*, London 1977. See also, however, the reply to this critique: E. Farjoun, in Mandel (ed.).

9. We do not wish to suggest that the various spheres of an economy are autonomous. In particular, it is clear that the conditions of production cannot be viewed simply as arising out of some autonomous technological development. They are certainly affected by various factors, including market conditions. However, conditions of production are virtually unaffected by the volatile 'microscopic' and short-term events in the sphere of circulation and exchange. The market affects the evolution of input-output coefficients predominantly through its macroscopic global behaviour and long-term trends.

10. This, by the way, may offer us an insight into the difference between a capitalist economy and a Soviet-type economy. In the latter, the role of the market is much more restricted; the chaos of the market has been eliminated to a great extent and replaced by a plan that is ostensibly deterministic. However, due to the alienation of the function of planning from the immediate producers, and their consequent sullen resistance to its dictates, *the process of production itself becomes a locus of chaos*. Indeed, in those economies the relation between inputs and predicted outputs becomes chronically chancy, and at any rate much less certain than under capitalism. Thus chaos has not been totally eliminated but rather displaced to another sphere, and in being so displaced its character has also been transformed. (See also note 2 to chapter III.)

11. However, in the case of joint production it has been shown by Farjoun (in the essay cited in note 8) that under reasonable assumptions (which do not refer to labour) concerning the input-output matrix, labour has a distinct mathematical advantage as a measure of commodities. In the most general case of joint production, no universal input or factor of production other than labour or labour-power yields a positive measure. What distinguishes labour-power in this respect is that it is the only factor of production which cannot reasonably be regarded as produced jointly with other products in the same process.

12. In an economy that is capable of producing surplus, the labour-content of one unit of the commodity-type *labour* must be less than one unit, as we have shown above in connection with the example of petrol. Marx pointed out that this apparent paradox had misled Adam Smith and Ricardo, who occasionally confused a given amount of labour-commodity with its labour content, thus obscuring the origin of surplus. Partly, perhaps even mainly, in order to prevent this confusion, Marx introduced a terminological distinction between labour-as-a-commodity, sold and bought on the labour market, and labour as a universal input, absorbed into other commodities in the process of their production. He referred to the former as *labour-power* and to the latter as (*abstract*)*labour*. We shall adhere to this helpful distinction. The above-mentioned 'paradox' is now re-formulated, less confusingly, by the statement that the labour-content of one unit of *labour-power* is less than one unit.

13. We shall dwell on this matter in some detail in chapter VI, as part of our critical discussion of the so-called transformation problem.

14. Steedman and others also claim that labour-content is an incoherent concept, because allegedly it cannot be defined consistently for an economy in which joint production occurs. This claim, which smacks of 'sour grapes', is in fact erroneous. (For Steedman's claim and its refutation see the works cited in note 8.)

15. In the following quotation from Ibn Khaldun, the terms 'profit' and 'capital' must not, of course, be taken in their modern sense but as denoting newly created wealth and accumulated wealth, respectively:

'[Man] obtains [some profit] through no efforts of his own, as, for instance, through rain that makes the fields thrive, and similar things. However, these things are only contributory. His own efforts must be combined with them, as will be mentioned. . . . Everything comes from God. But human labour is necessary for every profit and capital accumulation. When [the source of profit] is work as such, as, for instance, [the exercise of] a craft, this is obvious. When the source of gain is animals, plants, or minerals, human labour is still necessary, as one can see. Without it, no gain will be obtained, and there will be no useful [result]. . . . [T]he capital a person earns and acquires, if resulting from a craft, is the value realized from his labour. . . . If the profit results from something other than a craft, the value of the resulting profit and acquired [capital] must include the value of the labour by which it was obtained. Without labour, it would not have been acquired. . . . It has thus become clear that gains and profits, in their entirety or for the most part, are values realized from human labour.' (Ibn Khaldun, *The Muqaddimah*, Franz Rosenthal trans., 2nd edn, London 1967, vol. 2, pp. 311-14.)

16. In the Soviet Union and other countries with a similar system, wage labour exists in outward form, but there is no free contractual relation between worker and employer (= the state). The former is legally coerced into the transaction (refusing to 'sell' one's labour power is a criminal offence) and the latter is constitutionally committed to making it. This compulsory purchase is not a true commodity exchange, and labour-power in such a system is not a true commodity.

17. In seventeenth-century England, wage labour was still generally regarded as a relation of personal servitude and the labourer was considered a dependent person, and hence unfree. This comes out clearly from the famous debates held by the revolutionary Parliamentary army in Putney in October 1647. The main question discussed there was that of the franchise. The Levellers' rhetoric seemed to suggest that they were in favour of manhood suffrage, but as a matter of fact they demanded that the vote be given only to 'freeborn Englishmen', which explicitly excluded paupers and wage labourers. These two groups, along with women and children, were considered to be economically dependent and hence personally unfree and unable to exercise a free vote. The most radical faction, the Diggers or 'True Levellers', who did demand manhood suffrage, agreed that wage labourers were unfree; they therefore demanded the abolition of wage labour. The idea that

a wage labourer can be a free person with equal political rights had not yet come into existence. (See Christopher Hill, *The Century of Revolution, 1603-1714*, Cardinal edn, London 1974, pp. 119-120.)

18. By the way, this simple observation seems to provide a solution to a conundrum that has puzzled many critical students of Marxian economics. Marx states that the normal level of wages is determined as the minimum necessary to maintain workers and their families, and thus to regenerate labour-power. However, he makes it quite clear that by the 'minimum' he does not mean some absolute biological minimum, but a standard of living determined by historical and social conditions, a standard of living that is *socially* regarded as minimally acceptable. However, it seems that the only reasonable way to determine this socially acceptable minimal standard is to equate it to that which can be procured with the prevalent level of wages. But this is a circular argument, and Marx's statement about wages appears to reduce itself to an irrefutable, and hence vacuous, tautology. In other words, it appears as though any wage level whatsoever, if prevalent in a given economy, would satisfy Marx's statement automatically, by definition; and a statement that does not exclude any conceivable scenario is vacuous. But as a matter of fact Marx's statement can be interpreted in a perfectly reasonable and non-tautologous way: both the prevalent level of wages and the minimally acceptable standard of living are simultaneously socially determined, and under capitalism they are determined subject to the constraint that the former should not exceed the latter. For, if too many workers were to receive wages in excess of what is required to secure a socially acceptable standard of living, and were able to save enough to become capitalists, the system would soon break down.

19. Adam Smith uses a similar argument to suggest that the ratio between the price of a given commodity and the [average] hourly wage in the same economy ('the quantity of labour which [the given commodity] can purchase') provides a yardstick for comparing the prices of commodities in different economies: 'Equal quantities of labour, at all times and places, may be said to be of equal value to the labourer. In his ordinary state of health, strength, and spirits; in the ordinary degree of his skill and dexterity, he must always lay down the same portion of his ease, his liberty, and his happiness. The price which he pays must always be the same, whatever may be the quantity of goods which he receives in return for it. Of these, indeed, it may sometimes purchase a greater and sometimes a smaller quantity; but it is their value which varies, not that of the labour which purchases them. . . . Labour alone, therefore, never varying in its own value, is alone the ultimate and real standard by which the value of all commodities can at all times and places be estimated and compared. It is their real price; money is their nominal price only. . . . Labour, therefore, it appears evidently, is the only universal, as well as the only accurate measure of value, or the only standard by which we can compare the values of different commodities at all times, and at all places.' (*The Wealth of Nations*, Harmondsworth 1974, pp. 136-40.) The snag with this measure, however, is that it ignores differences in the *relative* level of wages between different economies. If in one economy the

price of commodity A equals ten times the average hourly wage and in another economy the price of commodity B equals five times the average hourly wage, it does not necessarily follow that A is 'really' twice as expensive as B; it may be that the relative level of wages (compared, say, to the income of self-employed people and non-workers) is much lower in the first economy than in the second. So the comparison which Adam Smith suggests is not always meaningful. But the very argument which he puts forward does tend to show that *labour-content* is a reasonable measure of the social human cost of a commodity, a measure which provides a meaningful comparison of commodities in different economies. Indeed, although from the context of the passage just quoted it is clear that Adam Smith wants to argue that commodities should be compared in terms of the ratio between their prices and the average wage, the passage itself reads as though he proposes labour-content as a measure of the human cost of commodities.

20. This is the case generally, but not always. For example, when a number of commodities are sold together, as a package, it is often not obvious what price was paid for each item.

21. We do not wish to suggest that there is an absolute distinction between empirical and theoretical concepts. Only an extremely naive empiricist will claim that there is such a thing as a 'pure' empirical observation, unladen with any theory whatsoever. Rather, the distinction is relative: some things can be observed more directly than others, and some observations are more heavily laden with theory than others.

22. In the case of relativistic mechanics, this applies to the so-called rest-mass of the body.

23. It may be objected that today molecular biologists identify genotype with a given collection of DNA molecules, which is concrete. But this identification itself is a highly theoretical statement that is meaningful only in the context of a very elaborate theory. Besides, to claim that a DNA molecule is 'directly observable' is to stretch the meaning of this term beyond reasonable limits.

Chapter Five

1. The importance of the concept of specific price for a theory connecting prices with Marxian values was emphasized by R.H. Langston.
2. See Adam Smith, *The Wealth of Nations*, bk 1, ch. V.
3. A transaction may involve a commodity of one type, or an assortment of several items, each belonging to a different type. In the latter case—that of a package deal—the price of each item is in general not well-defined, because the buyer and seller agree only on the price of the whole package.
4. For a discussion of the so-called normal distribution see appendix I.
5. '*Separation* appears as the normal relation in this [capitalist] society. Where therefore it does not apply, it is presumed and, as has just been shown, so far correctly; for ... in this society *unity* appears as accidental, *separation* as normal; and consequently separation is maintained as the

relation even when one person unites the separate functions.' Karl Marx, *Theories of Surplus Value*, pt I, Moscow 1963, p. 409.

6. In what follows, we shall point out the junctures in the argument where each of these assumptions is used. It should be noted, however, that occasionally we use an assumption not because it is absolutely vital, but because it simplifies the discussion. Thus, we believe that most of our conclusions—in particular the one concerning the near-normality of the distribution of specific price—do not depend on the full force of our simplifying assumptions.

7. Theoretically, the right-hand side of (2) is an infinite series; but in practice the iterative procedure described in the text need only be pushed back a moderate number of stages, until the residual non-labour cost becomes negligibly small. In other words, very remote indirect inputs of C may be neglected, because their collective contribution to the series in (2) is negligible. For this reason we may assume in practice that the various indirect inputs whose contributions occur in (2) were all produced not long before the period T in which C itself is sold. If the economy is at or near dynamic equilibrium, we may assume that technological and economic conditions have not changed greatly in the meantime. Note however that even if we neglect very remote indirect inputs, the number of value-added terms in (2) is still quite large—hundreds if not thousands. This is because in reality the production of most commodities under modern conditions uses up very many, often hundreds, of different kinds of direct input. Thus even three or four iterations of the procedure will yield many hundreds of value-added terms.

8. This rather subtle point concerning the definition of the concept *labour-content* is discussed in appendix II.

9. See note 7 above.

10. Note that formula (9) refers to net prices, without indirect tax. In the presence of a flat-rate VAT, the right-hand side of (9) must be multiplied by the factor $(1 + t)$, where t is the rate of tax.

11. Formula (11) uses (9), and therefore depends on the assumption that there is no indirect tax, as well as on our other simplifying assumptions. On the other hand, (10) *does not* depend on these assumptions.

12. In deducing the equality or near-equality between e_0 and e_M, we have ignored direct and indirect taxation as well as the social wage. If we do take these factors into account, then the result must be modified as follows. First, indirect taxation by itself does not affect (13) but pushes $\mathbf{E}\Psi$ higher than $1 + e_0$ (see note 9 above). Hence the effect of indirect taxation is to make e_M greater than e_0. On the other hand, the relation between $\mathbf{E}\Psi$ and e_M (but not e_0) is affected by direct taxation and the social wage. In the presence of these, the total gross money wage N is no longer equal to $\pi(\mathbf{V})$. Direct taxes on wages push e_M upwards and the social wage has the opposite effect. According to the official ideology of the 'welfare state', the joint effect of taxation and the social wage is to make e_M smaller than e_0 because real income is supposedly re-distributed in favour of workers. But this is mere ideology. For one thing, the progressiveness of direct taxation is largely

illusory, because capitalists are structurally far better placed to avoid or evade taxation than workers. Also, while official ideology assures us that taxes are largely spent on social consumption that is of great benefit to workers and boosts their real income, the truth is very different. In fact only a relatively small part of tax revenue is spent on genuine social consumption such as public health; in most countries a far larger part is spent on the political overheads of class society—the elaborate and costly apparatus of repression, destruction and extermination. The rest is spent on ambiguous activities; for example, publicly financed education is partly social consumption and partly a vehicle for inculcating skills useful to capital and attitudes favourable to the existing order. All in all, it seems that in reality e_M must be somewhat greater than e_0.

Chapter Six

1. The controversy began in fact even before the publication of the third volume of *Capital* (1894). Engels, who edited and published the second and third volumes after Marx's death, posed the problem squarely in his preface to the *second* volume (1885), and promised that it would be resolved in the third. Engels's challenge was taken up almost immediately by the economist Lexis in his 1885 critique of the second volume, and subsequently by others. So by 1894 the controversy had been going on for eight or nine years, and Engels devotes to it a major part of his preface to the third volume. Throughout this chapter we use the term 'transformation problem' in the sense in which this term is normally understood by the participants in the controversy, and which goes back to Engels's formulation in his preface to the second volume: 'show in which way an equal average rate of profit can and must come about, not only without a violation of the law of value, but by means of it.' It is in this sense that we dismiss the 'problem' as a pseudo-problem. However, the term 'transformation problem' can be reinterpreted in a broader sense, namely, as the problem of elucidating the systematic connections between *value* (or labour-content) categories on the one hand, and price categories on the other. If taken in this broader sense, the problem is, in our view, not only real but very important. Indeed, much of what we do in the present work is directed precisely at this problem.

2. Methodological determinism used to rule *all* science (with the obvious exceptions of the theory of gambling and demography, in which probability and statistics, respectively, had originated) until the middle of the nineteenth century, when it was breached first in meteorology, then in genetics (Mendel) and in Darwin's theory of evolution (where the variability of heritable characteristics is an essential postulate) and, most comprehensively, in statistical mechanics, whose advent, incidentally, roughly coincided with the publication of *Capital* Volume I. Rejection of methodological determinism does not necessarily imply a rejection of ontological determinism.

3. Only in a deterministic theory is the deviation of real prices from some ideal mean regarded as 'noise', which can be ignored at a first approximation;

and ideal prices are assumed to have an existence of their own, and to be logically connected with other economic parameters. For us, deviation from the average is not 'noise'; nor do we regard the average itself as existing on its own, apart from the whole distribution. What can be related to the economic system as a whole is not the average—at least not directly—but the entire distribution.

4. While our own theory of prices does not require the notion of the labour-content of a unit of labour-power, Marx's theory certainly does.

5. Marx's own explanations concerning these modifications (in Part II of the third volume of *Capital*) are not formulated in a mathematically precise way, and are therefore in need of interpretation. The explanation given by us is what we consider to be a fair and reasonable rendering, in our own words, of what Marx had in mind.

6. Note that the new ideal prices, the so-called prices of production, are determined by labour-values, albeit indirectly. For prices of production are determined by the general rate of profit, which in turn is determined by labour-values through formula (3).

7. For modern treatments, see J.T. Schwartz, *Lectures on the Mathematical Method in Analytical Economics*, New York 1961; P. Sraffa, *Production of Commodities by Means of Commodities*, Cambridge 1960; M. Morishima, *Marx's Economics*, London 1973.

8. See Sraffa; also J. Robinson and A. Bhaduri, 'Accumulation and Exploitation: an Analysis in the Tradition of Marx, Sraffa and Kalecki', *Cambridge Journal of Economics*, vol. 4, no. 2, June 1980.

9. Here is a sketch of how this comes about. For each $i \neq 0$, one gets an equation for the unit price of C_i: this price is equal to the total price of the inputs used up per unit of output (given by the coefficients a_j^i), plus r times the price of the invested capital employed during one week per unit of output (given by the coefficients f_j^i). The unit wage is equal to the total price of the unit wage basket, given by the coefficients a_j^0, and this equation can be used to eliminate the unit wage from the system of equations. (In the alternative treatment mentioned in the text, where the unit wage is assumed to stand in a given proportion to the unit price of some other commodity-type, the unit wage can likewise be eliminated from the system of equations.) One ends up with a system of m equations involving the m unit prices of non-labour commodity-types and the rate of profit r. This system is linear in the (unknown) unit prices, with coefficients involving r. In order for this system to have a solution in the unit prices, a certain determinant involving r must be 0. This yields a polynomial equation of degree m in the unknown r. This equation can have up to m roots, but at most one of them is positive and allows a positive solution for the unit prices.

10. K. Marx, *Capital*, vol. 3, Ch. IX.

11. For a recent spate of the controversy, see I. Steedman and P. Sweezy, *et al.*, *The Value Controversy*, London 1981. Cf. also older contributions cited in that volume.

12. As for labour-power, our own results cannot be directly compared with the implications of Marx's first model, because our specific price

excludes labour-power. As we have pointed out, Marx's theory on wages presents a special difficulty, since it involves the problematic notion of the labour-content of a unit of labour-power.

13. For example, as mentioned in appendix I, the distribution of R for British private manufacturing industry in 1979 was approximately $\Phi(4, 20)$, so that the standard deviation of R was about half of the mean. On the other hand, in chapter V we argued that the standard deviation of Ψ is not more than about $\frac{1}{6}$ of its mean.

14. If the effects of direct taxation etc. are taken into account, then it seems that r_G as defined in (3) is somewhat greater than $E R$. The reasons for this are the same as those discussed in connection with e_M and e_0 in note 12 of chapter V.

15. The point of departure—both historically and substantively—of all political economy is the observation with which Adam Smith begins his *Wealth of Nations*: 'The annual labour of every nation is the fund which originally supplies it with all the necessaries and conveniences of life which it annually consumes, and which consists always either in the immediate produce of that labour, or in what is purchased with that produce from other nations.'

Chapter Seven

1. That certain macroscopic parameters—such as the ratio e_0 defined in chapter III—nevertheless remain virtually constant is an exceptional and remarkable phenomenon. Each such exception requires some explanation.

2. Here we are identifying the Marxian notion of *value* with our labour-content. The differences between the two (discussed in appendix II) are irrelevant to the present discussion.

3. Workers' resistance to strategy (iii), when used in its 'pure' form, is normally very great. Resistance to strategy (iv)—often stigmatized as 'Luddite'—is more easily overcome. In practice strategy (iii) is most often used in combination with, and as a corollary to, strategy (iv).

4. This will actually happen if the specific price of the new input is sufficiently lower than that of the old one. For example, suppose the specific price of the new input is one-third that of the old input. Suppose also that two dollars'-worth of the old input is replaced by one dollar's-worth of the new input. The *cost* of this particular item is therefore *halved*, but the *labour-content* is increased by a factor of one and a half, because each dollar's-worth of the new input has three times as much labour-content as a dollar's-worth of the old input. (For a general discussion of this point, see further on in the main text.)

5. In practice, the factor c is seldom too close to 1. A change of inputs normally implies that more or less drastic technical readjustments must be made, which involve certain transitional expenses. The change will be made only if the eventual saving in costs of production is sufficiently attractive.

6. The assumption that Ψ_1 and Ψ_2 have the same distribution would not

necessarily be reasonable if, instead of measuring commodities by their labour-content, we were to measure them by some other universal input, so that *specific price* would be the ratio between price and (say) plastic-content. A large continual increase in the use of plastic may well be part of the very mechanism for driving unit costs down. Here we use in a crucial way the peculiar properties of labour-content as a measure: for this measure only, the equality $E\bar{\Psi}_1 = E\bar{\Psi}_2$ has a definite socio-economic meaning, namely that there is no change in the global rate of exploitation e_M.

7. See appendix I. In any case, this result hardly requires proof: it is merely another form of a well-known fact about gambling. In each gamble in a casino, the house may make a positive gain or a 'negative gain' (that is, a loss, which is a positive gain for the gambler). In each gamble the probability of the house making a negative gain is by no means negligible; there is even some probability of the gambler winning a very large amount. Otherwise, few people would be tempted. But the odds are fixed so as to make the *expected value* of the house's gain, in each gamble, a positive number. As a result, the probability that the *cumulative* gain of the house, in a sequence of gambles, will be positive is very large; and as the number of gambles increases this probability approaches certainty. In the long run the house is almost sure to make a profit. Of course, *almost sure* is not quite the same as *certain*, and from time to time a gambler may 'break the bank'. But this happens very rarely indeed, whereas a gambler's ruin is commonplace.

8. The effect of strategy (iii) must, of course, be added as a contributing cause.

9. See our discussion of the Law of Large Numbers.

10. It is easy to show that this probability is, in any case, greater than $\frac{1}{2}$. For, by formula (5), the probability $P(\log H > 0)$ can be written as $P(\log C + \log\bar{\Psi}_2 > \log\bar{\Psi}_1)$. Since $\log C$ is always positive, this probability is *greater* than $P(\log\bar{\Psi}_2 > \log\bar{\Psi}_1)$, which, for reasons of symmetry, is exactly $\frac{1}{2}$. (Since we are assuming that our random variables have smooth distributions, the probability $P(\log\bar{\Psi}_2 = \log\bar{\Psi}_1)$ is 0. Hence $P(\log\bar{\Psi}_2 > \log\bar{\Psi}_1)$ and $P(\log\bar{\Psi}_2 < \log\bar{\Psi}_1)$ add up to 1, and since by symmetry these two probabilities are equal to each other, they both equal $\frac{1}{2}$.) Economically speaking, this means that in a *single* change of inputs the odds that labour-content (per unit of output) is reduced are better than even.

11. In this calculation we use the fact that, for any random variable X, the variance $V(-X)$ is the same as VX. This follows from the general theorem (see appendix I) that $V(cX) = c^2 VX$, where c is any constant. In the present case we take $c = -1$.

12. In the limiting case where $\bar{\Psi}_1$ and $\bar{\Psi}_2$ are degenerate, they are reduced to a constant, which must be the same for both. Then (5) reduces to the equality $\log H = \log C$, so that $\log H$ is always positive (that is, the probability of its being positive is 1). This degenerate case corresponds to Marx's unmodified model, in which the law of decreasing labour-content is almost self-evident.

13. We may assume that these inputs are enumerated in the order in which they were actually purchased.

256

14. It seems highly plausible that as time goes by the standard deviation σ tends to diminish (very slowly, to be sure) due to the growing number and diversity of different inputs used up by most modern processes of production. This tendency is perhaps helped along by the very operation of the law of decreasing labour-content: the decline in the 'weight' of each individual input item may encourage the number of items to grow.

15. Cf. note 14 to chapter VI.

16. At this stage we are only interested in the logical aspect of the whole argument. Our critique of its factual aspects will come later.

17. This does not bother those later Marxists who believe in the tendency of r_G to fall as a purely metaphysical potentiality, which may never be actualized. But, as we have stressed, Marx himself quite clearly held that the tendency is a factual one, at least in the long term.

18. Thus, for example, at the very end of Chapter XV of the third volume of *Capital*, Marx mentions 'the growth in capital values ... growing far more quickly than the population' as the cause of crises.

19. For example, near the beginning of Chapter XIII of the same volume, Marx says: 'Moreover, it has been shown to be a law of the capitalist mode of production that its development does in fact involve a relative decline in the relation of variable capital to constant, and hence also to the total capital set in motion. *This simply means that the same number of workers or the same quantity of labour-power* that is made available by a variable capital of a given value, as a result of the specific methods of production that develop within capitalist production, sets in motion, works up, and productively consumes, within the same period, an ever-growing mass of means of labour, machinery and fixed capital of all kinds, and raw and ancillary materials—in other words, *the same number of workers operate with a constant capital of ever-growing scale.*' (Our emphases.) In this passage we find not only a conflation between the growth of q_G (that is, k/v) and that of k/N, but also the source of Marx's belief in the inexorable growth of both these ratios. He assumed that a purely physical increase in the means of production must almost always (excluding what he calls 'exceptional cases') be accompanied by a growth in their aggregate *value* (labour-content). This assumption is quite unfounded. Besides, the very notion of physical growth of the means of production is ill-defined and quite inapplicable in the long term, as we have argued.

20. This does not mean that there were no significant changes, still less that such changes are completely ruled out for the future. But, as we shall argue below, changes in global organic composition q_G and in the quantity (measured in terms of labour-content) of capital per worker k/N are *severely restricted* by the inner structure of capitalism. Thus, one cannot rule out changes of, say, 20 to 40 percentage points in q_G as a result of economic development. But it will be impossible for q_G to grow, even in the long term, to three or four times its present level. This is basically because the distribution of the rate of profit cannot move too far down, being quite low already. Notice again that while some of these considerations are in line with the traditional labour theory of value (cf. E. Mandel, *Late Capitalism*,

London 1975, pp. 199-222) they make little sense if one assumes a uniform rate of profit. This assumption puts no restriction on the distribution of organic composition (and virtually none on its global value), because it does not recognize any correlation between organic composition and the rate of profit.

21. This is an instance of what is known in traditional logic as *the fallacy of composition*.

22. For a discussion of the gamma family of distributions, see appendix I.

23. In our illustrative scenario we have assumed that the standard deviation of R declines in the same ratio as the mean $\mathbf{E}R$. If—as seems to be more realistic—the standard deviation falls less rapidly than the mean, then the dire consequences appear still earlier, and are more dramatic.

24. For example, in the early stages of a recession, as production begins to contract, capitalists react by laying workers off. But fixed plant cannot be reduced so quickly, and consequently k falls less rapidly than N. This pushes k/N further *upwards*, which exacerbates the recessionary process.

25. The government can aid recovery by encouraging or undertaking labour-intensive projects, which tend to push k/N downwards.

26. It is quite possible that at some early stage of English industrial development the average rate of profit did undergo a long period of decline. This phenomenon may have been observed by the classical economists (particularly Ricardo), who extrapolated it into a general law of development. Later, Marx attempted to provide an explanation for this supposed law within his own theoretical system.

27. For exactly the same reason one must distinguish between the labour-content counterparts of $1/\mathbf{E}Z$ and $\mathbf{E}Q$, namely the *global* organic composition q_G and the *average* organic composition. It seems that Marx does conflate the latter two quantities and speaks of 'average organic composition' where the context actually indicates that he is referring to the global organic composition.

28. A standard calculation, whose details we omit, shows that if Z has the distribution $\mathfrak{G}(\alpha, \beta)$, then the p.d.f. of Q is given by the formula

$$f_Q(q) = \begin{cases} Cq^{-(\alpha+1)}e^{-\beta/q} & \text{for } q > 0, \\ 0 & \text{for } q \leq 0, \end{cases}$$

where C is the same constant as in note 3 to appendix I. The value of $\mathbf{E}Q$ is then found by integrating $qf_Q(q)$ from 0 to ∞.

29. A weaker conclusion in the same direction is reached by Ernest Mandel: 'It is hence impossible for automation to spread to the entire realm of production in the age of late capitalism' (p. 207). Notice however that this entire direction of analysis and prediction is inaccessible in a theoretical framework that assumes a uniform rate of profit. Mandel reaches his conclusion by a traditional common-sense use of the labour theory of value and by turning a blind eye to the implications of the uniformity assumption. On this and similar questions, a careful common-sense use of labour-value

categories—without the uniformity assumption—becomes theoretically justifiable on the basis of our probabilistic approach.

Chapter Eight

1. Taken from *Times 1000*, London 1972.
2. The scale of the graph was chosen to be such that the area under the theoretical curve is the same as that under the empirical one. This area represents the total amount of capital in question. These computer processed data sum up a rather large representative sample from the said sources.
3. Business Ratios division, *Industrial Performance*, London 1981.
4. E.G. Wood, *British Industries—a Comparison of Performance*, London 1975.
5. I. Steedman, *Marx after Sraffa*, London 1977, pp. 37-42.
6. Joseph Gillman, *The Falling Rate of Profit*, London 1957. Gillman's findings are discussed by Meghnad Desai, *Marxian Economic theory*, London 1974. As for the evolution of the average rate of profit—the main theme of Gillman's work—we agree with Desai's assessment that Gillman's findings show a decline in the period 1880-1919, but no general long-term trend.
7. E. Mandel, *Late Capitalism*, London 1975.
8. Ibid., pp. 165, 175.

Appendix I

1. The probabilistic notion of independence discussed here must not be confused with the notion of independence between parameters describing a microscopic state of a system, mentioned in connection with the number of degrees of freedom in the beginning of chapter III.
2. Cf. W. Feller, *Introduction to Probability Theory and its Applications*, vol. 2, New York 1966, p. 46 f.
3. The constant C is determined by the fact that the integral of f_X from 0 to ∞ must equal 1. It turns out that $C = \beta^a / \Gamma(\alpha)$. Here Γ is the so-called *gamma function*, defined by

$$\Gamma(\alpha) = \int_0^\infty x^{\alpha-1} e^{-x} dx.$$

It has the property that $\Gamma(\alpha) = (\alpha - 1) \Gamma(\alpha - 1)$ for all $\alpha > 0$; in particular, $\Gamma(n + 1) = n!$ for $n = 0, 1, 2, \ldots$
4. Empirical computation by the authors, based on *Business Ratios, Industrial Performance Analysis, a financial analysis of UK industry & commerce*, 6th edn, Business Ratios division of Inter-company Comparison Ltd, 1981.
5. E. Lukacs, *Third Berkeley Symposium on Probability and Statistics*, vol. 2, 1956, pp. 195-214.
6. For example, see Feller.

Appendix II

1. See, for example, Catherine Colliot-Thélène's 'Afterword' to Isaac Ilyich Rubin, *A History of Economic Thought*, London 1979; also see older literature cited by her.

2. This can be done by comparing the prices of commodities whose process of production uses capitals of equal organic compositions (as measured by the amount of invested capital per worker).

3. See discussion of this point in Colliot-Thélène, pp. 390 ff.

4. Let us illustrate this point by a simple counter-example. In the following illustration, 'price' means *ideal* price; and the 'distorting effect' of the supposed tendency of the rate of profit to equalization is discounted. For the sake of simplicity, let us assume there are just two types of labour — simple labour, with skill coefficient 1, and one type of skilled labour, with skill coefficient c, whose numerical magnitude is for the moment unknown. Consider three commodities, C_1, C_2, C_3, of different types. The total labour required to produce C_1 is one worker-hour of simple labour plus four worker-hours of skilled labour. The production of C_2 requires one worker-hour of simple labour and one of skilled labour. Suppose that the price of C_1 is three times that of C_2. Then the *value* of C_1 must likewise be three times that of C_2, and from the data we have assumed it is easy to calculate that the skill coefficient c must be equal to 2. Next, consider C_3. Suppose that to produce this commodity four worker-hours of simple labour and one of skilled labour are needed. Then the *value* of C_3, is twice the *value* of C_2 (and $\frac{2}{3}$ that of C_1). The theory that (ideal) price is proportional to *value* therefore predicts that the price of C_3, should be twice that of C_2. This prediction is certainly not tautologous, but depends in an essential way on the theory in question (proportionality of price and *value*) in conjunction with the doctrine of skill coefficients. If one believes that the notion of ideal price has some empirical content (as the long-term average of market prices, for example) then the above prediction concerning the price of C_3 is likewise empirically non-vacuous. Of course, one may reject the notion of ideal price in the first place, as we do; but this is a different matter.

Note that our counter-example is by no means a freak. The same situation would arise in general, provided the number of different commodity-types is larger than the number of different skills—clearly, a realistic assumption.

More generally, it should be pointed out that there is nothing necessarily wrong with a 'circular' definition, in which two entities are defined in terms of each other. Logically speaking, this amounts to an implicit simultaneous definition of the two entities. Such a definition is perfectly acceptable, provided it is consistent and imposes a sufficiently strong constraint on the *definienda*. As a simple example, suppose we define a number x by saying that it is twice as large as another number y, and then define y as being smaller than x by 3. This 'circularity' amounts to postulating a simultaneous system of two equations, $x = 2y$ and $y = x - 3$, which in fact has a unique solution: $x = 6$, $y = 3$.

5. Or, to take a more 'shocking' example: one hour's work done by a skilled air pilot is taken to create the same amount of labour-content as an

260

hour's work done by an air steward or by a porter who loads luggage onto the plane.

6. The reasons for the relative scarcity of certain skills are diverse. In many cases the development of such a skill requires long years of schooling or apprenticeship, or the possession of some rare innate capability. But this is by no means always so. The number of people allowed to acquire or practise certain skills is strictly controlled, whether by guild-like unions or by other means. As for the amount of work needed to maintain a skill—this is, in most cases, not very great. Most skills are kept up by their very application in ordinary work.

7. As we remarked at the end of chapter III, empirical evidence suggests that this balance does not lead to a narrow distribution of R, as predicted by existing theories, or to a narrow distribution of W, but to a narrow distribution of the random variable $X = R/Z$ (the ratio between profits and labour-costs in the firm space).

8. Needless to say, in speaking about the 'contributions' of various types of labour we are referring to contributions in the narrow sense, to the quantitative economic measure of commodities. This does not necessarily imply that all skills and all types of work are equally valuable in some broader social or moral sense. We leave out of consideration the contribution made by this or that category of workers to the general welfare of humanity.

9. It seems that Marx did make such a claim in his 1857 *Contribution to the Critique of Political Economy*, but in *Capital* this claim is retracted. On this point, see Colliot-Thélène, p. 390, n. 4 and p. 392.

10. Cf. discussion in Colliot-Thélène pp. 405-15.

11. Colliot-Thélène commits this error, ibid.

12. Ibid.

13. Karl Marx, *Capital*, Harmondsworth 1981, vol. 3, ch. X, p. 280.

14. Ibid., vol. 1, ch. I, s. 1, p. 45 f.

15. It is quite clear that Marx himself had precisely this argument in mind when he opted for the 'socially necessary', generic (as opposed to the actual and individual) determination of *value*. For, in connection with the last-quoted sentence, in which he stresses the generic character of *value*, he cites the following observation due to Le Trosne: 'Toutes les productions d'une même genre ne forment proprement qu'une masse, dont le *prix* se détermine en général et sans égard aux circonstances particulières.' (Our emphasis)

16. It is not hard to see that in the input-output theory of prices, where a uniform rate of profit is assumed, the numerical value of that uniform rate of profit depends quite strongly on the mode of aggregation of commodities into types—rendering such a numerical result fairly meaningless.

Appendix III

1. I. Steedman and P. Sweezy, *et al.*, *The Value Controversy*, London 1981.

2. I. Steedman, *Marx after Sraffa*, London 1977, p. 180.

3. E. Farjoun, in Mandel (ed.).

4. Steedman p. 20.

5. Ibid., footnote.

6. Ibid., p. 205

7. E. Farjoun, in Mandel (ed.).

8. Geoff Hodgson, 'Critique of Wright, 1. Labour and profits', in Steedman and Sweezy, pp. 75-99.

9. P.Sraffa, *Production of Commodities by Means of Commodities*, Cambridge 1960, p. 91.

10. Erik Olin Wright, 'The value controversy and social research', in Steedman and Sweezy pp. 36-74.

11. Marco Lippi, *Value and Naturalism in Marx*, London 1979, p. 50.

Index

Entries for subjects, abbreviations and symbols refer only to the places
where they are defined, explained or substantively discussed.

Printed in the United States
by Baker & Taylor Publisher Services